Stand and Proclaim…

Enough Is Enough!

**Experience the Presence, Power, and Love
of God to Transform Your Life**

Stand and Proclaim...

Enough
Is
Enough!

Experience the Presence, Power, and Love
of God to Transform Your Life

By David Carlson

Enough Is Enough!
©Copyright 2005 - Rev. Dr. David Carlson
ISBN 0-9764536-0-6

Published by
Victory Publications
Maplewood, MN 55119
USA

Take note that the name satan and related names are not capitalized. We choose not to acknowledge him, even to the point of violating grammatical rules.

Editorial Consultation: Laura Bonne
White Bear Lake, MN

Sarah Fairrow
St. Paul, MN

For Worldwide Distribution

Impreso en Colombia
Printed in Colombia

Dedication

I dedicate this book to all Christians who are in a battle for their health, their peace of mind, and prosperity in all things. There is a burning fire deep in my soul, where my spirit yearns to see God's people experience His presence. Brothers and sisters in Christ, we are to be God's representatives in this world, reflecting His Kingdom in all that we do.

The Church is under siege, being tormented and destroyed by sin and the effects of sin. It should not be this way. Jesus did not die in vain! This book derives from my desire to see the Body of Christ empowered with the fullness of the Spirit and Truth, "running toward the giant" much like David did when he faced Goliath. King David's words are echoed today, *"Is there not a cause?"*

Arise today, with a declaration in your heart that *Enough is Enough!* and establish the truth of God's Word in your life. The victory *IS* yours. Step into the New Covenant promise and experience your miracle today.

Acknowledgments

To my beautiful wife Julie –

You are wonderful! Thank you for always believing in me. Your love, faith, support, and confidence form a constant rock in my life. I love you so much!

Dad and Mom –

Thank you for your love and support and the countless proofreads in the preparation of this book. Your faith and love have been foundational in my life. God bless you!

Maxine Roeske –

Thank you for your love and support. Your strength and courage have been important to me. May our Father in Heaven continue to bless you.

Dale Sides –

Thank you for being a committed spiritual father and mentor. Your guidance, love, and support have made this book possible. Words cannot express how thankful I am. I am a blessed man to have the opportunity to learn from you and experience the blessings of being your spiritual son. May your faithfulness to the Kingdom of God be richly rewarded.

Laura Bonne –

You are truly a blessing from God! Thank you for your faithfulness to God's Kingdom. Your sacrifice of time and resources through the editing process will be rewarded! You are an excellent, gifted editor and your services will continue to bless authors around the world for many, many, years to come! May God continue to pour out His blessing into your life!

Joel and Dawn Kaul –

Thank you so much for your friendship and the time you sacrificed to proofread and critique this book. Your input and suggestions were important. God bless you and your wonderful family.

Richard and Sarah Fairrow –

Thank you for being faithful to God's call! You are dear friends, and it is because of your gift that this book has been printed. Sarah, thank you so much, for the time spent editing this book. You are truly a blessing. May both of you reap a great harvest to your wonderful seed. You are a blessing to all who know you.

In memory of my father-in-law, Vern Roeske,
who fought the good fight.
God bless you, Vern.

Table of Contents

Introduction

God is Calling

Vernon William Roeske was my father-in-law. He fought cancer courageously for three long years before surrendering his earthly life to be with the Father. As his family, we prayed, confessed, and believed for the miraculous healing in the body of this tremendous man, in the end only to experience the disappointment of his death. I know from experience there are two choices Christians can make at such a time: 1) blame God and turn from the truth of His Word, or 2) press in for more understanding of His truth, never compromising the promises given to us. I chose the latter and this book is the fruit of what I have learned of God's faithfulness to His promise and covenant with His children.

When my father-in-law went home prematurely to be with Jesus, a fire consumed my soul that prompted me to dedicate my life to learn and experience the truth of our complete redemption and atonement through Jesus Christ. I made the decision not to allow my faith in God's Word to be undermined and destroyed. Instead, I would rise up and demonstrate that the Kingdom of Heaven is at hand and the Gospel of Jesus Christ is truly the Good News! A consuming fire drives me to experience the very presence of God in all I do. I hope to share this desire and fire within the pages of this book so that *all* who are sick, *all* who are oppressed, and *all* who are tormented may experience the truth of freedom in Jesus Christ.

We have a God-given promise, one that extends beyond any human intellect or understanding -- a promise directly related to our prosperity and health while we're on this earth. My life's mission is to preach, teach, and demonstrate the Gospel of the Kingdom, revealing the truths of God's Word so every one of His people may step into a new understanding of the complete price Jesus paid for mankind.

This book was designed to bring you into the fullness of God's glory, its framework the result of hours involved in studying the Word, seeking and hearing from God, and boundless prayers for those who are sick, tormented, and oppressed. My sincere prayer is that you will be empowered to receive the miracle your heart desires. God has equipped you to manifest His fullness in your life. He has given you the gift of living perfectly redeemed, dwelling in the blessings of His Kingdom through His Spirit.

I spent much time on my knees following my father-in-law's death, asking God why he died and why our prayers, fasting, supplication, confessions of faith, and thanksgiving failed to manifest a healing miracle. I asked God why Vern's life was stolen from us and why my children would have to grow up without the privilege of experiencing their "Papa." The answer I received changed my life forever, and I pray it will bring change to your life as well. God's revelation to me is wrapped in the pages of this book in a manner that will allow every reader to hear God speaking to his or her heart. God is calling you! He is calling His people to commit themselves to His Truth and His Word. Brothers and sisters in Christ, we can either manipulate God's Word to try to fit our limited understanding and worldly experiences, or we can come to a place in our lives where we are changed, transformed to fit God's Word and God's Kingdom. He is calling you and me to a place where we may fully experience His Kingdom NOW, in this life.

Are you ready to answer the call? There comes a point in a Christian's spiritual walk where heart and soul become aligned with the heart and soul of God, when all that God loves, he loves, and all God hates, he hates. A fire must arise in man's soul, a righteous anger, a hatred toward the kingdom of darkness and all that it represents. The defining moment comes when the Christian stands and proclaims "Enough is Enough!" rising above the darkness of this world and taking authority over it in the Mighty Name of Jesus Christ. It is then that an unquenchable fire burns deeply in the heart and releases the determination, confidence, and faith that terrifies and disables the kingdom of darkness and releases the powers of Heaven.

Biblical truths of the New Covenant promise lay the foundation for this book, equipping and empowering you, the reader, to accept and establish truths in your daily life. This book focuses on providing a clear portrayal of the promise of the New Covenant as it exists for us today. A careful reading and application of the following chapters will enable you to destroy the schemes of the enemy in your life and for others for whom you pray. This book unveils the full measure of the truth of the blood covenant that separates us unto God – the very covenant that releases us into a new understanding and a glorious new life.

I am excited for what God's Word can do in your life and for the transformation available to you. May God bless your coming and going and everywhere that your feet may tread. Enjoy, and be blessed.

In the divine promise of healing and miracles,

Dave

1

Living in the New Covenant Promise

Anyone who has rejected Moses' law dies without mercy on the testimony
of two or three witnesses. Of how much worse punishment, do you suppose,
will he be thought worthy of he who has trampled the Son of God underfoot,
counted the blood of the covenant by which he was sanctified
a common thing, and insulted the Spirit of Grace?

Hebrews 10:28-29

A Faith God Honors

It was 4:45 p.m. on a Friday evening in March, just about the end of my workday
in our home office in the basement. The sounds were comforting and familiar –
light taps on the keyboard, soft music, and joys from above as my wife, Julie,
tended to our children. In a heartbeat, however, the atmosphere would be
drastically altered. Above my desk I heard my wife run from the kitchen to the
family room. The Holy Spirit confirmed in my heart that something was wrong,
and I ran up the stairs.

As soon as I reached the doorway, the urgency was clear. Our beloved Andrew,
only 15 months old, lay limp in Julie's arms after striking his head on the coffee
table. He inhaled for a deep breath, one certain to erupt into a loud scream.
Instead, nothing came. Our little boy had stopped breathing. His heart stopped
beating and his life was gone.

Without hesitation, Julie and I joined as one in faith, rebuking the spirit of death
and commanding the spirit of Life to return to Andrew's small frame. We
engaged in full-fledged spiritual warfare for our son's life. Suddenly, Andrew
opened his eyes. But just as quickly as they'd opened, they would shut again, and
he was gone. What I didn't know then was that Julie could actually feel
Andrew's spirit leave, re-enter his body, and then leave once again.

Julie dialed 911 as I laid Andrew's lifeless body on the floor, and with every
ounce of my faith I spoke Life into him. At that moment, Andrew gasped for air
and life re-entered his tiny body. Because he had died for a span of five to ten
minutes, doctors requested to see Andrew at the emergency room to make sure

everything was restored properly. And there doctors confirmed what we knew to be the miraculous restoration of Andrew's precious life. The doctors could find nothing more than a good-sized bump and a laceration on his head. We were cautioned about the effects of a concussion and Andrew was released. When he awoke the next morning, there was no indication of a concussion, bruise, cut, or bump on his head. By God's power, he was completely healed and restored! Halleluiah!

Through God All Things Are Possible

She approached me following a prayer meeting and asked if I would pray for her. A woman with a deep desire to be a mother, she and her husband had tried to have a child, but the cysts the doctors found on her ovaries made it impossible for her body to produce an egg. The prognosis was bleak, and the doctors offered her no hope. She was acting on her God-given faith when she came to me and stated emphatically, "I am ready to give this oppression back to the devil, be healed and conceive a child!"

I laid my hands on her and we began to pray as two firmly standing in one accord. Together, we witnessed the mighty power of God enter her body as she proclaimed, "I am healed!" I was made to rejoice a year and half later when I met her beautiful eight-month-old daughter, Hannah. Praise God, the Giver of Life!

The New Covenant Established

The young man seated with his parents in my office had scheduled the appointment for the purpose of praying for his health, having recently received the doctor's devastating news. His symptoms, the lesions on his brain, and the test results all pointed to one very gloomy conclusion – the onset of Multiple Sclerosis. We prayed the prayer of faith that day and proclaimed the truth of the New Covenant established by the blood of Jesus Christ, the Son of God. The healing power of the Holy Spirit was manifested in this young man's life, and he and his parents went home confessing, believing, and *knowing* he was healed.

For the next 40 days, they continued to walk in faith and performed Holy Communion in belief of his healing. When he attended the next scheduled medical appointment for further testing, what they discovered was a dramatically different diagnosis: the doctors were unable to find any sickness or disease in the young man's brain. He was healed! Praise God forever.

* * *

Each of the testimonies above demonstrates God's presence and promise by and through the realistic accounts of what it means to live a "normal" Christian life. Why is it, then, that we marvel at such occurrences? Could it be we have failed to demonstrate the fullness of God's presence in all we think, say, and do?

God's purpose and the promise of His New Covenant with us is revealed in the midst of each of these testimonies. He is faithful in upholding His promises – those of health and prosperity to spirit, soul and body! Our Father, Yahweh, has made a New Covenant with His children, an everlasting covenant deemed "New" because it was built upon the fulfillment of the Old. We have been elected through the blood of Jesus Christ to reign as kings and priests today in this world! The blood covenant that sanctified us, separating us unto God, is bound by God's promise and oath. Jesus Christ offered the biggest sacrifice heaven and earth ever knew. On Him was laid the redemption of mankind. By His Spirit we are transformed into His likeness, filled with His very nature to reflect His image, character, and understanding.

And yet as I minister to the body of Christ, I observe Christians struggling daily with divorce, mental/emotional illness, physical sickness and disease, and all forms of oppression. Tragically for some, the struggle ends in premature death, while for others torment and strife pollute and steal the quality of life given to them through the blood of Jesus Christ. Certainly, Jesus' sacrifice, death, resurrection, and ascension were not in vain. Why, then, is the Church, the very Christian faith, not experiencing the full redemption and blood-covenant promise sealed by the Holy Spirit of God? It is essential that we gain a better understanding of God's promises so that we may appropriate the New Covenant into our individual lives. Simply, we must walk, talk, and experience that which God deems the accepted, indeed *expected*, everyday, normal Christian life.

The Christian Faith Today is Missing Something

I had the privilege of visiting a polio orphanage in South India. There were 45 children in this special orphanage, each suffering some form of oppression, infirmity, or sickness. My heart wept for those special children who were made to endure the curse of polio and its crippling effects. My heart ached for the truth of God's promise to be experienced there in its fullness.

Sitting near the entrance to the facility, I was able to see the attendance board on which was listed the background of each child enrolled in the orphanage. I noticed that of the 45 total orphans, 22 were of the Christian faith. I began to seek God on how this could be. How could there be as many Christians sick with polio in that orphanage as there were of those who had not accepted Jesus Christ as their Redeemer and Lord? It occurred to me that something is missing in today's Christian faith. We have taken the blood covenant of our Savior Jesus Christ, the very promise of our sanctification and redemption, and made a "common thing" of it. We *are not* experiencing the fullness of the promise of the New Covenant established by the blood of Jesus, the Lamb of God. We *are not* experiencing and living the life God has set before us.

Many Christians today find it difficult to open their hearts to the truth of complete and full redemption through Jesus Christ. We have a tendency to bring the truth of the Word of God to the level of our own limited experiences, instead of bringing our experiences up to the level of God's Truth. As such, whether resulting from the lack of knowledge or a conscious choice not to live in the fullness of the New Covenant, sin, sickness, and death are allowed to control and influence our minds and bodies. By our lack of faith, we render Jesus' ultimate sacrifice powerless, even meaningless. Fellow believers, we are the intended recipients of the Lord God Almighty's New Covenant. As His chosen ones, we should be experiencing life's fullness right now, on earth, as it is already done in Heaven. It's time this promise be manifested through our faith!

Receive Your Healing or Miracle

Even though we have been completely redeemed, set apart unto God as holy and acceptable through a new and living covenant of Truth and Power, we have yet to appropriate the power of God's oath into our Christian lives. The Bible says, *"To whom much is given, much is required."*[1] We are called, therefore, to be responsible, committed, and disciplined to God's Word and Spirit that we may fulfill all He has called us to fulfill. The power to transform life's circumstances lies in the understanding that God's grace is released only by our faithfulness to His Word.

> *Blessed be the God and Father of our Lord Jesus Christ, who has blessed us with every spiritual blessing in the heavenly places in Christ, just as He chose us in Him before the foundation of the world, that we should be holy and without blame before Him in love, having predestined us to adoption as sons by Jesus Christ to Himself, according to the good pleasure of His will, to the praise of the glory of His grace, by which He has made us accepted in the Beloved.*[2]

---

[1] Luke 12:48
[2] Ephesians 1:3-6

God our Father has already given us every spiritual blessing in the heavenly places in and through Jesus Christ. It has already been done, the Father having fulfilled the promise. We have been accepted *in* the Beloved. We are *in* the Beloved! We are exhorted to *give thanks to the Father who has qualified us to be **partakers of the inheritance** of the saints in the light. Our Heavenly Father, through His Son, has delivered us from the power of darkness and **translated us into the kingdom of the Son** of His love.*[3] The word "translated" derives from the Greek word *methistemi*, which means to be deposited, transferred, or exchanged. Our Heavenly Father has positioned us to live an abundant, triumphant life in this world. Is it not time we begin to live triumphantly, right where we are, dwelling in the Beloved?

Without a doubt, there will be times when sickness, disease, strife and/or oppression will come against us. After all, they are schemes the devil uses to tempt God's children away from the Truth. The demonic kingdom tests our faith and our faithfulness to God's Word and the promise of the New Covenant. The enemy continually schemes to effectively minimize that which Jesus has already accomplished for us. The demonic forces know they are defeated and their only hope is to divert our thoughts, words, and actions away from the truth of the Word of God. A veil of deception is created and strongholds are built to keep God's promise from being fulfilled. Through our faith we must learn to keep our eyes on Jesus, and off our circumstances, as the storms of life try to separate us from the love of Christ.

We have been deceived by the enemy of our God into believing and accepting the oppressions of this world. We have developed an understanding that accepts and even rationalizes sickness, mental and emotional strife, and premature death. We have reduced the blood of the covenant to communion rituals and we fail to live by its sanctifying powers. We "hope" for cures. Falling short of experiencing the full measure of God's promise, we wander aimlessly through life, often keeping our fingers crossed that we do not fall into the depths of the enemy's wiles. As a result, we have counted the blood of the covenant by which we have been sanctified a common thing and we have insulted the Spirit of Grace.

Jesus was rejected at the Cross and became the curse for all of mankind, breaking the stronghold of satan and his kingdom over our lives forever. By His sacrifice, the chains that bind God's children were forever destroyed that we may be heirs to His Kingdom in this world. Yet we continue to compromise His Word, His Promise and Truth and have trampled underfoot the Son of God. How much more could we possibly grieve the Holy Spirit of our Father?

---

[3] Colossians 1:12-14 (emphasis added)

Beloved, we are His chosen ones. Let us align our wills with God's and press on. All the glory and power that Jesus knows at the throne of God, all the wonders of His overcoming grace, all the marvel of the greatness of His power is yours and mine to *receive* through faith in the Son of God, yours and mine to *expect* through faith in the Son of God, yours and mine to *possess* and *enjoy* and *reveal* - - all to the glory of our Heavenly Father. We are called today to be His ambassadors in this world. We are called to be His sons and daughters, a full representation of His Kingdom in all that we do.

Enter the Promised Land

The revelation of living a "normal" Christian life will empower us to break free from the deception the devil holds over us. Establishing a consciousness of the presence of God in our lives transforms our whole being, providing an exodus by which our spirits may enter the Promised Land that was purchased for God's people. Health, healing, and prosperity to our spirits, souls, and bodies have already been achieved. It is our responsibility to appropriate them into our lives through faith and trust in the Holy Spirit of God living in us.

Do not allow yourself to be deceived by fear, doubt, and worry! Stop right now and allow the Holy Spirit of God to penetrate your heart and release a new understanding of your authority, dominion, and power over the strife and oppression of this world. The devil is defeated! Jesus came as the second Adam to reclaim man's authority over the works of the devil. In truth, the devil and his kingdom tremble at the understanding that God is the great *I AM*, that Jesus holds all power and authority over both heaven and earth, and that all His power and authority has been given to all those who believe that Jesus Christ is the Son of God through the Holy Spirit of God dwelling in us.

Something prompted you to pick up this book. Maybe a desire to be healed, delivered, restored, reconciled in a relationship, freed from oppression, or a driving hunger and passion to release the power of God in your life to minister to others. It is my sincere belief that if you take the time right now to write down on this page the desire of your heart, you will see that desire become a reality. Journey with me through these pages and take the time to meditate on God's Word, allowing it to build your faith and release your miracle today. Lay your cares on your Father's altar and believe Him for your miracle. He is faithful in ALL that He has promised.

Reflection Verse: *Hebrews 10: 28-29*

> *Anyone who has rejected Moses' law dies without mercy on the testimony*
> *of two or three witnesses. Of how much worse punishment, do you suppose,*
> *will he be thought worthy of he who has trampled the Son of God underfoot,*
> *counted the blood of the covenant by which he was sanctified*
> *a common thing, and insulted the Spirit of grace?*

Thought for Reflection:

The word "everlasting" or "eternal" is defined as a period of time without a beginning or an end. It is literally now and forever. Therefore, the New Covenant promise and guarantee is for all Christians to experience NOW and forever. God has already given us all spiritual blessings in the heavenly places through the New Covenant. God's Word implores us not to grieve the Holy Spirit, but to be a demonstration of a victory that has already been won! How does this truth affect your life today? How have you made the New Covenant promise a common thing in your life? Jesus said, "Repent, for the Kingdom of Heaven is at hand."

Daily Confession:

I am more than a conqueror! I am victorious over all trials and tribulations in my life through Jesus Christ my Lord and the New Covenant He established for me through His blood.

2

The New Covenant Truth

Christ in you, the hope of the glory.

Colossians 1:27

House Under Construction

A man built a big, beautiful house on a lake, and he and his family were very excited to make it their home. Once construction was completed, they moved all their belongings into the house and became comfortable. Until, that is, six months later when a crack developed on a wall in the lower level, extending from the ceiling all the way down to the floor.

A diligent homeowner, he contacted his contractor and immediately a Sheetrock man was sent out to repair the damaged wall. Ten days and one huge mess later, the Sheetrocking was completed and the wall looked as good as new.

Two months later, the crack reappeared, and the now-frustrated owner again contacted the contractor. This time a carpenter was sent to the house to replace the studs behind the Sheetrock. Once the carpenter was done, the Sheetrock man returned to finish the wall. One month and another large mess later, the family once again could enjoy their house on the lake.

Six months later, however, the same pesky crack was found on the same wall. The now-impatient owner contacted the contractor once again and the heated argument provided some gratification, but it didn't fix the crack in his wall. This time, a team of construction workers arrived and spent several hours looking into a remedy to permanently repair the crack. The bad news was delivered within a few hours.

Originally, they explained, it appeared the crack was a surface problem and simply repairing the Sheetrock would fix it. Then they thought perhaps the crack originated from the framed walls just behind the surface, so they'd tried to fix that. Now, however, they were sure the problem stemmed from a faulty foundation that developed as the house continued to settle. Over time, more cracks were certain to occur throughout the house. The family was forced to move so the foundation could be replaced.

A Faulty Foundation

Much like the house, many of our Christian beliefs are built upon faulty foundations. We have developed an understanding of the New Covenant and God's will for the Christian life based on man's doctrine and traditions rather than on a careful understanding of God's Word. As a result, more than a few cracks line our basic structure. We look only at the surface, or perhaps just a little beyond, to "fix" the cracks or problems, but they continue. Eventually, they become even worse. Paul's words, through the Holy Spirit, speak directly to the Christian faith today:

> *For since the creation of the world His invisible attributes are clearly seen, being understood by the things that are made, even His eternal power and Godhead, so that they are without excuse, because, although they knew God, they did not glorify Him as God, nor were thankful, but became futile in their thoughts, and their foolish hearts were darkened. Professing to be wise, they became fools, and changed the glory of the incorruptible God into an image made like corruptible man.*[4]

Our faulty foundations have diminished the glory of the incorruptible God to images of a corruptible man. Are we any worse than the children of Israel who spent forty years wandering in the wilderness? Have we not created "a golden calf" from our "Christianized" monuments and the idols of our hearts, and have we not worshiped and honored them more than we've honored God Himself? The cracks in our structures result from a confused and darkened foundation, one reinforced by futile thoughts and foolish hearts.

"He was in the world, and the world was made through Him, and the world did not know Him. He came to His own, and His own did not receive Him."[5] I wonder how the Christian faith lacks the fullness of Jesus Christ and the New Covenant established by His blood and sealed by the Holy Spirit of God? Jesus suffered, died, rose, and ascended into Heaven for us preparing a way full of victory and abundance, and yet His own do not know Him. Our foundations are unstable, and the structure of the entire Christian faith is threatened.

---

[4] Romans 1:20-23
[5] John 1:10-11

God Wills to Keep His Promise

The very reason many Christians are sick or oppressed is because of their lack of knowledge regarding the New Covenant promise established through Jesus Christ. God spoke through Hosea and declared, "*My people are destroyed for lack of knowledge.*"[6] Jesus said, "*If you abide in My word, you are My disciples indeed. And you will know the truth and the truth will make you free.*"[7] God is calling His people to know and understand His Word that all may receive the promise of His fullness. God's desire is to keep the New Covenant promise with His children that we may be filled with all the fullness and abundance of His Kingdom.[8] The early Church and apostles understood this truth of God's love for mankind. Their entire lives were dedicated to living out and being an example of the new and living way – a Kingdom example of the New Covenant in this world. The Apostles lived and died by the truth of the New Covenant: "*Christ in you, the hope of the glory!*"[9]

Acts 20:7-12 demonstrates this truth:

> *Now on the first day of the week, when the disciples came together to break bread, Paul, ready to depart the next day, spoke to them and continued his message until midnight. There were many lamps in the upper room where they were gathered together. And in a window sat a certain young man named Eutychus, who was sinking into a deep sleep. He was overcome by sleep; and as Paul continued speaking, he fell down from the third story and was taken up dead. But Paul went down, fell on him, and embracing him said, 'Do not trouble yourselves, for his life is in him.' Now when he had come up, had broken bread and eaten, and talked a long while, even till daybreak, he departed. And they brought the young man in alive, and they were not a little comforted.*

I wonder how we would respond to the same circumstances had they occurred in our church gatherings today. We probably would have called 911 and said some prayers, like "God, let your will be done," the pastor possibly concerned about lawsuits, and the family members contacting loved ones to give them the "horrible news." I recall a time when I was driving down a busy highway in Clearwater, Florida, one Sunday morning when I noticed a fairly large church and its filled-to-capacity parking lot. What grabbed my attention about this

---

[6] Hosea 4:6
[7] John 8:31,32 (author's emphasis)
[8] Ephesians 3:14-19
[9] Colossians 1:27

church was the fact that there was an ambulance with emergency lights on right outside the front door! Sadly, we lack Kingdom faith.

A Christian woman truly in love with Jesus proclaimed to me recently that she is wrestling with God to receive her blessing, just as Jacob did at Peniel.[10] As Christians, we do not have to wrestle with God for our blessings, because the Father has already given us all spiritual blessings in the heavenly places![11] It is this lack of knowledge that prohibits the manifestation of God's promise in the Christian life. At what point will we step into the promise of God's covenant and completely trust and rest in Him?

Psalm 91: 1-2 states, "*He who dwells in the secret place of the Most High shall abide under the shadow of the Almighty. I will say of the LORD, 'He is my refuge and my fortress; My God, in Him I will trust.'*" God promises us if we make our habitation in Him and put our complete trust in Him, He will heal, deliver, and forgive us.

*Because you have made the LORD, who is your refuge, Even the Most High, your habitation, no evil shall befall you, nor shall any plague come near your dwelling; for He shall give His angels charge over you, to keep you in all your ways. They shall bear you up in their hands, lest you dash your foot against a stone. You shall tread upon the lion and the cobra, the young lion and the serpent you shall trample under foot. (*Then God speaks), '*Because you have set your love upon Me, therefore I will deliver you; I will set you on high, because you have known My name. You shall call upon Me, and I will answer you; I will be with you in trouble; I will deliver you and honor you. With long life I will satisfy you, And show you My salvation.*[12]

What a faithful God we have! Unlike Jacob, we do not have to wrestle with Him for our blessings; Jesus Christ died, arose, and ascended into Heaven that we may completely possess His glory and blessing today. All God asks is that we simply trust and abide in Him.

The Father's desire is that we dwell in Him, abiding in the supernatural, experiencing His presence, His promise of the New Covenant, and the power of His love now and forever. The Christian faith is founded upon the supernatural act of the resurrection of Jesus Christ, and yet many Christians struggle to experience the miraculous in their lives today. Why is God's miraculous power limited today? The answer is simple: Our faith is not anchored upon the full

---

[10] Genesis 32:22
[11] Ephesians 1:3
[12] Psalm 91:9-16 (emphasis added)

assurance of the New Covenant promise through Jesus Christ. We allow doubt, fear, and worry to influence our thoughts and actions, and in time of adversity, when our faith is being tested by satan's kingdom, we cave to the pressure and fail to stand on the true promise of God's Word, the true promise of our complete redemption through Jesus Christ.

Deception

Brothers and sisters in Christ, we continue to be deceived! The father of lies, the devil,[13] has placed a veil of deception over our eyes, perverting and preventing the New Covenant truth from being manifested. The body of Christ is under siege, and sadly, it was never intended to be this way. Jesus could not have been clearer when He declared: *"On this rock I will build My church, and the gates of Hell shall not prevail against it."*[14]

Gates are designed to be defensive in nature in order to protect from an attack. Gates are used both for keeping something in and for keeping something out. As a Church, as members of the body of Christ, we have a responsibility to war against the gates of hell. These gates are located in our souls and minds through the thoughts that invade our consciousness. We are exhorted to battle against these thoughts by renewing our minds and taking every thought captive to the obedience of Jesus the Christ! The Church is built upon the revelation of Jesus Christ and the power of the Holy Spirit dwelling in each believer. Still, many Christians today have adopted an attitude that compromises and accepts the lies and deceit of satan and his kingdom. Therefore, the Church is under the siege of an already defeated foe!

A friend of mine is a substitute teacher. A video about King Arthur and the Knights of the Roundtable was played during a class in which he was subbing. "God" was mentioned in the video and a boy stood up to proclaim that "God" could not be talked about in school. The teens in the class whom the teacher knew to be Christians lowered their heads and looked at the ground in an obvious effort to disappear. Ironically, later that day the school celebrated Halloween.

Enough is Enough! We have allowed a defeated foe to kill, steal, and destroy for far too long! We <u>must</u> receive the revelation of who Jesus Christ is in our lives today and reclaim what satan and his kingdom have stolen. Jesus said, *"On this rock I will build My church."*

---

[13] John 8:44
[14] Matthew 16:18

"This rock" refers to the revelation of the overcoming Christ in our lives. Christ is not Jesus' last name. The definition of "Christ" is the anointed and His anointing.[15] The word "anointed" derives from the Greek word *chrio*, which means to consecrate or provide graciously with power to fulfill God's will on earth.[16] *Christ in us, the hope of the glory*, means that the anointed and His anointing, the very power of the Kingdom of God, dwells in us. Halleluiah! "Christ in us" is the promise that we have been equipped and provided with the power of God to fulfill His will.

The word "hope" means to have an expectation or to be confident.[17] Christ in us creates a confidence, an expectation, for the release and promise of His glory and power in all that we do! Our lives should fully demonstrate His anointing and His glory as we walk in faith, living in the Spirit, and fulfilling His will.

The Word of God is clear: A spiritual battle rages for every spirit, soul, and body, and we can either be a target or a warrior.[18] Satan's kingdom is not blatant in its attacks against the children of God, but subtle, shrewd, cunning and crafty. The kingdom of darkness delights in lies, using deception to lure God's children into believing and living a lie that will become their reality. There is very little satan and his kingdom can do in a believer's life without first creating deception in some manner. Certain things we do and attitudes we hold tend to open our minds to satan's lies and make us more susceptible to deception. 2 Corinthians 2:11 states, "*in order that no advantage be taken of us by satan; we are not to be ignorant of his schemes.*" We are to walk in the Spirit and not the flesh, to be on guard, vigilant, sober in our Christian lives.[19] It is our responsibility to make ourselves a living sacrifice, holy and acceptable unto God![20]

Deception laid the foundation for the fall of man, and it is the evil root preventing full manifestation of the New Covenant in our lives today. From the time man was created, satan has used deception to destroy God's will on earth. Adam and Eve were deceived into believing that God's Word was not truth.[21] As subtle as a snake, satan prodded Adam and Eve to choose to deny God's Word. He does the same thing today, deceiving Christians into believing that the New Covenant pertains only to life after death. Many people have spent a lifetime blaming God

---

[15] (1999) Bible Research Systems, *Strong's Concordance Dictionary*, Version 6.3
[16] Strong's Concordance Dictionary
[17] Strong's Concordance Dictionary
[18] John 10:10; 1 Peter 5:8; 2 Corinthians 10:3-5; Ephesians 6:10-18; 1 Timothy 6:12
[19] Romans 8:4; 1 Peter 5:8
[20] Romans 12: 1,2
[21] Genesis 3:1-8

for every negative circumstance experienced in their lives, when in truth, their suffering is a result of the enemy's deception.

It was Jesus who said, *"I am the light of the world. He who follows Me shall not walk in darkness, but have the light of life."* [22] Many believers struggle with their walk in the Light of life. We must be able to "see" through the darkness of deception in order to allow the light of Jesus Christ to be manifested.

Five basic false belief systems have twisted God's truth and prevented the body of Christ from living fully in God's promise. Such twisted truths come in the form of:

1. "Maybe it isn't God's will for me to be healed."
2. "Perhaps this sickness is for God's glory."
3. "God is using this sickness to chastise or punish me."
4. "Be patient in your sickness until God wills you to be healed."
5. "The day of miracles and healing went out with the Apostles and the early Church ."

I ministered to a woman who was very angry with God because her husband had died. She wondered how I could possibly believe in a God who would allow this world to be so corrupt, ugly, and sick. If God were real, she said more than once, He would have answered her prayers and her husband would still be alive.

I also ministered to a man struggling with severe, disabling back pain. He believed he was being tormented because, for whatever reason, God was calling him to move from glory to glory. In his opinion, he had to suffer the pain until God decided it was time to be healed. He was deceived into believing God's will was for him to be sick and to suffer so that he could be a "better Christian."

I ministered to a person suffering from lymphatic cancer. Sadly, her faith rested in the doctors and not in the New Covenant promise of healing and restoration. She could not bring herself to a place of true faith and believe that a miracle of healing was available to her. Instead, she stated, *"I'm sure the doctors will take care of me."*

Why is it so difficult for Christians to believe that God desires that we be healed? Is not the New Covenant a promise of health and prosperity?

---

[22] John 8:12

Understanding From Above

If then you were raised with Christ, seek those things, which are above, where Christ is sitting at the right hand of God. Set your mind on things above, not on things on the earth. For you died, and your life is hidden with Christ in God.[23]

The New Covenant is founded upon the ability of the believer to seek those things which are above, being confident in God's promises and believing in the supernatural authority established through the indwelling Holy Spirit. The key to truly manifesting the Kingdom of Heaven lies in a firm belief in the promises of the New Covenant. The secret to being healed and to release God's miraculous power rests upon our ability to be mindful of the things of God and not of the things of man. Once fully focused on Him, we are brought to a place of rest in the household of God, where we experience His glory.

A well-known minister once said, "I am not moved by what I see. I am not moved by what I feel. I am moved by what I believe."[24] *If God is for us, who can be against us?*[25] Receive by faith the truth of the power of the New Covenant and allow the spiritual awakening to release into your life a redeemed promise!

The New and Living Way

Is anyone among you suffering?[26] *Is anyone among you sick?*[27] If your answer is "yes," there is only one cure for complete deliverance and healing. Look at the foundation of our Christian belief system and how it is developed upon the faith of God's people. The Christian faith is to be concrete and unmovable free of all doubt. This type of faith will produce divine healing and life for those who believe. Hebrews 10:14 states, *"For by one offering He has perfected forever those who are being sanctified.*

We have been perfected through the blood covenant of Jesus Christ, our Redeemer! "Perfected" is past tense. God's living Word reminds us that believers being sanctified have been perfected forever. Galatians 2:20 states, *"I have been crucified with Christ; it is no longer I who live, but Christ lives in me; and the life which I now live in the flesh I live by faith in the Son of God, who loved me*

---

[23] Colossians 3:1-3
[24] Wigglesworth, Smith, *Wigglesworth on the Anointing*, Whitaker House, New Kensington, PA
[25] Romans 8:31
[26] James 5:13
[27] James 5:14

and gave Himself for me." We have been perfectly redeemed by the blood of Jesus Christ and now live in a New Covenant promise of Divine Health and even greater Divine Life; a God kind of life, wanting and desiring nothing. We are to live a life of abundance.

Praise God for His mercy and faithfulness! Our Father has empowered us, by a perfect and complete redemption, to fulfill and live in His Divine Life. No other belief system or religion in this world offers the same promise of partaking in the Divine Life of God. But because we, as the Church, have failed to demonstrate God's redeeming power through the Holy Spirit, Christians are renouncing their faith to chase false teachings. Enough is Enough! Praise God for the Great Carpenter who has provided a solid foundation for us to build our house.

The New Covenant Fulfills the Old

A covenant is a big deal to God. The word "covenant" derives from the Greek word *beriyth*, which means dividing something in two, an arrangement between two people.[28] The Hebrew word for covenant means "cut where blood flows." This is the strongest word for agreement in any language. The Scriptures demonstrate that God's covenants with Abraham and Moses and through Jesus were all sealed by blood, indicating the importance and "life" of the covenant promise. A covenant in itself is greater than a contract. A contract can be dissolved if one party does not adhere to the terms, but a covenant cannot be broken unless both parties agree. The promises contained in a covenant may be unfulfilled because one party failed to adhere to its terms, but it can only be broken if both parties agree to break it.

The Covenants established by God can never be broken or dissolved, because God will not break His promise. He cannot lie.[29] God will remember His covenant forever, the word that He commanded, for a thousand generations.[30] Both Old and New Covenants are realities in lives of Christians today because our Creator issued a promise that endures for all time.

Often when I ask people whether they feel it is God's will that they be healed, many respond that they simply do not know. I ask then if it is God's will to keep His promise. By the oath of our Father, a New Covenant was established over the Old. He is waiting for His children to appropriate their part under the terms of the agreement.

---

[28] Strong's Concordance Dictionary
[29] Hebrews 6:18
[30] Psalm 105:8; Psalm 106:48

The New Covenant is situated last in the eight great covenants of Scripture, marking the fulfillment of them all. The New Covenant is more excellent than the Mosaic Covenant because it is established upon better a promise. Under the Mosaic Covenant obedience sprang from fear, and under the New Covenant obedience comes from a willing heart and mind. The New Covenant secures the personal revelation of Jesus Christ to every believer. It assures the complete destruction of sins and it rests upon an accomplished perfect redemption. Finally, it secures the future conversion and blessing of a repentant Israel, with whom the New Covenant is yet to be ratified. So what does all this mean for the Christian faith?

The New Covenant – A Living Covenant

God's covenants were established for the purpose of appropriating God's will into man's heart in order to fulfill His desire of Heaven on earth. The Messianic Covenant (the New Covenant) was established that God would put His laws into our hearts, that He would write them on our minds, and our sins and lawless deeds He would remember no more.[31]   Through His perfect sacrifice, Jesus established a new and living way that allowed all believers the right and privilege to enter into the Most Holy Place, the throne of God. He made it very clear: *"Hear Me, everyone, and understand: There is nothing that enters a man from outside which can defile him; but the things which come out of him, those are the things that defile a man. If anyone has ears to hear, let him hear."*[32]

The New Covenant is written upon our hearts that we may develop a conscious relationship with the Father. It is in our hearts that the issues of life reside and we are commanded to guard our hearts with all diligence by placing our focus on the things of above, not on the things of this world.[33] God makes Himself to dwell "in" man and to empower man with His Spirit, to become intimate with His beloved. The New Covenant gives life in accordance with the measure of a believer's faith, its fulfillment conveying God's mercy, grace, and blessing to those who will receive.

The law now written upon our hearts, our focus is upon the ever-present, living nature of God, on drawing near to Him, experiencing the abundant joy and peace of His intimate presence, and resting in the truth of our redemption and empowerment through the New Covenant. Whereas the Mosaic Covenant established divine order, the New Covenant releases God's glory. And once that

---

[31] Jeremiah 31:33,34; Hebrews 10:16
[32] Mark 7:14,15
[33] Proverbs 4:23

glory is revealed, great blessings follow. God is faithful when our focus is upon Him, upon the things of above by which all things are possible. It is for that reason we are instructed not to conform to this world, but to be transformed by the renewing of our minds through God's Living Word.[34] Jesus gave His life that we may be partakers of God's Divine Life. We must be willing to die to self and allow God to possess our entire being that we may receive God's promise of a new and living way.

Each of the covenants demonstrates God working to transform man's heart in order that man be empowered to fulfill God's will. He wants a personal, intimate relationship with all His children, much like the one He had with Adam. The Father has provided for His children that His promise may be fulfilled. Jesus cautioned, *"Not everyone who says to Me, 'Lord, Lord,' shall enter the kingdom of heaven, but he who does the will of My Father in heaven. Many will say to Me in that day, 'Lord, Lord, have we not prophesied in Your name, cast out demons in Your name, and done many wonders in Your name? And then I will declare to them, 'I never knew you; depart from Me, you who practice lawlessness!'"*[35] We have been clearly instructed that God wants more than our works. He wants our hearts. The new and living way is a heart issue, and our focus must be placed on the things of above.

God has done His part. He has fulfilled His obligation of atoning mankind from sin and the effects of sin so that His Holy Spirit, His very essence, may dwell within us to draw us closer to Him. He has created a new and living way in which He dwells in the heart of man. What an awesome and glorious revelation that the very Kingdom of God dwells within us![36] The New Covenant fulfills the will of God and brings us into a fellowship and union with Him that transcends our wildest imaginations.

The Kingdom of Heaven Is at Hand

The New Covenant promise is quite simple: *"Christ in you, the hope of the glory!"*[37] We have the hope of life after death, eternal life, experiencing the intimacy and love of God forever. What we fail to recognize is the hope we have of His glory allowing us to experience His intimacy and love. God has called us to be Holy as He is Holy[38] and to be free from sin, sickness, and death that He

---

[34] Romans 12:2
[35] Matthew 7:21-23
[36] Luke 17:20-21
[37] Colossians 1:27
[38] 1 Peter 1:16

may re-establish His relationship with man as ordained from the beginning. *"And you, who once were alienated and enemies in your mind by wicked works, yet now He has reconciled in the body of His flesh through death, to present you holy, and blameless, and irreproachable in His sight."*[39] God is light and in Him there is no darkness.[40] It is our reasonable service to present ourselves holy and acceptable unto Him.

Christ is in us. Living in the New Covenant truth means standing against the lies and the works of the devil and instituting the truth of the hope and glory Christ has bestowed on us. We have been perfected through the New Covenant established by the blood of Jesus Christ and sealed by the Holy Spirit of God that we, the children of the Most High, may demonstrate and live the kingly nature of the Son of God.

The New Covenant truth has set us free from sickness, mental and emotional oppression, poverty, and death. It's a truth that will never change. Yet, to appropriate this truth into our daily lives we are called to allow His Spirit and Truth to inhabit our souls. *Christ is in you.* Have hope in the truth that He has empowered you with His Glory, His Holy Spirit, His very Kingdom to be more than a conqueror in all that you do. *Christ in you, the hope of the glory* is an eternal truth that declares that the Kingdom of God and all of His resources are at your disposal through your faith in Him! This is our New Covenant promise. Stand today with a fire within your soul that declares your inheritance of the New Covenant promise! You are Abraham's seed and an heir according to the promise![41] Step into your Promised Land today for it is flowing with the riches of God's Kingdom.

---

[39] Colossians 1:21,22
[40] 1 John 1:5
[41] Galatians 3:26-29

Reflection Verse: Colossians 1:27

Christ in you, the hope of the glory.

Thought for Reflection:

Is your Christian faith on a solid foundation? Recall that "Christ" means the anointed and His anointing. The anointing of God's Kingdom is in you! Romans 8:11 states, "But if the Spirit of Him who raised Jesus from the dead dwells in you, He who raised Christ from the dead will also give life to your mortal bodies through His Spirit who dwells in you." The New Covenant promise is God's presence, His anointing, His very Spirit dwelling in and upon you. We are told to have a confidence, an expectation of God's glory, His splendor and power dwelling in us through the Spirit of God and His anointing. Jesus said, "In this world you will have tribulation, but be of good cheer for I have overcome the world!" The power of the revelation that Christ is in you and you are hidden in God is a foundational truth that cannot be shaken. Are you unshakeable in your faith in God's New Covenant promise established for you?

Daily Confession:

Jesus Christ, the Son of God, is my refuge and my fortress; My God, in Him I will trust. Surely He has delivered me from the snares of the enemy and has covered me with His feathers. Under His wings I take my refuge; His truth is my shield and buckler. I am healed, delivered, and forgiven through the power of Jesus' blood and through the promise of the New Covenant now and forever.

3

The Will of God

Thy Kingdom come. Thy will be done on earth as it is in heaven.
Matthew 6:10

God's Will Has Not Changed

Have you ever wondered what the will of God is? The Scriptures mention "the will of God" twenty-two times in the New Testament, all referring to Christians fulfilling and knowing His will. Yet a majority of Christians today do not have a clear understanding of God's will for their lives.

Hebrews 10:36, for example, states, *"For you have need of endurance, so that after you have done the will of God, you may receive the promise."* If we do not fully understand what the will of God is, how can we do His will and receive His promise? 1 John 5:14 reminds us: *"Now this is the confidence that we have in Him, that if we ask anything according to His Will, He hears us."* And Matthew 7:21: *"Not everyone who says to Me, 'Lord, Lord,' shall enter the kingdom of heaven, but he who does the Will of My Father in heaven."* The Word of God is clear that the will of God is crucial and fundamental to our lives as Christians.

The truth of the New Covenant on which the Christian faith is established reveals the will of God. We ask "Why do some people get healed and others do not?" and "Is sickness and disease, strife and oppression the will of God?" The answers to these questions lie in the One who paid the price for our freedom and redemption. Many people are chasing the healing and not the Healer. They work so hard to believe, pray, and "do the right thing" that they make a law out of healing and fail simply to rest in the truth of God's Word and "receive" what God has already established for them through the New Covenant.

In order to understand the will of God, you will need to exercise your faith in His Word and His New Covenant. God cannot and will not change. *"For I am the LORD, I change not."* (Malachi 3:6). He has established covenants and specific spiritual principles from which all life evolves, and He will not compromise His righteousness and holiness in order to accommodate mankind. Your faith in the Word of God will allow you to fully understand your purpose and your identity through Jesus Christ.

I have heard all the arguments about the Word of God, from "Some of it is true and some is not," to "You can't believe everything the Word of God says." The truth lies in the Bible: *"All Scripture is given by inspiration of God, and is profitable for doctrine, for reproof, for correction, for instruction in righteousness."*[42] The word "ALL" means just that —ALL! John 1:14 backs it up clearly, *"And the Word became flesh and dwelt among us, and we beheld His glory, the glory as of the only begotten of the Father, full of grace and truth."*

The Greek definition of "word" is *logos*, and it means "the written word." Jesus became the written Word of God. This truth alone illustrates God's will for man. Jesus was a full demonstration of the will of God, because He only did and said what the Father told Him to do or say.[43] Further, the Scriptures state, *"I will worship toward Your holy temple, and praise Your name For Your loving kindness and Your truth; for You have magnified Your word above all Your name."*[44] To say that any words or accounts of the Bible are false is to deny the life of Jesus Christ and God's unfailing love for us. We cannot pick and choose parts of the Bible we want to believe. Either the whole thing is false or the whole thing is true. The decision is ours.

The New Covenant Reveals the Will of God

"For God so loved the world that He gave His only begotten Son, that whoever believes in Him should not perish but have everlasting life."[45] The word "life" at the end of this verse is defined as a "Zoë Life, a God kind of life, life real and genuine, a life active and vigorous, devoted to God, blessed in all."[46] The word "perish" means to destroy, to put out of the way entirely, abolish, and put an end to or to ruin.[47] "Everlasting" means "now and forever – time without beginning or end"![48] A contemporary translation of John 3:16 might read: "For God so loved the world that He gave His only begotten Son, that whoever believes in Him will not be destroyed, abolished, or ruined but will enjoy a Zoë Life, a God kind of Life, and be blessed, active, vigorous, and devoted to God, NOW and forevermore!"

---

[42] 2 Timothy 3:16
[43] John 14:10,11
[44] Psalm 138:2
[45] John 3:16
[46] Strong's Bible Dictionary
[47] Strong's Bible Dictionary
[48] Strong's Bible Dictionary

Imagine … God sent His only begotten Son not only to save the world, but also to empower His children to fulfill His will! *"He chose us in Him before the foundation of the world, that we should be holy and without blame before Him in love, having predestined us to adoption as sons by Jesus Christ to Himself, according to the good pleasure of His will."*[49]

The word "adoption" derives from the Greek word *huiothesia*, which means a placing as a son. It's a word not so much based on relationship as it is on position. A regenerated Christian receives the nature of a child of God, and in adoption he receives the position of a son of God. Therefore, *"we have received the Spirit of adoption by whom we cry out, 'Abba, Father.' The Spirit Himself bears witness with our spirits that we are children of God, and if children, then heirs – heirs of God and joint heirs with Christ."*[50] As sons and daughters of the Most High God, we have been predestined, chosen before the foundations of the world, to fulfill the will of God through the New Covenant. As a Christian, we dwell NOW in the household of God and are entitled to all of His glory and splendor.

Establishing God's Will on Earth

According to 1 John 3:5,8: *"And you know that He was manifested to take away our sins, and in Him there is no sin...He who sins is of the devil, for the devil has sinned from the beginning. For this purpose the Son of God was manifested, that He might destroy the works of the devil."* God's will in 1 John 3:8 is crystal clear. He sent His only begotten Son that He might destroy the works of the devil. The entire redemptive work of Jesus Christ was accomplished by destroying the works of the devil, and in doing so, He saved and set apart God's children!

In Jesus' own words, *"The thief does not come except to steal, and to kill, and to destroy. I have come that they may have life, and that they may have it more abundantly."*[51] The meaning for "life" here is the same as that mentioned in John 3:16. Jesus came to give all Christians abundant, God kind of life, Zoë Life, for the sole purpose of establishing Heaven on earth by destroying the works of the devil. The whole purpose of the manifestation of Jesus Christ, the Son of God, was to destroy the works of the devil that all of God's children would be healed, delivered, saved, freed and empowered to carry out the primary mission of the will of God. Jesus released His followers to go and preach that the Kingdom of

---

[49] Ephesians 1:4-5
[50] Romans 8:15-17
[51] John 10:10

Heaven is at hand![52] It is clear throughout Scripture that God's will is to establish His Kingdom here on earth.

The Will of God from the Beginning

God defined His will from the beginning of time when He first created man.

> *Then God said, 'Let Us make man in Our image, according to Our likeness; let them have dominion over the fish of the sea, over the birds of the air, and over the cattle, over all the earth and over every creeping thing that creeps on the earth.' So God created man in His own image; in the image of God He created him; male and female He created them. Then God blessed them, and God said to them, 'Be fruitful and multiply; fill the earth and subdue it; have dominion over the fish of the sea, over the birds of the air, and over every living thing that moves on the earth.*[53]

Man was created in God's image for the sole purpose of establishing a close fellowship, union, and relationship with Him that would exist forever. He created man to be a partaker of His Life. How important this relationship is to God is apparent when we remember that God and man walked together through the Garden of Eden, working together to create Heaven on earth. When Adam transgressed, that pure and perfect relationship with God was destroyed and man became separated from God. Yet God tore the veil of separation when Christ died to bring God's children back into holy relationship with Him.[54] His primary purpose and will is that every Christian abide in Him and He in them and that the intimate, perfect relationship that was established from the beginning be restored.[55]

It is through this relationship that God can fulfill the second aspect of His divine will for the body of Christ. God commanded Adam to "*be fruitful and multiply, fill the earth and subdue it.*"[56] God created man in His image to subdue and fill the earth. Subdue it from what? From satan and his works! The whole purpose of the Garden of Eden was to produce Heaven on earth. If Adam would have listened to God's command, he would have eaten of the Tree of Life,[57] stayed

---

[52] Matthew 10:7
[53] Genesis 1:26-28
[54] Matthew 27:51
[55] John 15:4
[56] Genesis 1:28
[57] Genesis 2:15

33

away from the Tree of Knowledge of Good and Evil,[58] and would have multiplied, filled, and subdued the earth from the works of the enemy. Following God's command would have allowed Adam and Eve to extend the boundaries of the Garden of Eden, and Heaven would have filled all the earth.

Since the creation of man, God's will has always been to establish Heaven on earth for the purpose of creating and establishing a perfect and pure relationship with His children. *"Then God saw everything that He had made, and indeed it was very good."* [59] From the beginning of time, everything God created was very good! Sin, disease, premature death, division, mental illness, bitterness, strife, anger, hatred, isolation, and oppression failed to exist. It was God's will that man live in love and harmony with one another partaking of His Divine Life.

God's will to establish Heaven on earth through the Garden of Eden was delayed when one man transgressed and the world fell under sin. Our good and gracious God, however, provided a way for man to overcome the transgression and sin of the flesh through the prophetic word and promise of His Son. God cursed the serpent, the devil, and assured him that one day the power and authority which he stole would be reclaimed forever! God said, *"And I will put enmity (hatred, adversity, strife) between you and the woman, and between your seed and her Seed (Jesus); He (Jesus the Redeemer) shall bruise your head, and you shall bruise His heel."*[60] By His omniscience, omnipotence, and love for creation, God put into motion through His spoken prophetic word the redemption of mankind and the reestablishment of His will on earth. Throughout history we see God striving to bring His children back under His banner, His provision, His peace, but time and again man has turned his back on God's will and become a slave to darkness and deception.

Oh, but God is so merciful and faithful! He has created a New Covenant that promises divine healing, health, and life. It is by virtue of this New Covenant that the sons and daughters of God have been empowered to fulfill and establish God's will on earth. Jesus said, *"Thy Kingdom come, Thy will be done on earth as it is already done in heaven."*[61] It is God's will to create Heaven on earth.

---

[58] Genesis 2:16
[59] Genesis 1:31
[60] Genesis 3:15 (parenthetical emphasis added)
[61] Matthew 6:10 (paraphrased)

The Will of God ~ Our Primary Mission

And the prayer of faith will save the sick, and the Lord will raise him up. And if he has committed sins, he will be forgiven."[62]

This verse demonstrates that through faith the healing promise released through Christ will raise man up from any attack of the devil. At the same time, if man has committed sins, he shall be forgiven. From Genesis to Revelation, God demonstrates that He wants to remove all sin and the effects of sin from man's spirit, soul, and body. The effects of sin are sickness and death. The salvation of God's Church, therefore, is not for the spirit alone, but also for the soul and body.

The threefold atonement for man's salvation and perfect redemption through Christ was prophesied in Isaiah 53:5: *"But He was wounded for our transgressions, He was bruised for our iniquities; the chastisement for our peace was upon Him, and by His stripes we are healed."* This verse is broken down into three different acts of atonement by Jesus Christ our Redeemer.

> First, He was wounded for our transgressions and bruised for our iniquities. This fulfills the promise of atonement for our spirits.

> Second, the chastisement of peace was upon Him. This fulfills the promise of atonement for our souls.

> And third, "through His stripes we were healed" fulfills the promise of atonement for our bodies.

The work of the Cross, the victory of Jesus' resurrection over death, and the ascension of Christ to the right hand of the Father has empowered us with the Holy Spirit of God and has permanently established His Kingdom in our lives.

God's will has always been that His people be cleansed, made holy and righteous for His name's sake, empowered to fulfill His primary mission of destroying the works of the devil, and establishing Heaven on earth. Psalm 110:1 states, *"The LORD said to my Lord, 'Sit at My right hand, until I make Your enemies Your footstool.'"* Hebrews 10:12-13 states, *"But this Man, after He had offered one sacrifice for sins forever, sat down at the right hand of God, from that time waiting until His enemies are made His footstool."* Both of these accounts demonstrate that Jesus Christ, the Son of God, is seated at the right hand of God *waiting* to return until His enemies are made His footstool. I wonder then, whose

---

[62] James 5:14-15

responsibility is it to make the Lord's enemies His footstool and prepare an atmosphere from which the glory of the Lord will be pulled into this world?

2 Peter 3:11-12 state, *"Therefore, since all these things will be dissolved, what manner of persons ought you to be in holy conduct and godliness, looking for and hastening the coming of the day of God."* "Hastening" means to desire earnestly. This idea is strengthened by the concept of preparing oneself to receive. Therefore, the Bride of Christ ought to be earnestly desiring, preparing herself for the coming of the day of the Lord, the return of the Bridegroom. Is the return of the King of kings and Lord of lords dependent upon the Bride of Christ making herself presentable to the Bridegroom? I have heard it said that there is a level of perversion to the thought that the Bridegroom is responsible for getting the Bride ready for the wedding day. Could it be that Jesus the Christ, the Bridegroom, is waiting for a people who will make His enemies His footstool, removing the blemish and stain from the Bride's wedding dress, creating a pure and beautiful expression of God's love on the wedding day?

Could it be that Jesus Christ is waiting until we, the Body of Christ, rise up against all the works of the devil? Every generation of men and women of God active in doing the will of God believed their generation would usher in the return of Jesus Christ. They believed this because they were entrenched in the fulfillment of God's will, destroying the works of the devil and preparing the Bride of Christ for His return. The demonstration of God's love flowed all around them. In reality, therefore, Heaven was open all around them. One of John G. Lakes prophecies reveals that "there will be a universal sound of praise in which angels and men, all creatures in the earth, the sea, and the sky, will eventually join, becoming one when the consciousness of the overcoming Christ has dawned upon man and possessed his very soul."[63]

We are the generation where the prophesies of the past shall come to manifestation. The will of God is that the universal sound of praise be established now in this land and in this time!

The Great Commission commands us to go into all the world teaching the Gospel of Christ.[64] The Golden Rule challenges us to do unto others as we would like done unto us.[65] In Jesus' own words, *"My food is to do the will of Him who sent Me, and to finish His work. Do you not say, 'There are still four months and then comes the harvest'? Behold, I say to you, lift up your eyes and look at the fields,*

---

[63] John G. Lake Prophesy: *John G. Lake – His Life, His Sermons, His Boldness of Faith* – page 61, Ft. Worth, TX, Kenneth Copeland Publications, Copyright 1994.
[64] Matthew 28:18-20
[65] Matthew 7:12

for they are already white for harvest! And he who reaps receives wages, and gathers fruit for eternal life, that both he who sows and he who reaps may rejoice together. For in this the saying is true: 'One sows and another reaps.' I sent you to reap that for which you have not labored; others have labored, and you have entered into their labors."[66]

Brothers and sisters, it is our responsibility to submit to the primary mission of the will of God and become co-laborers with Jesus Christ in developing, sustaining, and manifesting a culture of God's love by destroying the works of the devil.[67] That is the will of God and the calling of every proclaiming Christian in this world. Can you imagine the effect of every Christian deciding today to destroy the works of the devil? Sin, sickness, disease, premature death, strife, division, isolation, separation, and all oppression would be wiped out! People would want to be Christian, because God's provision and presence would be revealed. Are you willing to submit to the primary mission and become a co-laborer with Jesus Christ to fulfill the will of God on earth as it is already done in Heaven?

> *Be doers of the word, and not hearers only, deceiving yourselves. For if anyone is a hearer of the word and not a doer, he is like a man observing his natural face in a mirror; for he observes himself, goes away, and immediately forgets what kind of man he was. But he who looks into the perfect law of liberty and continues in it, and is not a forgetful hearer but a doer of the work, this one will be blessed in what he does. If anyone among you thinks he is religious, and does not bridle his tongue but deceives his own heart, this one's religion is useless.*[68]

God's will is that all those striving to be Christ-like utilize the power of the Holy Spirit within them to be doers of His Word and not hearers only. Be faithful and courageous. Step out into the world and begin destroying the works of the devil by proclaiming and demonstrating the truth, dominion, and power of the Word of God. We were called into the Lord's army the day we accepted Jesus as our Lord. Now is the time to stand and activate our faith by works. Let us be the generation that ushers in our King of kings and Lord of lords by keeping the enemy under Christ's feet and manifesting Heaven now.

---

[66] John 4:34-38
[67] 1 Corinthians 3:9
[68] James 1:22-27

The Kingdom of Heaven Is NOW at Hand

God's desire is to become "one" with His children. All of God's covenants with man, old and new, have been instituted to enable man to partake in God's Divine Life. Jesus stated,

> *I pray for them. I do not pray for the world but for those whom You have given Me, for they are Yours. And all Mine are Yours, and Yours are Mine, and I am glorified in them. Now I am no longer in the world, but these are in the world, and I come to You. Holy Father, keep through Your name those whom You have given Me, **that they may be one as We are**.*[69]

When the Christian faith claims this truth, there will be a shift, a transformation in the spirit realm that will establish God's Kingdom in this world. Sickness, disease, strife, and oppression are of this world, brothers and sisters in Christ, we are not! We have a new and living way that promises us a God kind of life. We have been called to be partakers in God's Divine Life to be one with the Father, the Son, and the Holy Spirit and lay hold of the New Covenant life now and forever. Arise and fight the good fight of faith and establish the will of God on earth as it is already done in Heaven.

Reflection Verse: *Matthew 6:10*

> *Your kingdom come. Your will be done on earth as it is in heaven.*

Thought for Reflection:

The will of God is to create Heaven on earth. Jesus Christ came to separate man unto God that we would be His ambassadors in this world, striving to create His Kingdom on earth NOW and forever. If it is God's will to have His Kingdom represented in this world, then who is responsible to carry out that will? Jesus defeated all the works of the devil and created a New Covenant promise that you may be partakers in God's Divine Life NOW.

Daily Confession:

For God so loved me that He gave His only begotten Son that I would not be destroyed or perish, but that I would have a life full of abundance, not only in heaven, but NOW. My Heavenly Father always leads me into triumph through Jesus my Christ.

---

[69] John 17:7-11 (emphasis added)

4

The Suffering Question

The Spirit bears witness with our spirit that we are children of God.
And if children, then heirs of God and joint heirs with
Christ, if indeed we suffer with Him, that we may also be glorified together.

Romans 8:16-17

The Doctrine of Suffering

There is a certain doctrine in the Word of God and throughout the Body of Christ, one rarely discussed or taught. Ironically, though, it yields as much power and truth to the freedom and liberty of the Christian life as does the doctrine of prosperity. This chapter stems from the revelation I received from a teaching entitled, *The Doctrine of Suffering,*[70] authored by my spiritual father and mentor, Rev. Dr. Dale M. Sides.

We look around this world, both in and out of the Church, and we see great suffering. The suffering question, in fact, is probably one of the greatest issues presented to the Church by non-Christians and Christians alike. They ask: "Why would a God who loves us allow us to suffer so much?" or "If there is a God, why is there so much suffering in this world?" The suffering question, for many people, becomes the basis and foundation of their belief and faith in God and His Living Word. The suffering question is such a powerful phenomenon that it has persuaded men to develop their own doctrine around the Word of God. It is, therefore, imperative that as children of God we understand the truth behind suffering question and how it applies to God's true will.

The doctrine of suffering is founded upon the proclamation and demonstration of the truth of the Gospel of Jesus Christ, no matter the consequences. *"Blessed are those who are persecuted for righteousness' sake, for theirs is the kingdom of heaven. Blessed are you when they revile and persecute you, and say all kinds of evil against you falsely for My sake. Rejoice and be exceedingly glad, for great is*

---

[70] Dr. Dale Sides, Doctrine of Suffering, *Liberating Partners*, LP/Tape 004 (Bedford VA: L.M.C.I).

your reward in heaven, for so they persecuted the prophets who were before you."[71]

Christians are instructed not to compromise the Word of God and be persecuted for the sake of Jesus' name. When we make the blood covenant a common thing and compromise the Gospel of Jesus Christ, we begin to live a double standard. True Christians are separated persons, separated forever unto God. Scripture demonstrates that true suffering comes from living a Christ-like life and allowing His Spirit to pour from us into the lives of others. Paul was a man who suffered for the Gospel of Jesus Christ, yet he did not suffer through sickness, disease, infirmities, or turmoil, as some would believe. Many believe that the "thorn" in Paul's flesh was a physical ailment; however, as you will see later on in this chapter, that is a deception from the enemy to twist Scripture and undermine our faith.

Paul suffered the effects of persecution. Take, for example, the account in Acts 14:19-20, which states, *"Then Jews from Antioch and Iconium came there; and having persuaded the multitudes, they stoned Paul and dragged him out of the city, supposing him to be dead. However, when the disciples gathered around him, he rose up and went into the city. And the next day he departed with Barnabas to Derbe."*

Paul was stoned to death, his weary, lifeless body then dragged by the Jews of Antioch and Iconium and dumped outside the city. The disciples gathered around Paul, activated their faith, and ministered the Spirit of Life (the promise of the New Covenant) back into Paul. The result of their faith was that Paul rose up and went into the city! Praise the Lord!

Paul was just one of many Christian martyrs. The truth is, ten out of the twelve disciples died a marytr's death. Of the two remaining, Judas hung himself and John was boiled alive and sentenced to live the remainder of his life in exile on the Island of Patmos. The doctrine of suffering is about standing up for the Gospel of Jesus Christ, not compromising the Word of God. It is about fulfilling God's will in all we do -- no matter what! The New Covenant promise hinges upon our ability to live uncompromised lives and destroy the lies of the devil.

In the book of Daniel we find three men who were persecuted and suffered for the sake of God and His Word.[72] Shadrach, Meshack, and Abednego refused to defy the God of Israel even when the consequence was death. In Daniel 3:25 we

---

[71] Matthew 5:10-12
[72] Daniel 3:1-30

see King Nebuchadnezzar looking into the furnace, astonished not only to see the three men completely intact and alive, but also a fourth man, one whom the King called the Son of God. *"Look!" he answered, "I see four men loose, walking in the midst of the fire; and they are not hurt, and the form of the fourth is like the Son of God."*[73] *And the satraps, administrators, governors, and the king's counselors gathered together, and they saw these men on whose bodies the fire had no power; the hair of their head was not singed nor were their garments affected, and the smell of fire was not on them."*[74]

The fire had no power over Shadrach, Meshack, and Abednego because the Son of God was there to protect them. The same is true today for all Christians. The fire of persecution today has no power over all those who believe in the Son of God, because the Son of God has given the very Spirit of God to empower and protect us!

The New Covenant established for all of God's children is a promise and guarantee of a life full of the riches and glory of God's Kingdom. And as believers in Jesus Christ, we must draw this truth close to our hearts and defend it with our very lives. *"For to me, to live is Christ, and to die is gain."*[75] The irony of Christianity and the fulfillment of the desire of our hearts lies in our ability to completely surrender to the Father's will. We prosper when we come to the complete understanding that it is not us who prospers, but He who has empowered us to prosper.

Jesus, the Example of True Suffering

> *The Spirit Himself bears witness with our spirit that we are children of God, and if children, then heirs of God and joint heirs with Christ, if indeed we suffer with Him, that we may also be glorified together.*[76]

We have heard this verse many times, but often without its ending. Read in its entirety, Romans 8:16-17 demonstrates that Christians will be joint heirs with Christ *"**if** indeed we suffer with Him."* The true Christian is called to suffer with Jesus. *"For to you it has been granted on behalf of Christ, not only to believe in Him, but also to suffer for His sake."*[77] True Christians are called not only to believe in Jesus Christ, but also to suffer for Him. *"If you are reproached for the*

---

[73] Daniel 3:25
[74] Daniel 3:27
[75] Philippians 1:21
[76] Romans 8:16-17
[77] Philippians 1:29

41

name of Christ, blessed are you, for the Spirit of glory and of God rests upon you."[78]

The Spirit of glory and of God rests upon us when we suffer for His namesake. The first martyr, Stephen, experienced God's glory and the heavens opened up when he refused to compromise his faith in Jesus Christ.[79] Suffering for the sake of Jesus simply means that we are not to compromise the truth of the Word of God to satisfy the lusts of this world. We are not to compromise the promises of our Heavenly Father simply because others might disagree. Jesus' persecution came from the hands of the elders, chief priests, and scribes of that day. He made the choice not to compromise God's will for His life, and He suffered terribly in order that all of mankind would be saved and empowered forever. Jesus Christ is the example of how we are to suffer with Him.

"And He took with Him Peter and the two sons of Zebedee, and He began to be sorrowful and deeply distressed. He went a little farther and fell on His face, and prayed, saying, 'O My Father, if it is possible, let this cup pass from Me; nevertheless, not as I will, but as You will.'"[80] Jesus entered into the Garden of Gethsemane in deep emotional turmoil and sorrow, seeking comfort from His Father. How easy it would have been for Jesus to slip out the backside of the Garden undetected and free from the persecution that lay ahead. Instead, He boldly proclaimed *"Father, if it is Your will, remove this cup from Me; nevertheless not My will, but Yours, be done!"* And He laid down His life for the will of the Father.

The example of Jesus' suffering is founded upon His surrendering to God's will. His betrayal and arrest demonstrate His willingness to fulfill the purpose of His calling. Jesus, the perfect example of suffering, paid a price that we do not have to duplicate. We suffer through affliction and torment because we compromise the truth of God's New Covenant, whereas Jesus suffered and died establishing the New Covenant through His blood because He did not compromise! Today's Church suffers the effects of sickness, disease, division, oppression, torment, affliction, and premature death because we have compromised the truth of the Word of God and His promise for our complete redemption. We have adopted a lie regarding the New Covenant under which we live, and as a result we suffer from our lack of faith.

---

[78] 1 Peter 4:14
[79] Acts 7:54-60
[80] Matthew 26:37,39

A distinction needs to be made about the concept of suffering and the means by which it has been twisted over time to benefit the thief, enabling him to steal, kill, and destroy.

The current suffering question established within the Church is founded upon fear, lack of knowledge, and lack of faith. It has eroded the true power of the doctrine of suffering. God did not call the Body of Christ to suffer sickness, infirmity, mental and emotional turmoil. If He called Christians to suffer in this manner, for what reason did He send His Son Jesus Christ to suffer and die for us?

The concept of suffering becomes confused when man confuses a biblical term with a worldly one. Generation after generation we have attributed the concept of biblical suffering to a worldly definition that includes sickness, disease and mental or emotional turmoil. *Suffering,* in a worldly sense, is attributed to the trials and tribulations experienced in this world. However, true biblical suffering is one of persecution and self-denial all for the name and glory of Jesus Christ. God did not create man that he should suffer at the hands of the devil. As God's children, we have been empowered with dominion, authority, and power over the enemy and his demonic kingdom that nothing by any means shall hurt us.[81]

"Let him ask in faith, with no doubting, for he who doubts is like a wave of the sea driven and tossed by the wind. For let not that man suppose that he will receive anything from the Lord."[82] We have been deceived into believing that we are to endure "worldly" suffering, and as a result we have allowed doubt and fear to enter into our confessions and beliefs about the New Covenant promise. We approach the throne of God with timidity and uncertainty, like waves of the sea driven and tossed by the wind. And we miss the inheritance of the Kingdom of God that has already been bestowed on us.

"Finally, my brethren, be strong in the Lord, and in the power of His might. Put on the whole armour of God, that you may be able to stand against the wiles of the devil."[83] The word "wiles" in this verse means to deceive or to trick, to scheme, and that is exactly what satan has done to the Body of Christ in regards to the suffering question. For centuries, the cloak of deception has covered our eyes, obscuring the truth behind suffering. We fail to see that suffering for Christ's sake means not to carry the same cross Jesus carried, but to be willing to carry our own cross, our own purpose, no matter the cost! *"But even if you should*

---

[81] Luke 10:19; paraphrased
[82] James 1:6-7
[83] Ephesians 6:10-11

suffer for righteousness' sake, you are blessed. And do not be afraid of their threats, nor be troubled."[84]

To be like Christ or a joint heir with Him, we must be willing to lay down our lives for the Father's will. Jesus is calling us to be like Him, to follow His example and suffer for righteousness' sake. One pastor took that calling to heart, and he called his parishioners to take up the mantle of suffering for Jesus Christ. The whole of his church stood and proclaimed "We are willing to die for the Gospel of Jesus Christ." However, for many these commitments proved to be very shallow. A masked gunman burst into the church and instructed them that if, "Anyone who wants to save their own life they may get up and leave the sanctuary now. However, in doing so you will renounce Jesus Christ as your Lord and Saviour. If you decide to stay, you will be killed."

Eighty percent of the church got up and left. The gunman made the call one more time stating, "This is the last call. Anyone who wants to save their own life, leave now. If you stay, I will kill you." Of the twenty percent remaining in the church, ten percent ran for safety.

With the remaining ten percent of the congregation still on their faces, the gunman removed his mask and revealed that he was their pastor. He wanted to demonstrate that taking the mantle of suffering for Christ is a heart decision, not a head decision. We are called to stand for the truth of the Gospel of Jesus Christ and not waver in our commitment.

The Deception of Suffering

It is imperative that you receive this revelation into your spirit. Please take the time to ponder and pray about this next statement:

> *We are deceived if we believe we must bear the same cross Jesus bore. That cross has already been carried.*

We live in a world dominated by sin, corruption, sickness, and death, and yet *"God so loved the world that He gave His only begotten Son that whosoever believes in Him will not be lost, ruined, or destroyed, but experience a Zoë Life, a God kind of life, a life of abundance, NOW and forever."*[85] We are called to suffer for the Gospel of Jesus Christ because we will not compromise the truth of our redemption, the truth of the New Covenant, and the gift of the Holy Spirit,

---

[84] 1 Peter 3:14
[85] John 3:16, paraphrased

who is the promise of God's presence in us. We will not be deceived into accepting the lie that we must suffer through sickness and disease, turmoil, strife, and oppression of this world. Again, this "worldly suffering" is sprirtual deception, preventing God's children from experiencing their true inheritance in this world. The real question is whether we are willing to stand faithful for the truth of the New Covenant and not grieve the Holy Spirit by compromising the blood covenant established through Jesus, our Redeemer.

Every Christian has been perfectly and completely redeemed, bought back by the atonement of Jesus Christ and the shedding of His blood, that we may become the perfect sons and daughters of the Most High God. By virtue of Christ's sacrifice, resurrection, and ascension to God's right hand, we are empowered to finish what Jesus started.

As the Body of Christ, we need to create a culture where healing is expected with as much belief as the forgiveness of sin. Sickness, sin, and death are not a part of God's plan for His children, because the Word of God states that "*God is light, and in Him there is no darkness at all.*"[86] The promise of healing has been accomplished, it is already here, and as believers in Jesus Christ it is our responsibility to activate that healing through our faith. Stop asking God to heal, because He has already done it! Instead, thank Jesus for it.

Matthew 8:17 is clear: "*He Himself (Jesus) took our infirmities and bore our sicknesses.*" The blood of Jesus Christ has rid us of all sin, sickness, infirmity, and mental and emotional turmoil. We are not to compromise this truth!

Step through the veil of deception and claim your inheritance through Jesus the Christ. As a believer in Jesus Christ you are not to be experiencing the suffering of this world, but demonstrating the glory and power of God's Kingdom in your life.[87]

False Teaching Revealed

And His disciples asked Him, saying, "Rabbi, who sinned, this man or his parents, that he was born blind?" Jesus answered, "Neither this man nor his parents sinned, but that the works of God should be revealed in him."[88]

---

[86] 1 John 1:5
[87] Galatians 3:13,14, 26-29
[88] John 9:3

Many have twisted this verse to mean that God allows a person to suffer sickness so His glory may be revealed. What they fail to understand is that God does not need man to experience "worldly" suffering in order for His glory to be displayed. This kind of thinking is no worse than believing that God's will is for us to be sick. The truth of this account is simple: Jesus' disciples asked Him *who sinned, this man or his parents, that he was born blind?*

Jesus' responsed: *"Neither this man nor his parents sinned, but that the works of God should be revealed in him."* Jesus simply revealed that sin, generational or individual, was not the cause for this man to be blind from birth. The concept that God had something to do with the man's blindness is a result of twisting Jesus' response. The truth is that this man was born blind because of the fallen world in which he was conceived, but it was God, through His love, mercy, and glory, who healed and restored his sight. How much different is this blind man than the lame man at the Gate of Beautiful or the lame man at the pool of Bethseda? All were a result of a fallen world and all were a result of God's unfailing love and power being released to demonstrate that His Kingdom – the Kingdom of Heaven – is truly at hand!

This is but one example of how suffering is misunderstood in the context of God's New Covenant promise. The enemy has twisted several other Biblical teachings as well in order to confuse us and to steal the truth. It is our responsibility to divide, rightly, the Word of God and to firmly establish His truth in our spirits, souls, and bodies.

The Faith of Job

The devil has twisted the Word of God to deceive Christians into believing that suffering oppression, sickness, and torment are part of God's will for the testing of our faith. One of these accounts is found in the book of Job. How often we have heard suffering Christians recite: *"Naked I came from my mother's womb, and naked shall I return there. The Lord gave and the Lord has taken away; Blessed be the name of the Lord."*[89] It's all too common for people to relate their lives to Job's and justify their ailments or struggles based on how Job himself suffered. In so doing, they confess it as God's will that they suffer and that when and if God is ready, He will heal them. What a lie from hell! Jesus, the perfect Lamb of God, was the demonstration of God's perfect will, and through His will He has shown that His timing is NOW for the release of His glory.

---

[89] Job 1:21

The Book of Job is the earliest written book in God's Word. Job was a man who lived well before there was a written Word of God, and he was not a Hebrew (meaning he did not belong to the covenant of Abraham). Truth be known, God really did not even have an obligation to protect or cover Job, and yet we find that God placed a hedge of protection around Job because Job was a good man. Job knew God existed, through creation and all that life provided, he feared God and was blameless and upright – a moral man. Hence, God showed mercy and favor on him.

Job 1:7-8 seems to be a place where many people develop the conclusion that God ordered Job to be sick.

> *Now there was a day when the sons of God came to present themselves before the LORD, and satan also came among them. And the LORD said to satan, 'From where do you come?' So satan answered the LORD and said, 'From going to and fro on the earth, and from walking back and forth on it.' Then the LORD said to satan, 'Have you considered My servant Job, that there is none like him on the earth, a blameless and upright man, one who fears God and shuns evil?' So satan answered the LORD and said, 'Does Job fear God for nothing? Have You not made a hedge around him, around his household, and around all that he has on every side? You have blessed the work of his hands, and his possessions have increased in the land. But now, stretch out Your hand and touch all that he has, and he will surely curse You to Your face!' So the LORD said to satan, 'Behold, all that he has is in your power; only do not lay a hand on his person.' Then Satan went out from the presence of the LORD.*[90]

In this account, God is revealing what the devil had already planned to accomplish. *"And the Lord said to satan, 'from where do you come'*[91]*...Have you considered My servant Job?"*[92] Both questions are rhetorical. The Lord was and is omniscient, and He knew from where satan came and upon whom he was preying. God knows everything! He knew satan was scheming to kill, steal, and destroy everything Job possessed.

Satan responded to God, *"Does Job fear God for nothing*[93]*...Have you not made a hedge around him, around his household, and around all that he has on every side?"*[94] The devil is shrewd. He was making sure he had the legal right to attack Job, to build a stronghold of oppression in his life and destroy all he had. The

---

[90] Job 1:6-12
[91] Job 1:7
[92] Job 1:8
[93] Job 1:9

Lord responded: *"Behold, all that he has is in your power; only do not lay a hand on his person."*[95] Once again, God confirmed what was already a truth. He was saying to the devil, "Is not Job already in your power? Has he not already sinned, allowing you to come against him?" Again, a rhetorical question, and one by which the devil's scheme and deception were revealed. God was making the enemy aware that He knows what is going on. God did not point Job out to the devil; He is not in the business of destroying people's lives, but in rebuilding, restoring, reconciling, and healing.

Let no one say when he is tempted, "I am tempted by God"; for God cannot be tempted by evil, nor does He Himself tempt anyone. But each one is tempted when he is drawn away by his own desires and enticed. Then, when desire has conceived, it gives birth to sin; and sin, when it is full-grown, brings forth death.[96]

The word "tempt" stems from the Greek word *peirazo*, which means to test one maliciously, craftily by putting to proof his feelings or judgments; to try or test one's faith, virtue, character, by enticement to sin or through adversity.[97] God cannot tempt or test one maliciously through adversity. God is love, and there is no darkness in Him.[98] God is the giver of Life, not death. God says, *"Be not deceived, for every good gift and every perfect gift is from above, and comes down from the Father of lights, with whom there is no variation or shadow of turning."*[99] God could not have ordered satan to attack Job, because darkness is not in God! God does not need sickness, disease, or strife to prove his point or get someone's attention. Just ask Saul.

The truth found in Job Chapter One is that God brought the devil's scheme to light, revealing that Job had committed sin which allowed the devil to prey upon him. First Peter 5:8 states, *"Be sober, be vigilant; because your adversary the devil walks about like a roaring lion, seeking whom he may devour."* Job 3:25 informs us that Job lived in fear. *"For the thing I greatly feared has come upon me, and what I dreaded has happened to me."*[100] Job may have been a moral man, but he lived in fear. Fear is a sin, and living in fear was the reason the devil was preying upon Job and why God stated, *"Behold all that he (Job) has is in your power."*

---

[94] Job 1:10
[95] Job 1:12
[96] James 1:13-18
[97] Strong's Concordance Dictionary
[98] 1 John 1:6; 1 John 4:7
[99] James 1:17
[100] Job 3:25

Job allowed the continual attack to occur when he cursed the day he was born. He cursed his very own life![101] *Death and life are in the power of the tongue, and those who love it will eat its fruit.*[102] Out of his own mouth Job gave the devil permission to destroy all he had possessed.

In Job Chapters 3-38 we find men discussing the things of God, men who had neither the knowledge nor the understanding of God's covenant promises. A careful reading of these accounts reveals that the same statements made from the lack-of-knowledge perspective are the same statements so frequently made today. The schemes of the devil have not changed; they are just more refined and shrewd.

God steps into the picture for the first time in Job 38. His first question is *"Who is this who darkens counsel by words without knowledge?"* God is talking about the nonsense with which Job and his three friends were conversing. The real revelation in chapters 3-38 is this: Learn what not to say or do. We can learn from others' mistakes. Job and his friends spoke from a place of ignorance, a lack of knowledge, and it was this lack of knowledge for which Job had to repent in order to be delivered from the oppression of the devil.

Job 42 describes Job's deliverance. *"Then Job answered the LORD and said: I know that You can do everything, and that no purpose of Yours can be withheld from You. You asked, 'Who is this who hides counsel without knowledge?' Therefore I have uttered what I did not understand, things too wonderful for me, which I did not know. Listen, please, and let me speak; You said, I will question you, and you shall answer Me. I have heard of You by the hearing of the ear, but now my eye sees You. Therefore I abhor myself, and repent in dust and ashes."*[103] Once Job acknowledged his ignorance and his false words, he repented and God restored twice that which Job had lost. God is not the inflictor of suffering, He is the Great Deliverer.

To use Job in relation to the condition of suffering today is to be misguided and uninformed. Job's situation must be viewed in the light of the truth of the New Covenant. It is there we will see that God is the giver of life and that He desires to see all of His children free from the works and lies of His adversary, the devil.

---

[101] Job 3:1
[102] Proverbs 18:21
[103] Job 42

Paul's Thorn in the Flesh

Likewise, the assertion that Paul's "thorn in the flesh" was that he suffered from some form of ailment or sickness is not founded upon accurate study of the Word of God. This, too, is a twisted truth, a deception of the Word of God. Many have said Paul's "thorn in the flesh" was ophthalmis, an eye ailment that caused repulsive discharge and great eye pain, a foundation based on Acts 9 with Saul's conversion to "Paul," and on Galatians 6:11, which states, *"See with what large letters I have written to you with my own hand!"* Both such Scriptural references fall far short of substantitating that Paul suffered from an eye ailment.

Saul's conversion and his temporary blindness caused by looking on Christ's Glory was healed by the blood of Jesus Christ at the Cross. Ananias, a disciple of the Lord, had been commanded to impart faith and God's blessing of healing into Saul's eyes.[104] *"Immediately there fell from his (Paul) eyes something like scales, and he received his sight at once."*[105]

The healing blessing, appropriated through faith in the blood of the New Covenant, does not bring about partial healings. Paul was completely healed. The argument, however, is that Paul could not have received complete healing, because if he had he would have had no need to write to the Galatians "with large letters." Again, to make this assertion takes a great leap from a twisted truth.

Paul was not using the word "letter" to denote or bring attention to a "letter" of the alphabet, but in the "letter" or document that he had written to the Galatian church. The Greek definition of "letter" is *gamma*, and it means any writing; a document; or record.[106] The word *gamma* is also found in 2 Corinthians 3:6, which states, *"the letter kills, but the spirit gives life."*

What's more, the word "large" here derives from the Greek *pelikos*, which means a quantitive form; as in how much, not how big.[107] Paul's letter, therefore, was quantitatively large. It was lengthy. Clearly, Paul is saying that his letters (documents, writings) are large (quantity), or lengthy. Nowhere in Scripture can we substantiate an allegation that Paul's "thorn" was actually eye disease.
2 Corinthians 12:7-10 we are told what Paul's "thorn in the flesh" was:

> *And lest I should be exalted above measure by the abundance of the revelations, a thorn in the flesh was given to me, a messenger of Satan to*

---

[104] Acts 9:11,12
[105] Acts 9:18
[106] Strong's Concordance Dictionary
[107] Strong's Concordance Dictionary

buffet me, lest I be exalted above measure. Concerning this thing I pleaded with the Lord three times that it might depart from me. And He said to me, "My grace is sufficient for you, for My strength is made perfect in weakness." Therefore most gladly I will rather boast in my infirmities, that the power of Christ may rest upon me. Therefore I take pleasure in infirmities, in reproaches, in needs, in persecutions, in distresses, for Christ's sake. For when I am weak, then I am strong.

Read verse 7 again: *"And lest I should be exalted above measure by the abundance of the revelations, a thorn in the flesh was give to me, a messenger of satan to buffet me."* The thorn in Paul's flesh was a messenger of satan sent to buffet him from receiving the abundance of revelation from God. Why would God put a thorn in Paul's flesh to prevent him from receiving more of His revelation?

Further, the phrase "thorn in the flesh" has been used in God's Word to denote persecution or strife from others.

> *"But if you do not drive out the inhabitants of the land from before you, then it shall be that those whom you let remain shall be irritants in your eyes and <u>thorns in your sides</u>, and they shall harass you in the land where you dwell."* Numbers 33:55 (emphasis added).

> And Joshua 23:13: *"Know for certain that the LORD your God will no longer drive out these nations from before you. But they shall be snares and traps to you, and <u>scourges on your sides and thorns in your eyes</u>, until you perish from this good land which the LORD your God has given you."* (emphasis added)

> *"But the sons of rebellion shall <u>all be as thorns</u>."* 2 Samuel 23:6 (emphasis added).

Without exception, the "thorns" are personalities or people who laid snares (traps) and who were, overall, irritants to God's chosen people. Similarly, Paul's "thorn" also clearly was stated, "a messenger of satan." Paul's "thorn" was clearly the evil works and persecution of man that buffeted him. Everywhere Paul went he was pummeled by the persecution of man. Assuming, for the sake of argument, that Paul's "thorn" was an eye ailment or some form of sickness, how could such a condition buffet Paul? The word *buffet* here means "to strike with the fist or to give one a blow with the fist."[108]

---

[108] Strong's Concordance Dictionary

Throughout his writings, Paul defined the thorn in his flesh as a messenger of satan that used man's evil works to persecute him. If Paul had suffered from such sickness or disease, why did he not mention it in his accounts of the buffetings he endured? *In stripes above measure, in prisons more frequently, in deaths often. From the Jews five times I received forty stripes minus one. Three times I was beaten with rods; once I was stoned; three times I was shipwrecked; a night and a day I have been in the deep; in journeys often, in perils of waters, in perils of robbers, in perils of my own countrymen, in perils of the Gentiles, in perils in the city, in perils in the wilderness, in perils in the sea, in perils among false brethren; in weariness and toil, in sleeplessness often, in hunger and thirst, in fastings often, in cold and nakedness - besides the other things, what comes upon me daily: my deep concern for all the churches.*[109]

Paul mentioned also that he was *"reviled," "persecuted"* (1 Cor.4:12), *"defamed," "made as the filth of the world...the offscouring of all things unto this day"* (v.13). He endured much for the advancement of the Kingdom of God. Were it not for God's grace, Paul would have died sooner, because, in his own words, he "died often."[110] The claim that Paul's "thorn" and sufferings were a form of sickness is a lie to keep God's children sick, oppressed, and dying. We have tried to justify our sicknesses and diseases by twisting God's Word, when His Word is very clear that we have a New Covenant under which to live, one promising health, prosperity, and abundance!

The issue of suffering is a pervasive problem in the body of Christ because we have a difficult time explaining why some people are healed and others are not. Seeking comfort, we comb the Word for an inkling that sickness is justified. The devil used Scripture to tempt Jesus in the wilderness. He does the same to us today. Nowhere under the New Covenant established by the blood of Jesus Christ does the Word suggest we need to suffer sickness or oppression. Indeed, the Word of God instructs us to take authority over it in the Name of Jesus Christ!

Jesus Rebukes Worldly Suffering

We are called to suffer as Christ suffered, not to bare His Cross again. Jesus Christ already paid the full price for our complete redemption. We no longer need to walk that road. Praise the Lord!

---

[109] 2 Corinthians 11: 23-28
[110] 2 Corinthians 11:23

Jesus, Himself, conveyed to all that suffering is not through sickness, disease, or mental or emotional turmoil in the account of the young boy with epilepsy. [111]

> *Lord, have mercy on my son, for he is an epileptic and **suffers severely**; for he often falls into the fire and often into the water. So I brought him to Your disciples, but they could not cure him." Then Jesus answered and said, 'O faithless and perverse generation, how long shall I be with you? How long shall I bear with you? Bring him here to Me.' And Jesus rebuked the demon, and he came out of him; and the child was cured from that very hour. Then the disciples came to Jesus privately and said, 'Why could we not cast him out?' So Jesus said to them, 'Because of your unbelief; for assuredly, I say to you, if you have faith as a mustard seed, you will say to this mountain, 'Move from here to there,' and it will move; and nothing will be impossible for you.'"*

Here was a man whose son had suffered greatly at the hands of the devil. Jesus rebuked the demon, and it came out of the boy, and then He rebuked his disciples and followers because they failed to activate their faith in accordance with Jesus' teaching in order to remove the boy's affliction. *"O faithless and perverse generation, how long shall I be with you?"* Jesus asked. *"How long shall I bear with you?"* At some point, believers must activate their faith in the Word and liberate themselves from the deceptive affliction and torment of this world.

"Now the Lord is the Spirit; and where the Spirit of the Lord is, there is liberty."[112] The Spirit of the Lord lives and dwells in you. Be free, therefore, from the veil of deception and live in the victory of our Lord Jesus Christ!

Suffering as a Spiritual Weapon

The Word of God is abundantly clear on the topic of suffering. The problem does not lie in God communicating His truth, His promises and His principles to us; the problem lies in the Christian's attitude in comprehending and applying His Word. Our Father has provided us with protection from deception, yet the Church continues to suffer under the devil's hand. Biblical suffering, we need to know, is a weapon at our disposal for destroying the works of our adversary. However, the enemy has twisted its purpose to inversely destroy the Body of Christ and the New Covenant promise. The Word of God states, *"since Christ suffered for us in the flesh, arm yourselves also with the same mind, for he who*

---

[111] Matthew 17:15-20 (emphasis added)
[112] 2 Corinthians 3:17

has suffered in the flesh has ceased from sin, that he no longer should live the rest of his time in the flesh for the lusts of men, but for the will of God." [113]

Christians are advised to arm themselves with the same mind and attitude toward suffering that Christ endured for us. Suffering for Jesus' namesake means we no longer live in the flesh, for the lusts of men, but for the will of God. Praise God for His grace and everlasting love! If Christians choose to suffer for God's truth and refrain from compromising that truth, no longer will we live in lust. God desires that our suffering be generated as a weapon against the enemy's lies and for creation of heaven on earth. Suffering in the Word of God advances the Gospel of Jesus Christ, and that is the Good News!

And they overcame him(Satan) by the blood of the Lamb and by the word of their testimony, and they did not love their lives to the death. [114] God calls the Christian to love not life unto death. He is waiting for a people who are willing to lay down their lives for Him. Not just a call to martyrdom, it is a call away from conformity to this world, to be transformed by the renewing of our minds through Him. We are being called to die to ourselves and to this world, to suffer for Christ's sake.

Therefore submit to God. Resist the devil and he will flee from you. [115] Suffering becomes a spiritual weapon when it is an act of submission to God and His truth, and the devil will flee only when we resist his temptations, our flesh, and this world. We must take a stand to suffer for Christ and a stand against compromising our souls for the sake of avoiding persecution. Just as it was with Paul, God's grace is sufficient, for His strength is made perfect in our weaknesses. Praise God!

The Kingdom of Heaven IS NOW at Hand

Christians today suffer sickness, disease, infirmity, and emotional turmoil because they have compromised the established and sealed New Covenant promise. I truly believe that if we get back to living a life that demonstrates the Father's truth, power, and love without compromise, no matter the consequence "worldly" suffering at the hands of darkness will cease to exist. It is time we create a culture where God's Living Word and New Covenant promises have dominion over all things, where His glorious Spirit possesses man's whole being – spirit, soul, and body. It is here that the suffering question will no longer

---

[113] 1 Peter 4: 1-2
[114] Revelations 12:11
[115] James 4:7

destroy man's faith and life, but he will be empowered and edified through Christ in him.

Dear brothers and sisters in Christ, we will not experience Christ's victory until our souls arrive at the place where we are willing to die for our faith. When we reach that degree of consecration and determination, when we're no longer compromising the Word and the promise established through God's Son, then, and only then, will the Kingdom of Heaven be experienced and the supernatural power of God be released.

Reflection Verse: *Romans 8:16-17*

> *The Spirit bears witness with our spirit that we are children of God.*
> *And if children, then heirs – heirs of God and joint heirs with*
> *Christ, if indeed we suffer with Him, that we may also be glorified together.*

Thought for Reflection:

The suffering question is answered by the purpose of Jesus Christ and His complete sacrifice for all of mankind. Was all that Jesus endured done in vain that you must suffer the same affliction and torment that He bore on the Cross? True healing and deliverance are accomplished when revelation of the suffering question establishes a resolve to stand upon the promise of the New Covenant established by the blood of Jesus Christ and sealed by the Holy Spirit.

Daily Confession:

I am a child of God and joint heir with Jesus Christ! I have unspeakable joy in times of trial and tribulation because my faith and belief in the New Covenant promise is strong, unwavering. No longer will I be tormented or suffer by the works of a defeated foe. I will torment him and his defeated kingdom by demonstrating the Kingdom of God in thought, word, and deed.

5

Moving Past the Cross

*But God who is rich in mercy, because of His great love with which
He loved us, even when we were dead in trespasses, made us alive
together with Christ, and raised us up together, and
made us sit together in the heavenly places in Christ Jesus.*

Ephesians 2:4-6

A "Cross" Religion

It is with the utmost care that I desire to communicate this next chapter. The accomplishment of Jesus at the Cross is, without a doubt, vital to our salvation and freedom of being perfectly redeemed and sanctified unto God. However, what we must also realize is that it was but one step in the whole purpose of Jesus Christ. Unfortunately, the majority of the Christian faith has stayed focused on only one aspect of the whole purpose and gift of God's Son to mankind. In essence, we have come to the foot of the Cross and never left. As the Body of Christ we have been commissioned to move beyond the Cross and promote a movement of the Gospel for Jesus Christ. The Cross was not the end, but the beginning for God's Kingdom to advance throughout this world.

Our traditions speak of the resurrection and acknowledge that Jesus is Lord, but we have yet to step into the complete victory and position of authority that His resurrection and ascension established. Jesus' ministry has a five-fold purpose. Throughout Scripture the number five is representative of grace, demonstrating that God's only begotten Son was the fulfillment of God's grace upon this world.

Of the steps in Jesus' ministry, the first was accomplished when the Word was made flesh. Jesus' life is an epitome of God's will for this earth. Scripture states, *"And the Word became flesh and dwelt among us, and we beheld His glory, the glory as of the only begotten of the Father, full of grace and truth."*[116] Jesus was clear when He said He only did what the Father told Him to do,[117] thereby fulfilling and demonstrating the will of God through His life as the Son of Man. His life in the flesh also positioned Him as our High Priest in the Heavenly

---

[116] John 1:14
[117] John 5:19,20

Places because He endured every temptation of the flesh and overcame them all.[118]

The second step of Jesus' five-fold ministry was the sacrifice of Jesus on the Cross, where He endured suffering, rejection, pain, and bloodshed for all of mankind. Having become the curse for us, Jesus redeemed us from the curse of the law in order that the blessing of God's Kingdom might come upon those who believe and that we might receive the promise of His Spirit through faith.[119] It is through His sacrifice and the blood of Jesus that we have been bought back at a price. The Perfect Lamb of God surrendered His very life that we may be perfectly atoned, forgiven, and given a New Covenant from which to live.

The third step of Jesus' five-fold ministry was His death. His death represents the battle. In death Jesus was made to descend into hell to reclaim all that Adam had lost. He disarmed the principalities and powers and made a public spectacle of them, triumphing over them in His death, reconciling mankind back to the Father.[120] Through the death of Jesus, the kingdom of darkness was destroyed forever and God's Kingdom once again was established in this world.

Jesus' resurrection was the fourth step in His ministry, providing a complete and utter victory and triumph over the kingdom of darkness. The Resurrection established a living King at the throne of God and eternal life for all who dare to believe. Death was conquered and the veil of separation between God and man was completely destroyed, allowing man to establish once again an intimate, personal, and eternal relationship with the Father through His Holy Spirit abiding in us. *For the same Spirit of Him who rose Jesus from the dead dwells in you and giving life to your mortal body through His Spirit who dwells in you.*[121] It was through the resurrection of Jesus Christ that satan's power over mankind was completely destroyed. We have been liberated by the Spirit of God to live in Resurrection Power in all that we do. We were crucified with Christ, resurrected with Christ, and are seated with Christ in the Heavenly places. We are more than conquerors through Him who loves us!

The fifth step of Jesus' five-fold ministry was His ascension to the right hand of the Father. The Ascension served to empower the Body of Christ with the living Spirit of God that we might exercise Kingdom living in this world.[122] The Bible is clear that the whole purpose of Jesus' life, crucifixion, death, and resurrection

---

[118] Hebrews 8:26,27
[119] Galatians 3:13
[120] Colossians 2:15; 2 Corinthians 5:17-21
[121] Romans 8:11
[122] Acts 2:33

was to destroy all the works of the devil, redeeming and atoning mankind, that we would be purified to receive His Holy Spirit. The work of the Cross was not the end, but the beginning, ushering in the very essence of God to dwell in His people.

Yet the Word of God is clear that Jesus' ministry is still incomplete. Jesus' last call will sound the moment He returns as King of kings and Lord of lords and takes His position at Mount Zion for the millennial rule. All that Jesus endured in His life – the torture, persecution, the ultimate sacrifice, death, resurrection and ascension – were necessary so God's Spirit could be poured out for His children. Christ's mission was to reestablish mankind as God's own sons and daughters and to empower His children for the completion of His will on earth.

As the body of Christ, we have failed to comprehend the true revelation and the fullness of Jesus' ministry. Much of our faith lies at the foot of the Cross. We are shrouded by darkness, having allowed suffering, pain, rejection, isolation, sin, sickness, and death to overcome and possess us. We've lost the understanding and truth of who we are today through Jesus Christ. *God who is rich in mercy, because of His great love with which He loved us, even when we were dead in trespasses, made us alive together with Christ, and raised us up together, and made us sit together in the heavenly places in Christ Jesus.*[123]

Jesus Christ is alive! He has risen indeed! Our Lord and Savior sits at the right hand of the Father, interceding on our behalf, loving us with a holy, perfect kind of love that is unshakeable and unconditional. We are invited to be like Christ and take our position as ambassadors for Christ right here on earth, by and through our fellowship with the Holy Spirit. We were selected and positioned as sons and daughters of God to rule as kings and priests of this world and exercise the Kingdom of Heaven in our daily lives. *For if by one man's offense death reigned through the one, much more abundance of grace and the gift of righteousness will reign in life for those who believe through the One, Jesus Christ.*[124]

Indeed, it was Adam who brought about the offense that allowed death, through sin, to enter and control man's life. It is only by the Father's grace that death was conquered by the resurrection of His only Son. We were given the gift of complete righteousness through Jesus Christ. Rise up from the Cross and lay hold of the revelation of who you are in Christ Jesus! We have been invited to partake in a life of victory, triumph, and authority. As King David said to Goliath, *"for*

---

[123] Ephesians 2:4-6
[124] Romans 5:17

the battle is the Lord's, and He will give you into our hands."[125] The battle is the Lord's. He has achieved victory through His Son, Jesus Christ! You have victory in your life, because Jesus has gone before your trials and won your battles. Be of good cheer, Jesus has already overcome the world![126]

Perfected Through Him

Those who have made the decision to confess Jesus Christ as their Lord and Savior have been born again, separated unto God. The moment we experienced rebirth, the spirit man, the very essence of our lives, are born again unto the glory and righteousness of God. Our spirits come into oneness with the Holy Spirit of God, forever transformed, altered unto perfection, and set apart unto Him. 1 Corinthians 12:3 states, *"No one can say that Jesus is Lord except by the Holy Spirit."* We cannot confess that Jesus is our Lord without the faith of the Holy Spirit. Therefore, when we confess that Jesus Christ is Lord of our lives, God's Holy Spirit enters into our spirits and renews our hearts, separating us unto God's heavenly glory.[127]

In order to fully understand what it means to be perfected through Jesus Christ we need to understand that we are a triune being, ultimately created in the image of God. That is, we are made up of a spirit, soul, and body. [128] The spirit is the heart of man[129] and it is where the life of man resides.[130] It is the place where we have contact with the spirit realm[131] and where the will of God is established forever.[132] The soul is place of the mind. It is the center where our intellect,[133] imagination,[134] decision-making,[135] free will and emotions reside.[136] The body is the temple of God[137] and the house of the physical senses designed for a life in this world. Over time, we have lost the true depth and meaning of who we are in Jesus Christ because we limit ourselves to our physical bodies and the five senses. We have based our faith on a foundation that rests on our own souls and

---

[125] 1 Samuel 17:47
[126] John 16:33
[127] Titus 3:4-7
[128] 1 Thessalonians 5:23; Hebrews 4:12
[129] 1 Corinthians 2:9-11
[130] Genesis 2:6
[131] 2 Peter 1:21
[132] Romans 7:15-16
[133] Romans 12:2
[134] 2 Corinthians 10:5
[135] Psalm 139:14
[136] James 5:17; Acts 14:15
[137] 1 Corinthians 6:19

bodies. We have allowed senses and emotions to rule our faith, and in so doing, man's spirit has been quenched, prohibited from truly releasing the manifested glory of God. The perfected spirit, however, lies idly by, it's union with the Holy Spirit of God waiting for our minds and emotions to line up. *For by one offering He has perfected forever those who are being sanctified.*[138]

It is through the spirit that the breath of God created us in His image. We were created to live in the spirit realm. Adam was able to fellowshipped with, walked alongside of, and interacted with the Father of all creation. It was a close, personal relationship because Adam was created first and foremost a spiritual being. When he transgressed, the spiritual connection, the Holy Spirit, was broken and Adam (and thereafter mankind) was left to live on his own.

However, the instinct of the spirit of man is to stand righteous before the Creator, to interact and be intimate with Abba Father. It's an instinct that remains largely unchanged, because the cry that resonates from every human heart is to be connected with the Great I Am. It is God's Spirit speaking to ours that brings us to the point of transformation to become new creations in Christ, born again, refined, and renewed by the Holy Spirit. The innermost part of us aligns with His image, and His heavenly glory is forever established the moment Jesus becomes Lord of our lives. The born-again experience is a miraculous process by which regeneration of spirit sets into motion the regeneration of our whole being, where soul and body align with spirit to enable God's fullness and glory to be experienced.

Jesus demonstrated the truth of the born-again experience in His interaction with Nicodemus, a Pharisee and ruler of the Jews. Nicodemus came to Jesus one night and said to Him, "*Rabbi, we know that You are a teacher come from God; for no one can do these signs that You do unless God is with him.*" *Jesus answered and said to him, "Most assuredly, I say to you, unless one is born again, he cannot see the kingdom of God." Nicodemus said to Jesus, "How can a man be born when he is old? Can he enter a second time into his mother's womb and be born?"*

Jesus answered, "Most assuredly, I say to you, unless one is born of water and the Spirit, he cannot enter the kingdom of God. That which is born of the flesh is flesh, and that which is born of the Spirit is spirit. Do not marvel that I said to you, 'You must be born again.' The wind blows where it wishes, and you hear the

---

[138] Hebrews 10:14

sound of it, but cannot tell where it comes from and where it goes. So is everyone who is born of the Spirit.[139]

The "new creation" is born when man's spirit becomes one with God's Holy Spirit. *Therefore, if anyone is in Christ, he is a new creation; old things have passed away; behold, all things have become new.*[140] The old sin nature is destroyed by our spirits' regeneration through the Holy Spirit that we may enter into His courts without blemish. It is through this "born again" experience that the battlefield is established between our flesh and the regenerated spirit within us. We are encouraged not to be conformed to this world, but to be transformed by the renewing our minds that our souls and spirits may become one with the Holy Spirit, releasing the Spirit of God through us.

Releasing the Spirit of God in Us

God's Word clearly illustrates that for man to dwell in the secret place of the Lord, thereby releasing His Holy Spirit through us, we must be one with Him. Jesus said, *"Abide in Me and I in you that if you abide in Me, and My words abide in you, you will ask what you desire, and it shall be done for you."*[141] God desires that we become partakers of His inheritance in this world, that we represent His Kingdom in every aspect of our lives. We are born again, a regenerated people, through Jesus Christ and the Holy Spirit of God, that we may be more than conquerors because *Greater is He who is in us than he who is in the world.*[142] The Holy Spirit at one with us is the perfection of Christ Jesus in us. Yet the process of perfection takes place between soul and body, both of which must come under the authority and rule of the Holy Spirit. A process of sanctification occurs to our souls and to the thoughts and emotions we hold in our minds. We are called to *cleanse ourselves from all filthiness of the flesh and spirit, perfecting holiness in the fear of God.*[143]

Our responsibility is to draw near to God and the truth of His Word to allow the perfection to be released. Sickness, disease, turmoil, strife, and oppression cannot exist when we are in the holy presence and glory of God. We must press into His divine power, which *has given us all things that pertain to life and godliness, through the knowledge of Him who called us by glory and virtue, by which have been given to us exceedingly great and precious promises, that through these you*

---

[139] John 3:1-8
[140] 2 Corinthians 5:17
[141] John 15:4,7
[142] 1 John 4:4
[143] 2 Corinthians 1:7

may be partakers of the divine nature, having escaped the corruption that is in the world through lust.[144] It is this new divine nature that allows us to sit with Christ in heaven and to have at our disposal and for our use all power and authority of Christ Himself.[145]

He who is joined to the Lord is one spirit with Him[146]*and,* therefore, has the privilege to exercise the authority of being seated at the right hand of the Father. Jesus has been raised from the dead and seated at the right hand of the Father in the heavenly places, *far above all principality and power and might and dominion, and every name that is named, not only in this age but also in that which is to come. And He (The Father) put all things under His (Jesus) feet, and gave Him to be head over all things to the church, which is His body, the fullness of Him who fills all in all.*[147] We are the Body of Christ, and the fullness of Jesus Christ resides in us. And because we are the fullness of Jesus Christ, all things are under our feet and all spiritual blessings in the heavenly places are ours to appropriate for His glory.

To be Christ-like, then, is not only a goal, it's the foundation of Christianity. It's not a religion, but a promise and a truth established in eternal life. Christianity is much more than a belief system; it's a way of life, a *knowing*, a living in the fullness of God's promise now and forever. It is a relationship with the living God, who has blessed us by separating us unto Him and making us one with Him. Our ability to release God's manifested glory – His Zoë life – through our own life depends on how we bring our souls and bodies into alignment with His Spirit.

Christianity ~ Moving Past the Cross

There is perhaps no better demonstration of Christianity as a way of living in God's promise than the account of the lame man beside the pool of Bethesda.[148] *The multitude of sick people, the blind, lame, and the paralyzed, laid waiting for the moving of the water. For an angel went down at a certain time into the pool and stirred up the water; then whoever stepped in first, after the stirring of the water, was made well of whatever disease he had.*[149] This account is similar to what we experience in the body of Christ today. People are sick, blind, lame, tormented, oppressed and paralyzed, laying in wait for God to move so that they

---

[144] 2 Peter 1:3-4
[145] Colossians 3:1-3
[146] 1 Corinthians 6:17
[147] Ephesians 1:20-23
[148] John 5:1-17
[149] John 5:1

may be made well. Today's Church is making the same mistake as the lame man and all the others who were sick and tormented at pool of Bethesda. We are waiting for a movement, a stirring of the water. And as we wait, we fail to see the Promise that stands right before our eyes.

Now a certain man was there who had an infirmity thirty-eight years. When Jesus saw him lying there, and knew that he already had been in that condition a long time, He said to him, "Do you want to be made well?" The sick man answered Him, "Sir, I have no man to put me into the pool when the water is stirred up; but while I am coming, another steps down before me." Jesus said to him, "Rise, take up your bed and walk." And immediately the man was made well, took up his bed, and walked.

Jesus, the Messiah, the Miracle-Worker, the Promise, was in the midst of all these sick and tormented people, and yet their attention was on the stirring of the water, not on Jesus. The lame man whom Jesus healed did not even know who Jesus was: *"But the one who was healed did not know who it was, for Jesus had withdrawn, a multitude being in that place."*[150] How similar are we today to this lame man? We are "working" for a healing, deliverance, or miracle rather than resting in the knowledge that Jesus Christ has already accomplished the victory. By and through His flesh, Jesus destroyed the veil that separated man from the fullness of God. We need simply to step through the ripped veil and into His presence in order to seek His beautiful face and release His manifested glory.

Does it all seem unrealistic? Bear in mind that the whole foundation of Christianity is developed upon the supernatural. Christians have the power and the authority to change and transform circumstances in their lives. We possess the same Spirit that raised Jesus from the dead, the Holy Spirit of God.[151] The choice is ours to *fight the good fight of faith and lay hold of eternal life*[152] or to become lambs led to the slaughter. We must trust in the truth of our redeemed lives and exercise, by faith, the authority and power already bestowed upon all those who believe through the Spirit of Christ that dwells within us!

A Consciousness of the Overcoming Jesus Christ

The key to moving past the Cross is to develop a confidence in the overcoming Jesus Christ who has empowered us with the Holy Spirit to be partakers of His divine nature. *I am He who lives, and was dead, and behold, I am alive*

---

[150] John 5:13
[151] Romans 8:11
[152] 1 Timothy 6:12

forevermore. Amen. And I have the keys of Hades and of Death.[153] Jesus is triumphant. He is victorious! He has destroyed the kingdom of darkness and reclaimed the authority and power that Adam lost. And as sons and daughters of God – as joint-heirs to Jesus Christ – we too are triumphant and victorious through Jesus Christ our Lord.

The word "key" derives from the Greek word *kleis*, which means the one who holds the power and authority of various kinds.[154] Jesus has given the keys of authority to all who rely on and build their faith upon the revelation of Jesus the Christ – the anointed and the anointing. *And I will give you the keys of the Kingdom of Heaven, and whatever you bind on earth will be bound in heaven, and whatever you loose on earth will be loosed in heaven.*[155] The Body of Christ has been given the keys, the authority, to attack the kingdom of darkness and to create a Church on the revelation of Christ that dwells in all believers. *As He is, so are we in this world.*[156] Please take time to receive this revelation. As Jesus is today, so are we in this world right now and forever. We are empowered to be bondservants and ambassadors for the Gospel of Jesus Christ. We are no longer citizens of this world, but aliens, a chosen people set aside for the advancement of the Kingdom of God.

A key to receiving the promises of God's covenant in our lives rests upon the glory of God possessing our souls and establishing a consciousness of the overcoming Christ who dwells in each born-again Christian. *Consciousness* is a state of recognizing the existence, truth, or fact of something, being in the state of knowing what is going on around you. Consciousness is that which the soul knows, not that in which we believe or have existing faith for, or have hope for, but that which the soul has proven, which the soul knows, upon which the soul rests, the very thing which has become concrete in our lives.[157]

Our souls must come into alignment with the perfected truth of our spirits to ultimately release the power and glory dwelling within us. The purpose of the manifestation of Jesus in the flesh was to save God's children from all the works of the devil and to once again allow His children to draw into His presence, to be intimate and to be in fellowship with Him. Brothers and sisters in Christ, the Father is waiting for you and me to lay hold of the abundant life already given to us through Jesus our Redeemer. The truth of God's Word for our perfect

---

[153] Revelations 1:18
[154] Strong's Concordance Dictionary
[155] Matthew 16:18-19
[156] 1 John 4:17
[157] *John G. Lake – His Life, His Sermons, His Boldness of Faith* – page 63, Ft. Worth, TX, Kenneth Copeland Publications, Copyright 1994.

redemption has already been established. We must develop a conscious belief, a knowing, a rest that surpasses all logic or intellect. We must trust in what God has promised.

Catch the Revelation

Setting the truth aside will serve no useful purpose. Please, right now, before going any further, stop what you're doing and pray. Communicate with the Father for a deeper understanding and revelation about this next section, a message that could be the catalyst to propel you into complete freedom and victory.

Jesus has created a New Covenant from which we have been completely atoned. All sin transgressions, and iniquities destroyed, our perfect peace of mind has been restored, and our bodies have been completely healed. We have been separated unto God that His very Kingdom may dwell within us.[158] Please receive the revelation that is in these words,

> *"I have been crucified with Christ; it is no longer I who live, but Christ lives in me; and the life which I now live in the flesh I live by faith in the Son of God, who loved me and gave Himself for me.*[159]

All of our needs and desires, all of God's resources have been given to us that we may live and express His Kingdom in this world. As a Christian, it is no longer you who lives, but Christ who lives within you! The *anointed* and *His anointing* dwells in your very being! This is the glorious promise of our God. We already possess the ability to open the door of our hearts to release God's Kingdom in our lives. You and I have the promise and guarantee of the Father to experience the glory of His presence and His Kingdom.

If you truly desire to be a vessel for the manifested glory of God, to be free from sickness, disease, or death, then step into the Spirit and learn to see the world through spiritual eyes rather than through physical senses. *For faith is substance of things hoped for and the evidence of things not seen!*[160] The only way to truly appropriate the spiritual blessings in your life is to bring your soul into alignment with the Spirit.

---

[158] Luke 17:20-21
[159] Galatians 2:20
[160] Hebrews 11:1

When we learn to live according to the Spirit we begin to focus on things unseen, recognizing that things seen are temporary, but the things unseen are eternal.[161] When we live according to the Spirit, we are no longer moved by circumstances stirred up by the storms of life, but we elevate ourselves above the storm and into a place of rest, exercising Holy Spirit power and promise. We begin to appropriate the Kingdom of God that releases peace to tribulation throughout life. Press into God's presence now. Seek a deeper revelation. Experience the power and truth of Christ living in you. When we develop a keen consciousness of the overcoming Christ in us, we truly step into a new realm of being marked by triumph and victory!

The Kingdom of Heaven Is at Hand

Jesus was pierced for our transgressions, wounded for our iniquity, the chastisement of peace was upon Him, and through His stripes we are healed.[162] Jesus' selfless sacrifice and atonement for all of mankind has separated us unto God, presenting us as holy and without blame to the Father. We have been called to consecrate the spirit, soul, and body completely unto God. Opening our hearts and minds, we allow ourselves to be vulnerable in God's sight, and we step into the New Covenant promises and the powerful presence of the Father.

As a child of the Most High God, you have been empowered to live in victory. Exercise that truth by your every word and action. Develop a "throne mentality" by moving past the Cross up-holding the established New Covenant and standing on the power of the Holy Spirit within you. Move by faith to a place of oneness with the Father, the Son and the Holy Spirit always resting upon your Kingdom inheritance and the deep, unconditional love of the Father. Learn to fellowship with the Father, aligning your soul and body to the holy presence of Christ in you. Take your place at the throne of God and allow His love, greatness and glory to shine through you. You have been predestined to be an instrument God can use to establish His Kingdom on earth today.

---

[161] 2 Corinthians 4:18
[162] Isaiah 53:5

Reflection Verse: Ephesians 2:4-6

> *But God who is rich in mercy, because of His great love with which*
> *He loved us, even when we were dead in trespasses, made us alive*
> *together with Christ, and raised us up together, and*
> *made us sit together in the heavenly places in Christ Jesus.*

Thought for Reflection:

As Christ is today, so are we in this world. Christ is glorified! You are glorified through the Holy Spirit in you! Take the time and reflect on the implications of the truth that we are seated together with Christ in the heavenly places and have all of God's Kingdom at our disposal. What did Jesus mean when He said, "Seek first the Kingdom of God and His righteousness and all things will be added unto you?" How does the truth of you being seated with Christ in the Heavenly places affect your life today?

Daily Confession:

I am an instrument of righteousness separated unto God to be His ambassador in this world. Through Jesus Christ my Lord I have all authority and power to change my life circumstances today. I have been empowered to change the atmosphere in which I live through faith in the New Covenant of Divine Life, because the Kingdom of God is upon me. I have a Throne Mentality, for as Christ is today, so am I in this world! Greater is He who is in me than He who is in this world!

6

A Call to Holiness

Therefore, come out from among them and be separate, says the Lord.
Do not touch what is unclean, and I will receive you. I will be a Father to you,
and you shall be My sons and daughters, says the Lord Almighty.

2 Corinthians 6:17

What is Holiness?

A young monk approached his father superior one day, asking: "Father, what is it to be dead to self?" The father replied: "I cannot explain it now, but I have a duty for you to perform. Brother Martin died last week and is buried in the churchyard of our order. Go to his grave, standing close beside it. Repeat in a loud voice all the good things you ever heard of him. After this, say all the flattering things you can invent; and attribute to him every saintly grace and virtue, without regard to truth; and report the result to me."

The young monk went to do his bidding, wondering what all this could mean. Soon he returned and the father asked him what had transpired. "Why, nothing," replied the young man. "I did as you told me and that was all."

"Did Brother Martin make no reply?" asked the superior.

"Of course he did not, for he was dead," said the monk.

The elder shook his head thoughtfully and said: "That is very strange. Go again tomorrow at the same hour, and this time repeat at the graveside all the evil you ever heard concerning Brother Martin. Add to that the worst slander your mind can imagine and report the result to me."

Again the young man obeyed, and brought back the same report. He had heaped unlimited abuse on the head of Brother Martin and had received no reply. "From Brother Martin you may learn," said the father, "what it is to be dead to self. Neither flattery nor abuse has moved him, for he is dead. So the disciple who is dead to self will be insensitive to these things, hearing neither voice of praise nor retaliation but all personal feelings will be lost in the service of Christ."[163]

Very simply, holiness is a dying to one's self, being separated and sanctified unto God. God is calling His people to be holy as He is holy.[164] That is, we are to be separated *unto* God and away from the wretchedness of this world. We are called to be Kingdom children, heirs to the seed of Abraham, and there are things this world participates in from which we, of the Kingdom of God, must separate ourselves. The call to holiness positions us to step into God's throne room and hear from God's own heart. God is calling us to make ourselves – spirit, soul, and body – a holy and acceptable offering unto Him. He is waiting for His people to step into His holiness that we may share in His glory.

In both the Old and New Testaments, the same Hebrew and Greek words, in their various grammatical forms, translate into the English words "sanctify," "consecrate," and "holy." The one uniform meaning for all these words is "to be set apart for God."[165] The meaning of "holiness" is threefold when applied to the Christian life: We are redeemed through the blood of Jesus Christ, sanctified through the Truth, and separated unto God forever.

The first meaning of *holiness* is in relation to our position in Christ. Believers in Jesus Christ are eternally set apart unto God, redeemed, justified, and made righteous from all sin through the offering of His body once and for all.[166] Through the blood-covenant believers are "saints" and "holy" from the moment of believing.[167] The New Covenant states that the "old man" is dead and we have become a new creation through Him.[168] This truth in itself is liberating. When we focus on our position as sons and daughters of God, then holiness becomes a way of life, not a law. We begin to see ourselves differently and to live accordingly. We realize that there is no condemnation for those who are in Jesus Christ and we are forever free from the power of sin and death.[169] As we begin to understand completely the position we hold as children of God, then living holy through faith becomes a realization and a way of life. The revelation of our

---

[163] Roberts Liardon, *Smith Wigglesworth: The Complete Collection of His Life Teachings*, (Tulsa, Oklahoma: Albury Publishing, 1996), p. 125-126.
[164] 1 Peter 1:16
[165] Strong's Concordance Dictionary
[166] Hebrews 10:10
[167] Philippians 1:1; Hebrews 3:1
[168] 2 Corinthians 5:17
[169] Romans 8:1

position sharpens our senses to abide and live in the Spirit of God and experience His glory.[170]

The second meaning of *holiness* applied to the Christian life is in relation to our experiences in life. We are instructed that although we are born again and a new creation in Christ, there is a process of "putting off" the "old man" and "putting on" the "new man."[171] That is, we have a choice throughout life to be a blessing or cursing. The sanctifying truth of the Word of God and the Spirit of Truth abiding in us work together to bring spirit, soul and body into alignment that we may be holy and preserved blameless at the coming of our Lord.[172] We have been sealed with the Holy Spirit of promise, the guarantee of our inheritance until the redemption of the purchased possession arrives — the full measure of God and His Kingdom.[173] The process of sanctification, separating ourselves unto God, works to bring us to a place of oneness with the Father. Sadly, this process is one many Christians fail even to recognize. As a result, many good Christian believers are experiencing continual spiritual warfare. Once we understand that we must die to self and to the things of this world, then the appropriation of God's glory can be experienced.

Jesus boldly proclaimed: *"Do not lay up for yourselves treasures on earth, where moth and rust destroy and where thieves break in and steal; but lay up for yourselves treasures in heaven, where neither moth nor rust destroys and where thieves do not break in and steal. For where your treasure is, there your heart will be also."*[174]

The process of making soul and body holy, as He is holy, is the conscious act of establishing the treasures in heaven and not of this earth. Through our souls we begin to take every thought captive to the obedience of Jesus Christ until our obedience is fulfilled.[175] Yes, our spirits are holy the moment we receive Jesus as our Lord, but our souls still must align with the Spirit. Trusting God and making our habitation in Him is a choice, an act of obedience to God's Word.[176]

I have ministered to many people over the years who were chasing their need for healing, but failed to understand that the miracle of healing rests in their ability to trust God and to be completely separated unto Him. True victory over tribulation

---

[170] Romans 8:30
[171] Ephesians 4:21-24
[172] John 17:17; Ephesians 5: 25-26; 1 Thessalonians 5:23
[173] Ephesians 1:13-14
[174] Matthew 6:19-21
[175] 2 Corinthians 10:5
[176] Psalm 91

comes when the revelation of *Christ in us, the hope of the glory,*[177] becomes a reality. So often our thoughts, words, and deeds are focused on what the physical senses perceive, when in truth we are not to focus on the physical senses but on our spiritual senses and on the truth of the Word of God. Once our eyes are opened to the truth of God's Living Word, a real transformation develops deep within the consciousness of our understanding. Our focus shifts to the things above and the promises of the Father, established through Jesus Christ our Redeemer. The veil now removed, we see where our treasure lies. True holiness is established when our focus shifts from making treasures on earth to fulfilling the treasures of heaven.

I heard the testimony of a woman who was full of cancer and the doctors had sentenced her to die within two or three weeks. Not about to give up without a fight, she checked herself into a healing house for miraculous healing by the Holy Spirit. Because she was unable to walk into the healing house alone, the hospital escorted her there by ambulance. The beautiful saints of God who ran the healing house met her at the door and welcomed her there in the peace of Jesus the Christ.

Once situated in her own room, she took in the life-giving praise and worship music filling the air. Soon a volunteer had entered her room and prayed with her reading from Galatians 3:13-14, which states, *"Christ has redeemed us from the curse of the law, having become a curse for us (for it is written, Cursed is everyone who hangs on a tree), that the blessing of Abraham might come upon the Gentiles in Christ Jesus, that we might receive the promise of the Spirit through faith."* She read also from Deuteronomy 28:58-61, regarding the curse that would come upon man if he did not follow God's Word. And she then instructed the woman to read the Scripture references herself over and over again until she "got it." The sickly woman failed to understand what the volunteer meant by "getting it," but she was obedient and followed the instructions.

After several hours, the volunteer once again entered the patient's room to pray and read the same Scripture, again instructing that she "keep reading these Scripture references until she 'got it.'" Again, the patient was obedient. The whole process went on for three full days.

Early in the morning on the third day, the healing house staff was gathered in the kitchen eating their breakfast and fellowshipping with one another, when suddenly they heard what sounded like someone falling to the floor in a room upstairs. Then they heard little feet scurrying across the cold wooden floors,

---

[177] Colossians 1:27

coming down the steps, across the hallway to the kitchen. The kitchen door flung open, and there stood the woman who'd been dying, still as frail as could be, but now with a new and obvious light in her eyes. She looked at the healing house staff and proclaimed, "I have been redeemed from the curse by Jesus Christ. I am no longer under the curse of death or sickness. I am healed, praise be to God forever!" The volunteer who had prayed with the patient those long three days looked into the woman's eyes and said, "You got it! Praise the Lord."

The process of establishing holiness in our souls and bodies is about "getting" the truth of the Holy Scriptures into the depths of our consciousness that we may begin to live out the promise of the New Covenant. Holiness is not what we do, but who we are. Holiness is no longer about the law; it's about the treasures of our hearts. No longer are we a part of this world. Holiness is a rest in the truth of the Word of God and a trusting in God to be faithful to His promise. Holiness brings a person closer to the heart of God and allows man to experience the Father's glorious presence. All our thoughts, perceptions, and focus must be on the Kingdom of Heaven and all that it provides. Holiness is about getting our focus off this world and anchoring it securely, and permanently, onto God.

Applied to the Christian life, holiness relates also to the final and complete sanctification or separation unto God when Jesus appears the second time. On that return, Jesus will assume His position as King of kings and Lord of lords for the 1,000-year reign.[178] The Bride of Christ will be lifted out of the Body of Christ to take her position of rulership at the side of the Bridegroom for the 1,000-year reign.

Who is this Bride of Christ? The Bride of Christ is all those who have been diligent in striving to separate themselves from the world and to draw closer to God. The Bride of Christ will come out of the Body of Christ. "She" will be found blameless, without blemish, holy and acceptable to the Bridegroom. When Jesus, the Bridegroom, returns, He will be looking for those who have suffered for His sake. He is looking for those who have brought their spirits, souls, and bodies into one accord with His, into a oneness with the Father. On this great and glorious day, all eyes and understanding will be fully opened and a full measure of His glory shall fill all those who believe.

Holiness ~ a Heart Condition

Holiness is not about what we do, but who we are. In essence, the entire New Covenant established through the blood of Jesus Christ is built upon the

---

[178] 1 John 3:2

transformation of man's heart to be in a relationship with God. Holiness is a condition of the heart.

In Jeremiah 31:33, the Lord said: "*But this is the covenant that I will make with the house of Israel: After those days, says the LORD, I will put My law in their minds, and write it on their hearts; and I will be their God, and they shall be My people.*" The New Covenant, one of holiness and relationship, is established upon the heart of God's people. He has written upon our hearts a new and living way, a life established upon His love and faithfulness. *For this is the will of God, your sanctification: For God did not call us to uncleanness, but in holiness. Therefore he who rejects this does not reject man, but God, who has also given us His Holy Spirit.* [179] God's call to be holy is a call to the condition of our hearts, the innermost part of our beings, to that place where life itself dwells.

The Scriptures state, "*My son, give attention to my words; incline your ear to my sayings. Do not let them depart from your eyes; keep them in the midst of your heart; For they are life to those who find them, and health to all their flesh. Keep your heart with all diligence, for out of it springs the issues of life.*"[180] Holiness is an act of surrender and humility. It's about submitting to God's Word and applying it to the heart, striving to make our lives His Living Word. When our hearts are full of His truth and His Spirit, it becomes life and health to every aspect of our flesh. The heart is the dwelling place for the issues of life. Jesus states that "*a good man out of the good treasures of his heart brings forth good things, and an evil man out of the evil treasures of his heart brings forth evil things.*"[181] Therefore, we are told to "keep" our hearts with all diligence, because the heart is the dwelling place in which the issues of life reside.

Throughout His life and ministry, Jesus taught that holiness is a heart condition. Holiness is produced when we know the heart of God and our hearts become one with His. Jesus rebuked the scribes and Pharisees who were in Jerusalem, saying, "*Hypocrites! Well did Isaiah prophesy about you, saying: 'These people draw near to Me with their mouth, and honor Me with their lips, but their heart is far from Me. And in vain they worship Me, teaching as doctrines the commandments of men.'*" God is not interested in our works and "doing the right thing." He is interested in the condition of the heart, one that is separated unto Him.

Jesus was asked by a rich, young ruler, who lived a life of doing the "right thing" by obeying and following the law, how he could achieve eternal life. Jesus responded, "*You still lack one thing. Sell all that you have and distribute to the*

---

[179] 1 Thessalonians 4:3
[180] Proverbs 4:20-23
[181] Matthew 12:35

poor, and you will have treasure in heaven; and come, follow Me." But when the rich, young ruler heard this, he became very sorrowful, for he was very rich.[182] Jesus understood the condition of his heart and knew he was unable to focus on his treasures in heaven because his heart was focused on his treasures on earth. Jesus is looking for a holy heart, a heart separated from the affairs of this world and completely settled upon Him.

Jesus said to Martha, the sister of Lazarus, when He came to raise Lazarus from the dead, *"Did I not say to you that if you would believe you would see the glory of God?"*[183] The word "believe" derives from the Greek word *pisteuo*, which means to know to be true, to have confidence in.[184] The essence of holiness is having a heart condition that has confidence in God and is completely separated unto Him. When Jesus wept at Lazarus' tomb, it was not because of His sorrow for Lazarus' condition, but for the condition of the heart of the men around the tomb. They questioned not only the power of the Holy Spirit of God but also who Jesus represented. They cried out to Jesus, *"Could not this Man, who opened the eyes of the blind, also have kept this man from dying?"*[185]

Upon hearing these words, Jesus *"again groaned in Himself."*[186] He groaned because of the condition of man's heart, so defiled by doubt, fear, and unbelief. The people around Lazarus' tomb had the treasures of their hearts in this world and they failed to recognize and receive the revelation of the absolute greatness of God. How similar are we today in our hearts as compared to those around Lazarus' tomb? Did not Jesus say, *"If you would believe you would see the glory of God"*? Is it any different today? Is God the Father, Jesus Christ the Son, and the Holy Spirit of God any different today than they were around Lazarus' tomb?

Jesus made this comment to His disciples when they were unable to cast a deaf and dumb spirit from a young boy who had been tormented from childhood: *"This kind can come out by nothing but prayer and fasting."*[187] Jesus was speaking to the condition of man's heart, his holiness, and said, *"If you can believe, all things are possible to him who believes."*[188] This type of faith can only come from a holy heart, a heart condition that trusts and has confidence in the truth and power of God. Jesus instructs that through the act of prayer and

---

[182] Luke 18:18-30
[183] John 11:40
[184] Strong's Concordance Dictionary
[185] John 11:37
[186] John 11:38
[187] Mark 9:14-29
[188] Mark 9:23

fasting we can develop a heart condition that will allow the fullness of God to be poured out from us.

True holiness is the root to a faith that has confidence in the promises of God and the power of the Holy Spirit within us. The more we yearn to be closer to God, to know His heart, to know Him intimately, the more confident we become in the truth and power of His promise through the blood covenant of His Son, Jesus Christ. *Blessed are the pure of heart, for they shall see God.*[189] Through our obedience and discipline, because we desire to be closer to the Father, prayer and fasting teaches us how to align our souls and bodies to the promise of the Holy Spirit of God within us. True holiness is purifying our hearts that they become like the Father's heart. In doing so, we will see God in all we do. Jesus promises, *"If anyone thirsts, let him come to Me and drink. He who believes in Me, as the Scripture has said, out of his heart will flow rivers of living water."*[190] As we press in toward the holiness and oneness of Christ Jesus, we begin to experience the outpouring of our hearts, and rivers of living water touch everything surrounding us. Through the outpouring of living water we will see God in all we think, say, and do.

An Undefiled Heart

"Assuredly I say to you whoever does not receive the kingdom of God as a little child will by no means enter it."[191] Here, Jesus paints a verbal picture of the revelation of what God is looking for in our hearts. Our Father desires for His children to have a heart not defiled by traditions, intellectualism, religion, fear, doubt, worry, and the like. Often, however, as we mature and grow in this world, we develop a hardness in the heart established by mistrust in mankind because of the rejections and fears we have experienced. Left unguarded, our hearts tend to lose the purity and perfection of a childlike heart. But does it need to be this way? Did Jesus suffer and die in vain? On the contrary, He made it very clear that whoever does not receive the Kingdom of God as a little child will by no means enter it. It is important to get back to that place where we have a heart as trusting and loving as a child's.

> And He looked up and saw the rich putting their gifts into the treasury, and He saw also a certain poor widow putting in two mites. So Jesus said, "Truly I say to you that this poor widow has put in more than all;

---

[189] Matthew 5:8
[190] John 7:37-38
[191] Mark 10:15

> *for all these out of their abundance have put in offerings for God, but she out of her poverty put in all the livelihood that she had.*[192]

She was a widow, impoverished, and with a heart as pure as the most trusting child, full of faith and hope and love in God. She was more concerned about the state of her heart and her holiness than she was about her earthly condition. The act of giving her livelihood unto God was not an act that made her holy; rather, it stemmed from her holiness, from a pure and childlike heart. Jesus is telling us that holiness is who we are, not what we do. He demonstrated that it is not just the act that makes us holy, but the heart behind the act. *Be holy, as I am holy* calls for a union, a oneness with the Father's heart. This woman gave all she had because her heart was one with God.

Holiness is a heart condition that responds to the heart of God. It's one that obeys the promptings even when they don't make sense. Just ask the woman who stood doing dishes in the late hours of the night.

It was well past midnight, and she simply couldn't go to sleep with the sink of dirty dishes awaiting her in the morning. Her mind filled with thoughts and her arms deep in suds she felt a sudden tug on her heart. The Lord was directing her to pray for her beloved grandmother who lived alone in a townhouse some 1300 miles away.

Drying off her arms, the woman went to the living room where she sat down to pray, lifting her grandmother to the Lord. She prayed until she was certain the Lord had released her, that her prayers were sufficient. Curiously, she found herself asking Jesus to hug her grandmother for the both of them — that Nana would know it was her granddaughter sending love to her through the Spirit of God. It was a request that made no sense to the woman even as she prayed it, but she knew beyond a doubt that it was placed on her heart specifically, in detail, by the Lord. Although she wanted so desperately to hug her grandmother herself, she knew she could not because of the great distance between them. So she trusted Jesus that the promptings on her heart were placed there by Him and that He would fulfill the prayer request.

As she prayed the heartfelt prayer, and because she obeyed the unction and leading of the Holy Spirit, she actually felt the Spirit of God release from her and hug her grandmother. In her mind, the woman visualized Nana soundly sleeping, for it was well past midnight. In her spirit, though, Nana's softness, her petite frame, even her fresh, clean scent were as vivid as though they were in the same

---

[192] Luke 21:1-4

room. Through spiritual eyes, the woman saw Nana awake, sitting in her favorite chair in the living room.

The prayer done, she went back to washing her dishes and eventually retreated to bed. When the phone rang the next morning, the woman was pleasantly surprised to hear the sound of sweet Nana's voice. Nana seemed joyful, ready to tackle the day. And among the first words to follow, Nana was very interested to know, "What did you do last night?" It was a peculiar question.

"We just watched a movie," the woman began, trying to recall the details of her evening. She began describing parts of the movie she'd watched with her husband. But Nana interrupted, because that's not really what she meant: "I just had to call you," she began. "I happened to be up around midnight last night because I couldn't sleep. I was sitting in my chair, trying to find something to watch on TV, and I had the strangest feeling you were hugging me." The woman nearly dropped the phone!

Holiness is who we are, not what we do. Holiness is a heart condition that responds to the Spirit of God "tugging" on our heartstrings no matter the time or our geographic location. Holiness is being able to respond and fulfill the Father's desire. A defiled heart, on the other hand, prevents us from hearing God's heart, and as a result we miss the opportunity to truly experience God and bless others.

A Defiled Heart

The children of Israel experienced the mighty power of God when they were delivered from Egypt and crossed the Red Sea where they found the Egyptian army completely destroyed. They experienced the presence of God as Moses ascended Mount Sinai to receive the plans, direction, and divine order for God's people. The children of Israel experienced the presence of God as a pillar of fire by night and a cloud by day as His Holy presence directed and guided them to their inheritance of the Promised Land.

Yet God had not called the children of Israel out of Egypt to go to the Promised Land immediately. He called them to the wilderness, that He could establish an intimate personal relationship with them. God's heart desire was that every man, woman, and child experience His love and presence as Moses had. The Promised Land was a result, a reward of the intimate personal relationship that God desired to establish with His children. However, the children of Israel, because of their defiled hearts, chose to ignore God's calling and moved away from holiness and oneness with the Lord.

I wonder whether the great signs of deliverance that came against Egypt during Israel's departure were for the purpose of increasing the faith of God's people. Was God demonstrating His great love and faithfulness to the descendants of Abraham that they would follow Him and come into relationship with Him without question, regard, doubt, fear, or unbelief? Is this not what Jesus meant when He made the call "Follow Me"?

Yet we find that the Israelites, the very people who had experienced God's mighty works, had begun complaining to the Lord about their hardships. They began to whine and complain about the food (the manna) God miraculously produced for their benefit, because they wanted meat. They questioned the Lord "Why did you not leave us in Egypt where all the fish, cucumbers, melons, leeks, onions, and garlic were free and plentiful?"[193] They were blinded by their defiled hearts and their lack of faith and trust in their Father, the One who proved to be their Provider, their Banner, their Salvation, their All and All. Their treasure was of this world, not on the mighty, magnificent presence of God the Father and Creator of all things Who was within their midst.

Complaining Comes From a Defiled Heart

The interesting truth of this account is that God had promised health and prosperity to His children that none of the diseases of Egypt should come upon them. Not one person was sick or in need, and God supplied their every need. However, when they complained and exercised their irreverence toward the Lord, a great plague struck their camp and many died.[194] Complaining is an act of disrespect and irreverence in the face of God. It proclaims that we do not trust in the promises of the blood covenant given to us through Jesus Christ. Complaining comes from a defiled heart.

One of the greatest roadblocks to the manifestation of God's glory in the life of today's Christian is the whining and complaining spoken from their mouths. Complaining proclaims that God is not good enough to supply our needs. The saying "Life is not fair" is satanic! Jesus, a man perfect and sinless, suffered unexplainable pain and rejection on the cross, a cross destined for the cursed. *That* was unfair! The heart that claims life is unfair has been defiled. Jesus Christ has already redeemed us from the curse.

Holiness is a heart condition that surrenders to the will and promises of God no matter what our physical senses portray. Holiness is a trust, a reliance on the

---

[193] Numbers 11:1-23
[194] Numbers 11:33-35

Word of God and the blood that has redeemed us from the curse. We must step away from the old trap of complaining and begin rejoicing for the life we now live through Jesus the Christ.

Saul was a man with the potential to be a great leader. He was the man God had chosen to be a king over His nation. Yet his defiled heart led him astray, and he sought the things of the world instead of trusting in the promised Word of God. Saul's fall from holiness did not occur as the result of a single dramatic experience, but slowly, over time Saul made decisions that separated him from God's protection and blessing. He chose to ignore God's word and intruded into the priest's office to perform a sacrifice so he could go into battle and be successful. Saul waited seven days for Samuel, but when Samuel did not come on the seventh day, Saul lost patience and trust in God.[195] He made the decision to offer the burnt sacrifice himself. It would prove to be the act that defiled God's word and ignited the demonic assault against Saul's life.

Beloved, we must be determined and vigilant in protecting and guarding our hearts. Like Saul, we have been chosen to fulfill God's will here on earth. But we must make the choice to be humble and completely reliant on God for all things. *Therefore humble yourselves under the mighty hand of God, that He may exalt you in due time, casting all your care upon Him, for He cares for you.*[196] The Word of God is clear that when we humble ourselves under the mighty hand of God, He has promised to exalt us, lift us up, and increase our joy.[197]

A holy heart is humble, poor, and meek. King David was a man after God's own heart. He did not become king because of his diplomacy, but because of all the time he spent in the fields tending his father's sheep, fellowshipping, worshiping, honoring, and surrendering his life to the Lord. Interestingly, the difference between Saul and David came down to a matter of the heart. Saul never repented for his irreverence toward the Lord. David, on the other hand, made mistakes, but he always repented and accepted the consequences of his decisions. David trusted in the Lord with all his heart, surrendering all unto God and willing to die for God's truth and word. Holiness is a heart condition!

The Message on the Mount

Jesus has given us a clear revelation of what we must do to set ourselves apart unto God to be a vessel, a river of life, that releases the magnificent, life-

---

[195] 1 Samuel 13:8

[196] 1 Peter 5:6-8

[197] Proverbs 29:23; Isaiah 29:19; James 4:6; James 4:10

changing glory of God in all we do. Matthew Chapter Four describes Jesus in the wilderness overcoming and defeating the temptations of the devil and being released into His ministry.

In Matthew 4:17, Jesus makes a call to the condition of man's heart. He said, *"Repent for the kingdom of heaven is at hand."* "Repent" means to change, transform your way of thinking.[198] The fruit of repentance therefore, is a changed life, a life transformed in thought, word, and deed. Jesus proclaimed that the Kingdom of Heaven is at hand and that all of its promises, glory and splendor are available to those who humble themselves before God and change their way of thinking. By definition, "kingdom" refers to a king's domain, a king's rulership over a domain.[199] Jesus was saying that we must change our way of thinking in order to perceive the Kingdom of Heaven set before us. We must change the way we think about life and adopt a Kingdom perspective in order to experience the glory and power available to all who believe.

> *By faith Abraham obeyed when he was called to go out to the place which he would afterward receive as an inheritance. And he went out, not knowing where he was going. By faith he sojourned in the land of promise as in a foreign country, dwelling in tents with Isaac and Jacob, the heirs with him of the same promise; for he waited for the city which has foundations, whose builder and maker is God.[200]*

Abraham, the Father of Faith, set his heart, mind and eyes on the Kingdom of God and rested in God's promise. He focused on the foundations of a city whose builder and maker is God, and he focused on the Kingdom of Heaven promised to him and his descendants. Jesus made the same call in Matthew: "Change your way of thinking and place your eyes on me and you will experience the Kingdom of Heaven." We are called to renew our minds in order to perceive the Spirit of God and His truth.

Once Jesus made the call to repentance and declared that the Kingdom of Heaven is at hand, He went about all of Galilee, *teaching in their synagogues, preaching the gospel of the kingdom, and healing all kinds of sickness and all kinds of disease among the people. Then His fame went throughout all Syria; and they brought to Him all sick people who were afflicted with various diseases and torments, and those who were demon-possessed, epileptics, and paralytics; and*

---

[198] Strong's Concordance Dictionary
[199] Strong's Concordance Dictionary
[200] Hebrews 11:8-10

He healed them. And great multitudes followed Him - from Galilee, and from Decapolis, Jerusalem, Judea, and beyond the Jordan.[201]

The multitudes followed Jesus as He demonstrated that the Kingdom of Heaven is at hand. People from all over Israel walked off their jobs, left their homes and their cities to experience the presence of God through Jesus of Nazareth. Desperation pulled God's manifested glory and power into the reality of the Israelites' physical senses. Such is the craving God also desires in our hearts today. Holiness is to allow one's heart to be so hungry and desperate for the life and breath of the Holy Spirit that we pull the manifested glory of the Kingdom of Heaven into this earthly realm.

A pastor once said that the anointing experienced on ministry trips in other countries is no greater than the anointing found here in the United States. The only difference is that the manifested glory of God is in the measure of desperation from the people being ministered to. Our desperation and hunger for the promises of the Kingdom of Heaven enable us to pull into our existence and experience the glory and power of the Holy Spirit.

Once Jesus finished ministering and he saw *the multitudes, He went up on a mountain, and when He was seated His disciples came to Him. Then He opened His mouth and taught them*.[202] Please receive the revelation of Luke's statement in Acts 1:1: *"The former accounts I made, O Theophilus, of all that Jesus began both to **do** and to **teach**"* (emphasis added).

Jesus demonstrated first the Kingdom of God, and then He taught on the Kingdom of God. He sat down on the Mount and began to teach those who had gathered around Him about the tangible, living presence of God's Kingdom. He began with the Beatitudes illustrating God's will to establish His Kingdom on earth as it is already done in Heaven. He instructed all those who would hear how to live a Kingdom Life.

Blessed (happy) are the poor in spirit, Jesus was saying, for theirs is the kingdom of heaven.[203] He explained that those who received an outpouring of God's glory and power were the desolate, the desperate, those poor in spirit and hungry for a touch of God. It was through their broken spirit that the Kingdom of Heaven was released into manifestation in the physical realm. In essence, Jesus was saying that those who mourned were blessed, for they were comforted by the presence

---

[201] Matthew 4:23-25
[202] Matthew 5:1,2
[203] Matthew 5:3

and glory of God.[204] He was teaching about the conditions of man's heart that released the reality of the Kingdom Heaven into the reality of this world. The Beatitudes provide us with a model of the Kingdom of God. Happy is the pure of heart, for they shall see God. Holiness is a heart condition.

The Kingdom of Heaven *IS Now* at Hand

Our transformed lives provide us with the ability to manifest the Kingdom of Heaven in everyday life. The reality of the Kingdom of God is a present-day reality, one waiting for men and women of faith to arise and lay hold of the manifested truth of its existence, power, and glory. The only way this realm is accessible is through our holiness, our hearts' hunger to be one with the Father. Jesus made it clear: "*I am the true vine, and My Father is the vinedresser. Every branch in Me that does not bear fruit He takes away; and every branch that bears fruit He prunes, that it may bear more fruit. You are already clean because of the word, which I have spoken to you. Abide in Me, and I in you. As the branch cannot bare fruit of itself, unless it abides in the vine, neither can you, unless you abide in Me. I am the vine, you are the branches. He who abides in Me, and I in him, bears much fruit; for without Me you can do nothing.*"[205]

Holiness begins with surrendering to God and His Word. We are called to be one with the Father, through the Son and the Holy Spirit. Once our Christian faith understands the revelation of what it means to abide with Him, a great release of His power and presence will occur. We are taught to change our perspective by focusing on the Kingdom of God and striving with a hunger and desperation to abide and reveal His promise of the New Covenant through the Holy Spirit in us.

The full revelation and consciousness of Jesus Christ in our everyday lives provides a peace that rises above the tribulations and struggles of this world. When Jesus Christ becomes the breath of our souls and His presence possesses our entire beings, an eternal life fills our conscious minds and the weights of this world decrease. John 1:4 states, "*In Him was life, and the life was the light of men.*" From the soul of Jesus breathes a holy life of God that comes into the nature of man, quickens him by its power, and by God's grace Jesus resides in man, emitting eternal light and life. God's purpose through Jesus Christ is to defy the nature of man, forever changing man to reflect Christ, not only in outward appearance, but in nature and content, in spirit, soul, and body, as the Son of God Himself.

---

[204] Matthew 5:4
[205] John 15:1-5

We are called to produce good fruit for the Kingdom of God, for the Kingdom of Heaven is at hand. The ability to produce quality fruit hinges upon our ability to find a sustained level of consciousness of Jesus in our lives. The moment we realize the truth of the power of Christ, our spirits, souls, and bodies enter into a place of rest where doubt and fear cannot exist. It is then that the fruit of the Holy Spirit is released to grow abundantly. Holiness becomes a life-centered desperation for the Father's touch. The manifested glory and power of God flows through our beings like a mighty river of water freeing the lost, healing the sick, and delivering the tormented wherever our feet may tread.

Reflection verse: *2 Corinthians 6:17*

Therefore, come out from among them and be separate, says the Lord. Do not touch what is unclean, and I will receive you. I will be a Father to you, and you shall be My sons and daughters, says the Lord Almighty.

Thought for Reflection:

Holiness is who you are, not what you do. Holiness is a heart condition! Where is your heart today? When soul and body comes into alignment with the Spirit of God, holiness becomes a desire, a way of life. When Jesus Christ becomes the life and breath of your soul and His presence possesses your entire being, an eternal life fills your conscious mind and the weights of this world are released. There is great power in humility, in dying to oneself, and allowing the Holy Spirit of God to possess your very soul. The greatest form of worship is obedience! Submit to God today and allow His Spirit and Word to restore your life.

Daily Confession:

I seek first the Kingdom of God and His righteousness and all things will be added unto me. I draw near to my Father and He draws near to me, because all that I am, I am because of Christ in me. I am nothing without God's Divine Life dwelling in me, but with Him I am more than a conqueror! Today I confess that my treasure, my heart, and my focus are on the Kingdom of God, allowing His Spirit to possess my every thought, word, and deed.. I am a child of Yahweh, the Great I AM.

7

A Father's Love

But earnestly desire the best gifts. And yet I show you a more excellent way.
Though I speak with the tongues of men and of angels, but have not love, I have
become as sounding brass or a clanging cymbal. And though I have the gift of
prophecy, and understand all mysteries and all knowledge, and though I have all
faith, so that I could remove mountains, but have not love, I am nothing.

1 Corinthians 12:31-13:2

A More Excellent Way

In July of 2003 I was conducting a discipleship week with twelve young adults
and we were pressing into the presence of the Lord through worship, teaching,
and ministry. The theme for the week was "Draw Near to God" and each one of
the participants came out of the week with a new revelation of who they are in
Jesus Christ. They went home with a new understanding of the depth, height,
length, and width of how much the Father loves them.

During this discipleship week, a word came from the Lord regarding "the call" of
this particular generation in regards to being a "Joshua generation." The
revelation word was clear and precise, and it changed each of us participating in
the discipleship training. The Lord said, *"Before you can become a Joshua*
generation that takes up the sword and brings My people into the Promised
Land, you first must become an Isaac generation surrendering your life unto
Me." This word was so profound that it impacted each of our lives. As this
revelation unfolds throughout this chapter, your life also will be transformed.

This particular chapter is a prophetic word to the body of Christ. As I prepared to
write this chapter, the Spirit of the Lord was very clear as to the importance and
weight of the information that follows. Many people are struggling under the
yoke of oppression and affliction because they do not understand the depth of the
Father's love for them. The Church is crying out to God for healing, restoration,
and reconciliation, trying to understand how to release and receive the promise of
God's living Word. The answer is found in the Father's love for us, His beloved
children. The Lord says,

I am the everlasting God and I love you! Have I not provided you with all the provisions and blessing to fulfill and live in the New Covenant I have established for you? Have I not promised that you shall not perish because of the abundance of love I have for you? I tell you this day that I am not interested in your cries for help, because your hearts are far from Me. I desire all of your love because I love you. Do you not hear My words? I love you and I desire an intimate, everlasting relationship with you. Turn your hearts back to Me, take your focus off the things of this world for they are only temporal, and bring your focus back onto Me and you will experience My glory. I desire all your love. Can you not love Me? All that I am I have given to you because I love you; I have drawn you near and covered you with My promise that I, your Father, may demonstrate My love through you. My love is everlasting, it does not have a starting point and it has no end and I have given it all to you. Why would you doubt? Is not My love sufficient for you? Step into My love and receive the revelation of the depth of My compassion for you. Do not be deceived! My love is deeper then you could ever imagine and it is all for you, My children. You cry out for a renewal of My presence for this time, but I tell you today, that the blessed hope is not a blessed escape! I tarry My Son because you have yet to learn to love as I have commanded. You cry out for peace, and yet the peace I provide is in the assurance of My love for you. What is preventing you from experiencing the outpouring of My love? Wake-up! Love is the cornerstone to My Church. My Son was, is and will always be perfect love and My glory was upon Him because He trusted in My love. Why is it so hard for you trust in My love? My children hear My words, I AM your Father and I love you and I have given My Kingdom unto you. I have promised that when you step into the fullness of My love you will experience the fullness of Me. Repent for My Kingdom is at hand. Trust in My love, for you will experience a glory that cannot be explained; a glory that will be so overwhelming that it will pour from you like a mighty river of life transforming the lives around you. I love you My children, receive My fullness today as you bend your knees and minister unto Me with your whole heart, soul, and strength! Abide in My love and My love will abide in you. For did I not say that if you would believe in Me you would see My glory? I say today, Arise and demonstrate the love of the Father in all that you do.[206]

Praise the Living God!

---

[206] A Prophetic Word from God in preparation for this chapter; October 20, 2003

I challenge you, in light of the following word from the Lord, to receive the revelation of Genesis 22 where Abraham's faith was tested. Hebrews 11:17 states, *"By faith Abraham, when he was tested, offered up Isaac, and he who had received the promises offered up his only begotten son."* God was testing Abraham's devotion and love to Him, a love upon which the Father could then establish His Kingdom. Abraham's response to this test was a demonstration of faith, and it revealed his love and devotion to God and His word.

The Apostle Paul wrote to the Galatians church that *in Christ Jesus neither circumcision nor uncircumcision avails anything, but faith working through love.*[207] Paul was stating that faith can only work through a revelation of the Father's love and our obedience to abide in that love. The foundation of our faith rests upon the unseen life, death, resurrection, ascension of Jesus Christ into Heaven, and the promise of the Holy Spirit living in us. This whole redemptive promise came out of the abundance of the Father's love for us, His beloved. The test Abraham underwent is the same test we experience today on a daily basis. Are we willing to love God with our "whole" heart, soul, and strength no matter the consequence? Our response to this ongoing test is demonstrated through our faith. When we can stand in the promise of the New Covenant without wavering, without excuses, and without compromise, we demonstrate a faith rooted in the eternal love for the Father. Fear, doubt, and worry characterize a life that has yet to receive a revelation of the fullness of the Father's love. "Fear not," "Do not be afraid," and "Do not fear" are recorded in 26 books of the Bible and on 95 different occasions. God is exhorting His children to trust in Him and abide in His unfailing, everlasting promise of love.

Love and Faith

1 Corinthians 13:13 states, *"And now abide faith, hope, love, these three; but the greatest of these is love."* We cannot please the Father without faith, because all who come to Him must believe that He is, and that He is a rewarder of those who diligently seek Him.[208] We cannot love the Father without a fear of God for it is through the reverent respect and trust for Him that we hunger and thirst for His divine presence. Therefore, faith and love co-exist as mighty towers of spiritual truth in Scripture. That is, as we walk in love, we also walk in faith; as we walk in faith, we must also walk in love, because the one cannot exist without the other.

---

[207] Galatians 5:6
[208] Hebrews 11:6

When we as a Church come to the understanding where our hearts are open to the depth, height, width, and length of the Father's love, faith abounds and we reach that place of confidence in the promise of the New Covenant. For the most part, today's faith reaches only as high as our minds and intellect can reach. Once challenged or put to the test, such "faith" wavers and crashes with the force of waves on the sea. But God, throughout Scripture, calls us to have a faith rooted and grounded in our hearts by His unfailing love.

The love of the Father is a belief that rests upon His truth and the reverent respect of His magnificence. The divine revelation of faith and love co-existing as mighty spiritual towers of strength is validated by the counterfeit of the devil in this world. The father of lies and deception has used fear and hatred since the time of creation to counter the spiritual truth and reality of faith and love in the Kingdom of God. The defeated foe has offered a goal-line defense through the destructive seeds of fear, doubt, worry, bitterness, hatred, and unforgiveness that prohibits God's children from pulling the fullness of God's Kingdom into this world and living a "normal," anointed Christian life. A dark veil blinds us, enabling us to live contrary to the promise established by Jesus Christ. We have stepped out of the one commandment Jesus established through His thought, word, and deed. We allow our hearts to become hard and have, therefore, resisted the manifested experience of the Father's love for us, His children.

The Law of Christ

The new commandment established by Jesus Christ Himself, found in Matthew 22:37, states, *"You shall love the Lord your God with all your heart, with all your soul, and with all your mind. This is the first and great commandment. And the second is like it: You shall love your neighbor as yourself. On these two commandments hang all the Law and the Prophets."*

Abraham demonstrated this New Covenant love well before the Messiah, because God's love was deep within Abraham's heart. Abraham's love for his son, Isaac, foreshadowed the love the Father has for His children. The Father's love is so deep that He gave His only begotten Son to be sacrificed for all of mankind. God had prophetically demonstrated His love for mankind through the "test" of Abraham. On the day that Abraham stood ready to sacrifice his only son, the Father put into motion a promise of a new and living way anchored on the love of a Father and the sacrifice of His Son.

Abraham was willing to sacrifice his son Isaac for his love of God. All of Abraham's earthly desires were acknowledged through his son, and through his faith and love in God Abraham was willing to give them all up solely for the purpose of pleasing the Father. Abraham's reverent respect and deep adoration for the Father represent the same type of love God calls this generation to fulfill.

Genesis 22:5 demonstrates Abraham's faith in the love of the Father: "*And Abraham said to his young men, 'stay here with the donkey; the lad (Isaac) and I will go yonder and worship, and we will come back to you.*'" Abraham trusted the promises of God, that God, his Father, loved him and would not forsake His promise to him. Though he might not have understood why his God was asking him to sacrifice his only son, Abraham was obedient, trusting that God would allow both Isaac and himself to come down the mountain when the worship was completed. It's an account crucial even to the Christian faith today.

We are exhorted not to base our understanding on the things we see, but on the things which are not seen. Abraham demonstrated that faith is released when our focus is on His promise for us – the promise of the Kingdom of Heaven. Abraham believed that somehow God would make it possible for both Abraham and Isaac to come down from the mountain together. He believed in the supernatural. It's a faith only available when we come to a revelation understanding of the love of the Father.

Let's take a different look at this account as recorded in Genesis, from Isaac's perspective. Here is a young man, probably in his late teens or so, who has been asked by his father to join him in a worship service to the Lord. Isaac asks his father, "Where is the sacrifice?" and his dad responds, "The Lord will provide." They reach the place where the Lord had directed them to worship and they build an altar together, preparing the ground and the atmosphere for an encounter with the Almighty. Once they had prepared the altar, Isaac's dad looked at him and said, "Son, God has informed me that you are the sacrifice."

Isaac easily could have overpowered his father who was well over 100 years old and run from the situation, but he had developed a fear of the Lord and a trust in the provisions of God. I can imagine Isaac laying himself down on the altar, looking into his father's eyes and saying, "Father, not my will, but your will be done." Not many words were exchanged between father and son as they prepared themselves to be obedient to God's command. Because Isaac trusted his Heavenly Father, he was able to demonstrate complete trust also in his earthly father, and he positioned his chest to receive the blow of the knife lifted high above Abraham's head.

When viewed with spiritual eyes, the entire sacrifice scene actually reveals a level of love that has been absent from the Christian life far too long. Manmade traditions and rituals have caused us to ignore our Father's call to completely rely on His unfailing, unconditional love. Both Abraham and Isaac understood the love of the Father and the faithfulness that transcends through the unconditional, compassionate love God has for all His children. What must it take for this generation of God's children to come to the same revelation understanding of the Father's love for us today?

The Fullness of God Revealed

The new law of Christ is the divine love produced in the renewed heart by the Holy Spirit,[209] flowing out in the energy of the Spirit, unforced and spontaneous, toward the objects of God's affection. The Church is crying out to God for a revival, for a renewing of His Spirit for the desperate times our world is experiencing. The cries are similar to those heard in the early 1900s when a great revival of the Holy Spirit poured out upon the land. Still, I wonder: Should our cries be different? Why do we want the same thing that already has occurred? Should we not be crying out for something more?

Each generation in God's Kingdom should be building upon the previous, growing and expanding that one day the King of kings and Lord of lords may return in all His glory. If we look closely at the divinely inspired Word of God, we will see what God is calling this generation to release and experience. He is calling us to a renewal of His divine love where all His children may step into His experience of peace, liberty, and the fullness of His glory.

Pay particular attention to Ephesians 3:14-19:

> *For this reason I bow my knees to the Father of our Lord Jesus Christ, from whom the whole family in heaven and earth is named, that He would grant you, according to the riches of His glory, to be strengthened with might through His Spirit in the inner man, that Christ may dwell in your hearts through faith; that you, being rooted and grounded in love, may be able to comprehend with all the saints what is the width and length and depth and height - to know the love of Christ which passes knowledge; that you may be filled with all the fullness of God.*

What more must be said? In these five simple verses, God opened the heavens unto all who believe. Through faith we receive Jesus Christ into our heart, strengthening us according to His riches and glory that through the indwelling presence of Christ in us we become rooted and grounded with a full understanding of the Father's love. We receive access into the mysteries of the

---

[209] Romans 5:5; Hebrews 10:16

Word of God that enable us to comprehend with all the saints the width, length, depth, and height of the love of Christ that surpasses man's comprehension. The supernatural understanding of the Father's love bubbles to overflowing and we are filled with the fullness of God, the Father.

This is God's desire for a "normal" Christian life! This is what we are to experience on a daily basis. We are to commune with the Holy Spirit, thereby drawing closer to the heart of God and positioning us to pull down the heavens through our desperation and hunger to be filled with God's abiding love. God desires us to be filled with His fullness. Do you get this? God desires each one of His children to be filled with His fullness, to be a vessel from which He can pour out His glory upon all the earth. We cannot, however, be filled if we fail to understand how much the Father adores and loves His children.

> *As the Father loved Me, I also have loved you; abide in My love. If you keep My commandments, you will abide in My love, just as I have kept My Father's commandments and abide in His love. These things I have spoken to you, that My joy may remain in you, and that your joy may be full. This is My commandment, that you love one another as I have loved you. Greater love has no one than this, than to lay down one's life for his friends. You are My friends if you do whatever I command you. No longer do I call you servants, for a servant does not know what his master is doing; but I have called you friends, for all things that I heard from My Father I have made known to you.[210]*

Time and again throughout God's Word, we are exhorted to abide in the Father's love. Why do you suppose that is? Because only when we choose to abide in Him can God fully abide in us. He loves you and He desires an intimate, personal relationship with you! God our Father has promised that each of us would be filled with His fullness. The key to the fulfillment of this promise is the revelation understanding of the love of Christ. Jesus said we are His "friends" *if* we adhere to His command. Jesus had only one command, and that was to love. Beloved, we cannot experience the truth, power, and glory of the Kingdom of Heaven in this world without the revelation of the abundance of the Father's love for us.

---

[210] John 15:9-17

The Great Expanse of the Father's Love

Outside the Holy Spirit's wise counsel, is there any way we could comprehend the width, length, depth, and height of the Father's love for us? *And about the ninth hour Jesus cried out with a loud voice, saying, 'Eli, Eli, lama sabachthani?' (*that is, *'My God, My God, why have You forsaken Me?').* The anguish and suffering expressed in these words has shaken my soul and brought me to a deeper understanding of the covenant promise we are to be living and experiencing today as believers in Jesus Christ. The price Jesus paid is beyond human comprehension. We have yet to truly appreciate all that Jesus endured at Calvary. We have made the sacrifice Jesus endured at the Cross a common thing and denied ourselves the true transformation all Christians are challenged to press toward. We missed the truth of the abundant love that was expressed and released through "one sacrifice for the atonement of all."

Many books have been written on overcoming fear and pride, removing offense, bitterness, and unforgiveness in the Christian life. Sometimes we become so involved with "working" to be set free from different curses and a hardness of heart that we fail to see that what is right in front of our face: How can Christians hold in their hearts any bitterness or offense toward another when their hearts and souls are filled with the love and compassion of Jesus Christ? They cannot! Why are so many Christians crying out to the Lord for their joy to be full, when Jesus said *if you abide in My love, My joy may remain in you and that your joy may be full*? The answer is simple: Because Christians are not following the simple command of Jesus Christ to *"love one another as I have loved you."*[211]

We are not abiding in His divine presence. We desire for God's glory and power to be manifested in our lives, but we continue to ignore Him throughout the day. We find ourselves so caught up in this world that we neglect the Father who adores us beyond understanding. We are told to *count it all joy when we fall into various trials, knowing that the testing of our faith produces patience.*[212] When we place our faith and trust in the love of the Father, we find a place of rest where we can abide in peace and joy.

By definition, "joy" means to have confidence that God is with you![213] Galatians 5:22 lists the fruit of the Holy Spirit: *"love, joy, peace, longsuffering, kindness, goodness, faithfulness, gentleness, self-control. Against such there is no law."* Love is recorded first, because love releases all the other fruit in a Christian's

---

[211] John 15:12

[212] James 1:2-3

[213] Strong's Concordance Dictionary

life. People who struggle to see the fruit of the Spirit in their own lives lack revelation of the Father's love. Love is the cornerstone to the experience of God's divine presence in a Christian life. Therefore, count it all joy, because the Father's love is greater than anything this world can produce.

Wake Up

Jesus made it clear that the new and living way is a life of love. For whatever reason, Christians have stepped out of the truth of the Gospel of Jesus Christ. Christianity is about love, a supernatural love that goes beyond our understanding. Jesus has called us to love one another without regard. We are to abide in His perfect love, and in doing so we will experience joy. The joy of the Lord is our strength! God has exhorted us to "wake up," because we are missing His provisions and truth. We are to love as Christ loved. We are to be ready to lay down our own life for another. *God is love and love is God; and everyone who loves is born of God and knows God. No one has seen God at any time. If we love one another, God abides in us, and His love has been perfected in us. By this we know that we abide in Him, and He in us, because He has given us of His Spirit.*[214]

At the beginning of this chapter I shared with you a revelation I received during a discipleship week with young adults. The Lord said, *"Before you can become a Joshua generation that takes up the sword and brings My people into the Promised Land, you first must become an Isaac generation surrendering your life unto Me."* I made a bold statement then that as the revelation of this profound word unfolds throughout this chapter, your life would be transformed forever. I can make that statement because I believe in the truth and transforming power of the Word of God. Isaac was willing to lay down his life because he trusted and feared God. Isaac was willing to die because God had so commanded it. Are we willing to lay down everything for God, even life itself?

Because He established the New Covenant, God does not need to test our faith through adversity as He did with Abraham and Isaac. We do not live under the same covenant Abraham and Isaac experienced. God chooses to abide in us when we surrender our lives to Him. So the more we kick against the Word of God and the truth of the New Covenant promise, the more we experience the hardships of this world. God has provided for us a way to overcome all the trials and temptations of this world. When we abide in the fullness of His abundant love, we are filled with His glory, power, and magnificent presence, driving darkness from our atmosphere. We can then stand like Jesus, and proclaim, "Peace, be

---

[214] 1 John 4:11-13

still,"[215] and the storm will cease to exist, because the very essence of God's peace will be poured from our very being.

The Kingdom of Heaven Is at Hand

Beloved, we have the capability through the power of the Holy Spirit to create an atmosphere charged with the presence and glory of God. When our hearts are joined with the heart of God an atmosphere is created with the presence and power of God. It is through this presence that the supernatural is released. However, before God can release the supernatural in our lives, we first must come to the place of surrender for the love of God. We are nothing without God's abiding presence, but with His presence we are filled with His love, power, and glory that establishes dominion over the enemy.

The Apostles came under great persecution when John and Peter ministered healing to the lame man beside the Gate of Beautiful. Instead of running and hiding or questioning the Father's love for them they got into prayer and asked the Father for more of His abiding presence:

> *Now, Lord, look on their threats, and grant to Your servants that with all boldness they may speak Your word, by stretching out Your hand to heal, and that signs and wonders may be done through the name of Your holy Servant Jesus. And when they had prayed, the place where they were assembled together was shaken; and they were all filled with the Holy Spirit, and they spoke the word of God with boldness.*[216]

Maybe we are asking for the wrong thing. The apostles walked in such confidence in the Father's love that nothing shook their conviction to spread the Gospel of Christ. They had such a fire and love for mankind that they did not want to see one person perish for lack of knowledge. Their prayer was simple, and it was connected to the heart of God: *Give us more of You, that You may be glorified!* How desperate are you to be filled with God's fullness? Press into the revelation of the width, length, depth, and height of God's unfailing, unconditional love for you.

Some of you might say, "All this sounds good and I would like to be in God's presence, but I have experienced so much pain, rejection, and sickness in my life I do not know how to achieve God's love." The good news is that we do not have to achieve anything. It is given to us, and all we need to do is receive God's

---

[215] Mark 4:39
[216] Acts 4:29-31

unfailing love. Put down your concerns, your pains, and your sicknesses and open your heart for His love! Open your heart right now, lay yourself down on the altar as Isaac did and surrender everything you have unto God. Cry out from the depth of your heart for a revelation of His love. He desires to give it to you, but you must draw near to Him, and He will draw near to you.[217] Commune with your Father today and seek His unfailing love.

Reflection Verse: *1 Corinthians 12:31-13:2*

But earnestly desire the best gifts. And yet I show you a more excellent way. Though I speak with the tongues of men and of angels, but have not love, I have become as sounding brass or a clanging cymbal. And though I have the gift of prophecy, and understand all mysteries and all knowledge, and though I have all faith, so that I could remove mountains, but have not love, I am nothing.

Thought for Reflection:

The Law of Christ is love. On the Law of Christ hangs all commandments and laws of the Prophets. This love is founded upon the love of the Father that was demonstrated through the sacrifice of His Son that all of mankind would be healed, delivered, and saved. Love is the cornerstone necessary to release the power of God in one's life. Receive today the revelation that the Father loves you and has empowered you to be an overcomer, more than a conqueror in all you do.

Daily Confession:

I count it all joy when I fall into various trials, knowing that the testing of my faith produces patience. I know my Father loves me and has provided for me a perfect Lamb from which I have been perfectly redeemed. I know by faith that He will never leave me nor forsake me, and if my Father is for me, no one can be against me! I stand upon the unfailing love of my Father that I am an example of His love.

---

[217] James 4:7

8

The Mantle of Spiritual Dominion

Most assuredly, I say to you, he who believes in Me, the works that I do he will do also; and greater works than these he will do, because I go to My Father.

John 14:12

The Lord Speaks

In all humility the following is a word from the Father, and it is a word that must be heard:

Thus saith the Lord, *"You are My children and I love you and have empowered you to be overcomers and conquerors over the wretchedness and wickedness of this world. The Kingdom of Heaven is at hand. Trust in Me, and My Kingdom will be yours. I say repent, from the doubt, fear, and unforgiveness in your heart. It is sin, and it has hardened you and kept you from experiencing My glorious presence.*

For I have not left you an orphan in this world, but I have given you a Comforter, a Helper, Who desires to know you and assist you in all you do. Open your eyes and see, open your ears and hear, for My Kingdom is at hand and I have given you the authority that will unlock a power greater than you could ever imagine.

But first you must trust in Me, surrender all to Me, that you may be an empty vessel from which My Holy Spirit may inhabit and flow. Your doubt and fear in the supernatural is prohibiting you from truly experiencing My Awesome presence. Why do you question and doubt the power within you? Do you not believe that I can do all things? You must trust in Me and My Word. Then, and only then, will you experience My glory.

I yearn for a people who are willing to have faith in Me and ALL of my Word. I desire a people who will establish My Kingdom here on earth by exercising the authority and power I have given them. Where are these people who will reclaim, rebuild, fortify and inhabit my land through faith and trust in Me? It is time for all of My glory to fill the land and for My people to be filled with My Holy Spirit. Open your heart today and receive My abiding presence.[218]

Please take the time right now, before you go any further, and honor the Father's spoken word. Close your eyes and worship our Heavenly Father, inviting the Holy Spirit to come upon you and fill your heart with hope and faith to receive the words of life and restoration for all of God's children. Receive today a greater outpouring of His Spirit upon you and experience the power and freedom available to every Christian through the victory of our Lord, Jesus Christ.

The Mantle of Authority

There comes a point in a Christian's relationship with God where his heart and soul becomes aligned with the heart and soul of God, when all that God loves, he loves, and all God hates, he hates. There must arise in the soul of man an indignation, a righteous anger, a hatred toward the kingdom of darkness and all that it represents. This fire within the heart and soul of man releases a determination, confidence, and faith that satan's kingdom recognizes and runs in terror. This fire is a passion that resonates throughout the consciousness of man releasing the faith that exercises the mantle (the covering) of authority given to every believer by the blood of Jesus Christ.

Jesus "wore" a mantle of authority that every demon recognized, and they threw themselves down at His feet begging not to be tormented. Brothers and sisters in Christ, this mantle has been given to you and to me that we may *put on* the very power of the Kingdom of God to be displayed, honored, revered, and exercised. *For you are all sons of God through faith in Christ Jesus. As many of you who are baptized into Christ have **put on** Christ.*[219] The "anointed and His anointing" are ours to *put on* as we are immersed in His presence. The mantle of authority has been given to all believers as a gift propelling us to a level of existence beyond our comprehension. We are God's fellow workers in this world restoring His Kingdom throughout our lives.

The measure of God's supernatural power and glory that releases the Kingdom of God into this world derives from the authority we exercise by faith. If you are crying out to God for the release of more of His power and glory, you must, by faith, exercise a greater measure of spiritual authority at all times.

---

[218] Prophetic word from God: November 25, 2003 (in preparation for this chapter)
[219] Galatians 3:26-27

Such godly authority is not something to be obtained. The authority of Christ has already been given to us. It is up to us now to exercise that authority by faith. The more authority we exercise, the greater God's glory will be demonstrated. My prayer is that as you read this chapter, the fire deep inside your heart will be stirred and you will step into a place where you will exercise the mantle of authority by faith and release the power of the Holy Spirit. *Are you willing to receive this mantle and fulfill God's covenant in your life?*

Jesus commissioned each of us to take authority over the kingdom of darkness, over all of the principalities, powers, rulers of the darkness, and spiritual wickedness in high places. He has given us power, *dunimus* – Holy Spirit power – to exercise this authority over the enemy and He has promised that nothing shall, by any means, hurt us.[220] Yet so many of us fail to exercise this authority and lay hold of the *dunimus* power within us. We have yet to learn the fullness of the truth of our spiritual dominion and authority through Jesus Christ.

Jesus said, *And these signs will follow those who believe: In My name they will cast out demons; they will speak with new tongues; they will take up serpents; and if they drink anything deadly, it will by no means hurt them; they will lay hands on the sick, and they will recover.*[221] What Jesus is saying is that we have been commissioned by the mantle of authority through the Mighty Name of Jesus to cast out demons, speak the language of angels,[222] disperse and dethrone principalities and powers (serpents), be filled with the Spirit of Life that nothing shall hurt us,[223] and lay our hands on the sick and they will be healed! Jesus has commissioned all believers to exercise their spiritual mantle of authority that He suffered and died to provide. We have been given the power to break the enemies strongholds in this world.

Matthew 10:1 states, *And when He had called His twelve disciples to Him, He gave them power over unclean spirits, to cast them out, and to heal all kinds of sickness and all kinds of disease.* The word "power" in this verse derives from the Greek word *exousia*, which means authority.[224] Jesus has given all His disciples, all those who surrender their lives to Him, the authority to cast out demons and heal all kinds of sickness and disease. Fellow believers, do you see it? We have been given spiritual authority and dominion through Jesus Christ, the

---

[220] Luke 10:19
[221] Mark 16:16-20
[222] 1 Corinthians 13:1
[223] Romans 8:2
[224] Strong's Concordance Dictionary

Son of God, over the entire kingdom of darkness and over all of the works of the devil. *For Greater is He who is in us than he who is in the world!*[225]

This authority will not be exercised until the righteous fire burning deep inside our hearts and souls is released in a passion of faith, confidence, and determination to overcome. Then and only then, through the fire and conviction of our divinely appointed authority and dominion in this world, will the yoke-destroying power of the Holy Spirit be manifested to destroy the oppression that holds us in bondage.

"Is there not a cause?" King David cried out when he heard the curses of the Philistine toward the army of God. He was but sixteen years old, and the fire in his soul moved him to step out in faith. His confidence and determination prevailed against the uncircumcised Philistine, because David knew the power of God was far greater than the power of the enemy.

How about you? Can you make a similar cry today? Can you stand with authority and proclaim *"Enough is Enough!"* and receive your victory? Assume the mantle of authority and release the *dunimus* power to destroy the chains that bind. Stand in confidence and know that victory has already been achieved and exercise by faith your God-given power through the Holy Spirit.

Spiritual Principle of the Mantle

The Christian faith has been given a mantle, and we're to be consciously aware of its covering over us. The term *mantle* in God's Word literally means a cloak or garment that covers,[226] but the symbolic nature of the mantle in God's Word has always been the source for God's anointing upon man. From Moses to Elijah to Jesus Himself, God used a mantle of authority to carry forth His glory and anointing. Each time, the mantle was passed to the next generation or person whom God deemed worthy to advance His will.

The principle of the passing of the mantle has been established, and each time the mantle extends to the next generation a greater measure of God's anointing and glory is available to be experienced. As we look back and study the history of God's Word, we find that when many of the great prophets and men of God passed their mantle of authority to the next generation, in each case the mantle evolved into a greater anointing and power.

---

[225] 1 John 4:4
[226] Strong's Concordance Dictionary

The same principle applies to passing the mantle of authority in the New Covenant. That is, as the body of Christ, we have been given a mantle of authority that carries more power than has ever been experienced in the history of God's people. The mantle of Christ's authority has been passed to each and every Christian today. Individually, and in one accord, we have the power to exercise our spiritual authority over the world. How is it then, that the Christian faith is not moving from glory to glory, faith to faith, and strength to strength, demonstrating dominion and power over the kingdom of darkness?

Jesus proclaimed, "*Most assuredly, I say to you, he who believes in Me, the works that I do he will do also; and greater works than these he will do, because I go to My Father.*"[227] The mantle of authority passed from Jesus Christ to all Christians carries an expectation from the Throne of God to perform greater works than those Jesus performed. We have been given the authority of Heaven to exercise God's glory and power in all we do through our faith in the Son of God and the promise of our Father. The baton has been given to us to finish the last leg of the race and to create a culture where God can be God, His glory can reign, and His children at last may live in the Promised Land overflowing with health and prosperity – living in abundance!

The Passing of the Mantle

The passing of the mantle holds great promises for future generations, demonstrating the unfailing faithfulness, love, and sovereign power of God to impact this world through His people. The first miracle Jesus performed was when He turned water into wine, and it serves as a prophetic word for the mantle we bare as Christians today.[228] Once Jesus instructed the servants of the house to pour water into the water pots, He told them to draw some out and take it to the master of the feast. "*When the master of the feast had tasted the water that was made wine, and did not know where it came from, the master of the feast called the bridegroom. And he said to him, 'Every man at the beginning sets out the good wine, and when the guests have well drunk, then the inferior. You have kept the good wine until now!'*"[229] This account is a prophetic word that speaks of an even greater wine that will be given to all who hunger and thirst after His righteousness in these last days.

Throughout the Bible, *wine* is symbolic of the revelation of God's Word. We are promised that in these last days God will provide a deeper revelation of His Word

---

[227] John 14:12

[228] John 2:1-12

[229] John 2:9-10

than has ever been experienced. This "new wine" will strengthen and add to the depth of our understanding of the New Covenant – *Christ in us, the hope of the glory* – empowering us to create an atmosphere of His presence. More of His glory stands ready to be released as we exercise our authority through faith in His covenant promises. God is waiting for a generation to arise that will *put on* the garment of authority passed down from His Son and release His glory as never before. Jesus was sacrificed that we may be that generation, and God is waiting for us to unveil the power necessary to put every work of the adversary under the feet of Jesus Christ.

The Old Testament houses an entire history of God's people passing the mantle, the anointing of God, unto the next generation. It speaks of Moses, called by God to deliver the children of Israel out of Egypt and into the Promised Land. We know Moses did not bring the children of Israel into the Promised Land, but that the mantle of authority was passed to Joshua to fulfill God's plan. Similarly, with Elijah and Elisha the mantle of authority was passed that a greater work for that time could be accomplished and God's plan fulfilled. A closer look at both of these accounts demonstrates the principle of the passing of the mantle of authority that God's Kingdom may forever be established on earth.

Moses and Joshua

We find God visiting Moses for the first time in Exodus 3:3-4. God did not speak to Moses until he turned aside and noticed God's presence in the burning bush. It's a word of truth God has made very clear throughout the history of His people and He is saying the same thing today to all Christians: "Turn aside and look, draw near to me with a full assurance of faith, be not deceived or distracted by the world, for the great I AM is calling you."

We are being called to turn aside from the distraction of this world to lay hold of the truth of the New Covenant promise given to us through the sacrifice of Jesus Christ our Lord and become one with the Father. Only by turning aside and giving God our full attention will He begin to speak to us and instruct us on what to accomplish for His Kingdom.

Moses' submission, humility, and faith allowed God to provide him with the mantle of authority through his shepherd rod. [230] Moses was given clear instructions on how to exercise spiritual authority by exercising his faith. He was told to throw his shepherd rod to the ground, and when he did it turned into a serpent. God's miraculous power and anointing was released when Moses exercised by faith the spiritual authority given to him by the Father.

---

[230] Exodus 4:3

The Book of Exodus is full of instances where Moses' rod was used to demonstrate authority when Moses activated, through faith, the release of signs, wonders, and miracles of God.

God revealed that the dominion of Moses' mantle was established when Aaron threw the rod down and it turned into the serpent that swallowed all of Pharaoh's rods.[231] God was demonstrating not only His sovereignty and power over evil works of this world, but also that all things are possible through God if we believe and act in the authority provided.

The Spirit of the Lord is saying the same thing to us today. Our spiritual dominion has already been established through the life, death, resurrection, and ascension of Jesus Christ our Redeemer. Jesus has defeated the serpents of this world and put them under His feet. As with Moses, we need simply to exercise our authority through faith that Jesus the Christ is, was, and always will be triumphant over the kingdom of darkness. What's more, we are in Christ and He in us, establishing our dominion and authority over all the works of the devil.

Since the beginning of time God has proved to us that we are responsible, through our faith, to release the power of our spiritual dominion. This truth is revealed when God rebuked Moses on the banks of the Red Sea.[232]

Pharaoh's army was pressing in and the children of Israel had nowhere to go. Moses cried out, *"Do not be afraid. Stand still, and see the salvation of the LORD, which He will accomplish for you today. For the Egyptians whom you see today, you shall see again no more forever. The LORD will fight for you, and you shall hold your peace."*

God responded to Moses, *"Why do you cry to Me? Tell the children of Israel to go forward. But lift up your rod, and stretch out your hand over the sea and divide it. And the children of Israel shall go on dry ground through the midst of the sea."*

God instructed Moses to divide the Red Sea by lifting his rod and stretching his hand. It was up to Moses to exercise his faith in order to release the mantle of authority given to him by God.

The authority principle has remained the same throughout time. We must activate our faith to release the spiritual authority we have through Jesus Christ. Through

---

[231] Exodus 7:8-13
[232] Exodus 14:13-16

our authority, then, the Holy Spirit power is produced. We find, however, that Moses' rod got the children of Israel only as far as the Jordan River, and not quite into the Promised Land. *"Moses My servant is dead. Now therefore, arise, go over this Jordan, you and all this people, to the land, which I am giving to them, the children of Israel. Every place that the sole of your foot will tread upon I have given you, as I said to Moses."*[233] To fulfill God's will, Moses' mantle was passed to Joshua for a greater anointing to be released. Joshua was anointed by the Commander of the Lord's army, Jesus Christ Himself. Joshua was given a sword of authority, his mantle, empowering and commissioning him to conquer and reclaim the Promised Land for the children of Israel.[234] Joshua continued the effective leadership begun by Moses, and he did so demonstrating a measure of anointing great enough to effectively lead God's people into war and victory reclaiming the Promised Land for God's people.

Elijah and Elisha

So he departed from there, and found Elisha the son of Shaphat, who was plowing with twelve yoke of oxen before him, and he was with the twelfth. Then Elijah passed by him and threw his mantle on him. And he left the oxen and ran after Elijah, and said, 'Please let me kiss my father and my mother, and then I will follow you' And he said to him, 'Go back again, for what have I done to you?' So Elisha turned back from him, and took a yoke of oxen and slaughtered them and boiled their flesh, using the oxen's equipment, and gave it to the people, and they ate. Then he arose and followed Elijah, and served him.[235]

Elisha was busy plowing the fields when Elijah threw his mantle upon him. It was an act demonstrating that the time had come for a successor, one who could carry the mantle of authority, representing the Kingdom of God throughout the land, and advancing God's Kingdom and truth through the office of the Prophet.

Elisha received his new commission taking everything that represented his life and consecrated it unto God. The Lord expects no less of us today. He cannot use anyone who refuses to lay down his or her life by not loving that life unto death.

This is not a call only to martyrdom; we are to be transformed by the renewing of our minds through Him. We are called to die to self and to this world, that our past, present, and future be laid at God's altar and sacrificed for His glory. Only

---

[233] Joshua 1:2-3
[234] Joshua 5:13-15
[235] 1 King 19:19-21

then can God use us as instruments to victoriously carry the mantle bestowed upon us.

The garment passed from Elijah to Elisha was a double portion of the anointing that Elijah had carried. [236] Elisha was to accomplish a greater work than had his successor by calling the heart of man back to the sovereignty and love of God.

Both Elisha and Joshua received a greater revelation of the anointing of God to fulfill God's will. It is important for our edification to bear in mind that the source of their anointing (power) was the same as it had been for their successors for it came from the same Spirit. However, they were the next generation and it was their responsibility to build upon that which their successors had established. They were called to exercise a greater faith and a greater authority to accomplish that which their successors began. Remember, the anointing and power of God can only be released by the measure of authority a person exercises through faith. That is, the more faith we exercise the greater the anointing is released to fulfill God's will. This is a spiritual principle that will always be true. The more we give, the more we will receive.

The Mantle of Jesus Christ

The Messiah, the Anointed One, was and is the Word made flesh. Jesus dwelt among us that we might behold His glory, the glory received by the Father, full of grace and truth. He was and is the Lamb of God, the perfect sacrifice for all of mankind. His death on the cross was unavoidable redeeming man to become the Father's representatives in this world - bondservants and living epistles of His glorious Kingdom in all that we do.

Jesus hung on the cross accursed, naked, and broken, His blood spilling from the crown of His head to the soles of His feet. His blood was the only thing covering His body. Without a garment of any sort, He was displayed naked, covered in His own blood, and he was tortured to the point of death. The blood of Jesus Christ is the mantle given to all Christians. *"I have been crucified with Christ; it is no longer I who live, but Christ lives in me; and the life which I now live in the flesh I live by faith in the Son of God, who loved me and gave Himself for me."*[237] It is through the blood of Jesus Christ that the New Covenant promise has been fulfilled. Victorious, powerful, and redemptive, the blood of Christ has been passed on to all who believe, from generation to generation. Great authority rests in His blood.

---

[236] 2 Kings 2:1
[237] Galatians 2:20

God desires that we acquire the mantle of authority through the blood of Jesus. As the Lord revealed to us in the accounts of Moses, Joshua, Elijah, and Elisha, we are responsible for exercising this authority to release the anointing God and fulfill His will.

Exercising the Mantle of Authority to Release Power

John the Baptist was confused when he sent his disciples to question Jesus whether He was the Messiah, the Coming One. Jesus met his confusion with the Truth: *"Go and tell John the things which you hear and see: The blind receive their sight and the lame walk; the lepers are cleansed and the deaf hear; the dead are raised up and the poor have the gospel preached to them. And blessed is he who is not offended because of Me."*[238]

Jesus made it very clear that to believe in Him means we also must believe in the works He accomplished. He was not saying that the act of simply witnessing His miracles was enough. His message extends deeper into the revelation of how we may release the power that comes straight from the Throne of God. Through Jesus, the Kingdom of God is released. All the power of the devil cannot stop the dominion of God and His truth.

Many of us are familiar with the account of the lame man who was lowered through the roof of a house in which Jesus was ministering.[239] When Jesus blessed the crippled man, saying "Your sins are forgiven," the Pharisees and scribes called into question Jesus' authority to forgive sins. "God alone could only forgive sins," they argued. Jesus revealed that He knew the truth buried far beneath their words, saying: *Why are you reasoning in your hearts? Which is easier, to say, 'Your sins are forgiven you,' or to say, 'Rise up and walk'? But that you may know that the Son of Man has power on earth to forgive sins - He said to the man who was paralyzed, 'I say to you, arise, take up your bed, and go to your house.' Immediately he rose up before them, took up what he had been lying on, and departed to his own house, glorifying God.*[240]

Jesus demonstrated clearly that He not only had the power to forgive sins, but He also had the authority (*exousia*; power) to heal.

There comes with each mantle of authority a revelation, the truth of which, when fully received, helps each believer to release the yoke-destroying anointing over

---

[238] Matthew 11:4-6
[239] Luke 5:16-26
[240] Luke 5:22-25

their life. It is here that Christianity is elevated to a level far above mere religion, when it becomes a way of life to glorify the living and faithful God. For many churchgoers today, Christianity is merely religion, the performance of time-honored traditions and rituals that really offer no more than any other belief system available. The Christian faith has failed to lay hold of the life-transforming revelation of the mantle of authority that activates, through faith in Christ, the very power and glory of God's Throne.

> *When I consider Your heavens, the work of Your fingers, the moon and the stars, which You have ordained, what is man that You are mindful of him, and the son of man that You visit him? For You have made him a little lower than the angels, And You have crowned him with glory and honor. You have made him to have dominion over the works of Your hands; You have put all things under his feet.*[241]

King David prophesied the truth that man would be made a little lower than God. The word *angels* derives from the Greek translation *elohiym*, which means the supreme God.[242] There are 2,250 translations of *elohiym* throughout the Bible, and here, in Psalm 8, is the only place it was translated to mean angels. Man was created a little lower than God, and therefore has been given the responsibility to uphold His authority in this world. The prophecy in verse six depicts that God made man to have dominion over the works of His hands, that all things have been placed under our feet as stewards. We are empowered by the Holy Spirit and set apart by Jesus Christ to exercise the mantle of authority on earth.

When we rise up with the fire of God in our souls to reclaim the world and exercise the mantle of authority through faith, God's power will heal the sick, cast out demons, raise the dead, and destroy all the works of the devil! Then, and not before, will "religions" begin to notice that Christianity is founded upon a living God who is faithful to His promise, far greater than anything this world has to offer. It is time for believers to arise, take up the mantle of authority, wear it proudly and faithfully, and expose it so everyone may see the one true Almighty Father who was and is and forever shall be.

The Revelation of Holy Communion

Take, eat, this is my body broken for you; do this in remembrance of Me. This cup is the New Testament in My blood. This do, as often as you drink it, in

---

[241] Psalm 8:3-6
[242] Strong's Concordance Dictionary

remembrance of Me.[243] Jesus spoke these words at the Last Supper. They were words delivered in the heavenly realm, embracing the promise that Jesus' authority would be transferred to all believers. *"This cup is the New Testament in My blood"* was His proclamation and the establishment of a new and better covenant created for God's children. *"Take, eat, this is my body broken for you"* were words of transformation as Jesus broke the bread revealing that He, the Bread of Life, would destroy infirmities and bear all sickness for mankind. Through His words and His faith, Jesus established forever the redeeming healing power of the Bread of Life! When God's people partake of Holy Communion, through the elements of bread and wine, receiving the revelation of the overcoming Christ within us, the power of the Holy Spirit is released to heal, deliver, and save!

Jesus' blood became the foundation of the New Covenant from which the mantle of authority has been passed. The very act of Holy Communion harnesses the great power of the New Covenant and releases God's blessings into our lives. Partaking of Jesus' blood and flesh, through faith, releases Holy Spirit power to heal and deliver man from the wretchedness of this world. When Jesus said, *"This do as often as you drink it,"* He offered that every time we drink the element of wine and break the bread in remembrance of Him, the New Covenant is consecrated by faith, spiritual authority is exercised, and the yoke-destroying power of God's Holy Spirit is produced to set us free.

Partaking in Holy Communion is more than a mere ritual, it is the act of faith from the heart of man that releases the prophetic truth of our atonement, redemption, and inheritance through Jesus' sacrifice. We are warned that *whoever eats this bread or drinks this cup of the Lord in an unworthy manner will be guilty of the body and blood of the Lord. But let every man examine himself when he eats of that bread and drinks of that cup. For he who eats and drinks in an unworthy manner eats and drinks judgment to himself, not discerning the Lord's body. For this reason many are weak and sick among you, and many die.*[244]

The very act of partaking in Holy Communion is done from the heart of man whereby we examine ourselves before the Lord, opening heart and soul to the

Holy Spirit and embracing what Jesus endured on our behalf. The elements are more than just bread and wine; they are the very blood and broken body of Jesus Christ. Therefore, when you engage in Holy Communion, do so with reverence

---

[243] 1 Corinthians 11:24-25
[244] 1 Corinthians 11:27-30

that you may appreciate all Jesus endured for your complete redemption. Much of the sickness, disease, and premature death is a result of making the New Covenant a common thing and partaking in the Holy Communion as a religious ritual, not discerning what was accomplished for us. The body of Christ has yet to receive the full revelation of Holy Communion's power. Divine healing and restoration occur when we partake in Communion. The very act itself demonstrates the divine covenant established by Jesus' perfect sacrifice, one that renders mankind forever free from the chains that bind.

Holy Communion is an act of consecrating oneself before the Lord that we may exercise spiritual authority and assume responsibility for being an ambassador for Christ. The words Jesus spoke as He broke the bread and took the cup prophetically released the power of the Holy Spirit to establish now and forever the mantle of authority through His blood. *"This cup is the New Testament in My blood."* It is through His blood and broken body that we can boldly proclaim, *Christ in me, the hope of the glory*! Jesus was telling us to live in the New Covenant promise by exercising the mantle of authority given to all believers. His blood, shed for all mankind, became our cloak, the precious life-saving garment we put on when we seek Him as our personal Lord and Savior. We are to apply the blood of Jesus Christ to our lives and wear the mantle of authority with confidence, standing ready to exercise dominion over the kingdom of darkness at all times.

The Kingdom of Heaven IS AT HAND

The passing of the mantle to Christians simply means that we have the authority of Christ in our lives today. The spiritual authority we possess is activated by our faith, releasing Holy Spirit power. The key to releasing the power of God in our lives lies in exercising the authority given to us through the blood of Jesus Christ. A double portion of God's anointing and power is available to all Christians who are poised and ready to exercise their authority and dominion over the kingdom of darkness.

When Jesus stated, *"Freely you have received, freely you must give"*[245] He was referring to the power and anointing of the Holy Spirit in each Believer. The concept is simple: the more we exercise God's authority and power the more power and anointing we will receive. This process is similar to the strengthening of our muscles. When we exercise our muscles we break down muscle fibers to enable them to grow back stronger. The same is true with the power and anointing of Christ in us. The more we exercise the mantle of authority in our

---

[245] Matthew 10:7

lives, the more we will receive greater power and anointing of the Holy Spirit in us.

When we step out in faith and stand against the lies, deception, and works of the devil, a power to destroy those yokes is released by God through His Holy Spirit. The result is the Kingdom of God comes upon us, the blind see, the deaf hear, the lame walk, the sick are healed, and the dead are raised! *Now it came to pass, as Peter went through all parts of the country that he also came down to the saints who dwelt in Lydda. There he found a certain man named Aeneas, who had been bedridden eight years and was paralyzed. And Peter said to him, "Aeneas, Jesus the Christ heals you. Arise and make your bed." Then he arose immediately.*

Peter exercised his spiritual authority through Jesus when he spoke, by faith: *"Aeneas, Jesus the Christ heals you. Arise and make your bed."* They were but eleven simple words, yet spoken in faith they released the Kingdom of God upon the paralyzed man and the result was immediate. The man was completely healed! Brothers and sisters in Christ, we have the same mantle of authority and the same power and anointing to release the Kingdom of Heaven in this world. Prepare yourself today and take hold of the truth of the authority, power, and anointing that is in you, that you may fulfill the call to be the ambassador of Christ and His Kingdom.

The Apostle David Hogan gave a testimony once that will stretch your faith.[246] The testimony that follows is one that requires great faith, a conscious understanding of the overcoming Christ that resides in each of us. We must know that we have the authority and power through Jesus our Lord to release the power of the Kingdom of God in every situation we encounter.

A great plague had swept through a jungle village, and one resident in particular, a widowed woman, discovered that her only two daughters had died as a result of the disease. She went to her village leader to find assistance in caring for the dead bodies, but was told to go home, that they were too busy to help because so many people in the village had died. So she took the bodies of her daughters and laid them outside, side by side, on her front porch. She made her way then to the local store, where she bought two large sacks of limes for pouring over the dead bodies to stop the spread of the terrible sickness.

Her sad task completed, the woman packed a small bag of food and set out to locate the pastor of a small church, a journey that would take an entire day by foot.

---

[246] Source: David Hogan, Videotape *"The Power to Raise the Dead."*

Many hours later, tired and weary from lack of sleep, she reached her destination and walked into the small church where she was greeted by the pastor's wife. The woman was informed that the pastor was currently unavailable, because he was in the middle of a two-day prayer and fast and could not be disturbed. The tired woman described her situation, and the pastor's wife was happy to help. Soon the pastor emerged and spent time with the villager. After some conversation the pastor responded, "Tomorrow we will leave to minister to your daughters, but tonight we pray."

They began their travels back to the village early the next morning. A day later, the pastor, his disciples, and the heartbroken mother came upon the dead bodies. The girls had been dead for three days. The smell was overbearing and their bodies were already decaying from the heat of the sun. Nevertheless, the pastor took one girl while his disciple took another, and they began to pray, exercising spiritual authority through faith in the redeeming power of Jesus' blood. When the men finished praying, exercising their spiritual authority over the demonic kingdom, the Kingdom of Heaven was released and both girls were raised from the dead.

Fellow believers, this same miracle-working power is available to you and to me if we exercise the authority given to us by the blood of Jesus Christ. For truly the Kingdom of Heaven is at hand!

Reflection Verse: *John 14:12-13*

Most assuredly, I say to you, he who believes in Me, the works that I do he will do also; and greater works than these he will do, because I go to My Father. And whatever you ask in My name, that I will do that the Father may be glorified in the Son.

Thought for Reflection:

What was Jesus saying in these words: "He who believes in Me and the works that I do he will do also and greater works than these he will do"? Do you believe in Jesus Christ and the works He accomplished? If so, there is an expectation that you not only will do the same works, but a greater work! The blood of Jesus Christ is the mantle of authority that has been passed on to you. Only through your faith in God's Word and the completed work of Jesus Christ can you exercise your spiritual authority.

Daily Confession:

The peace of Jesus is with me and I receive and put on the mantle of spiritual authority in my life. The blood of Jesus Christ covers me and all areas of my life, empowering me with the Holy Spirit to fulfill God's will. The power of life, a God kind of life full of abundance and blessings, is in my tongue through the words I choose to speak. Today I declare that I am a vessel the Holy Spirit may freely use to accomplish all that God desires.

9

The Power of the Throne

You are of God, little children, and have overcome them, because
He Who is in you is greater than he who is in the world.

1 John 4:4

Greater is He Who Is in You

"If the gospel that is preached in most churches today were preached by Jesus, He never would have been crucified."[247] The Gospel of Jesus Christ is the gospel of truth, and it will confront the hearts of those who are far from God. There is no compromise to the Word of God and the New Covenant established by the blood of Jesus the Christ. We must hate that which God hates and love that which God loves, standing, therefore, ready to proclaim the truth and power of God's Word in this world.

1 Corinthians 4:20 states, *"For the Kingdom of God is not in word but in power."* That is, the Kingdom of God is not just fancy talk; it is living by God's power. Jesus never proclaimed the Kingdom of God through word only, but there was always a demonstration of God's power in all Jesus accomplished. The Gospel of Jesus Christ was never designed to be seeker-sensitive, but confrontational through the truth of God's word, a demonstration of God's power to those who refuse to adhere to the truth of His Word.

Please do not misunderstand me. There is great compassion, mercy, and love in the Gospel of Jesus Christ, but the message itself is one that should – and does — pierce the heart of man, driving the truth of God's Word into the very soul of those who have ears to hear. No longer can we simply put on the armor of God and uphold a defensive posture against the oppression in the land. We have to take up the mantle of authority that releases, through faith, the power of God's Throne and reclaim everything Christ died to provide.

The battlefield is our faith, and we must take the offensive and be aggressive in our stance as a child of God to overcome the wretchedness of this world. We

---

[247] Pastor Bill Johnson, *Healing our Neglected Birthright*, Tape Series, Bethel Church, Redding, CA

have been authorized to destroy the idols of man's heart by demonstrating God's Living Word. Jesus said, *And from the days of John the Baptist until now the kingdom of heaven suffers violence, and the violent take it by force.*[248] We are commissioned to exercise the authority and power of the Throne of God in this world by destroying evil and all that it represents. We are to become violent in the areas of sin, sickness, disease, turmoil, strife, and premature death. We are to aggressively take back God's land from the kingdom of darkness.

Many brothers and sisters in Christ suffer under the yoke of oppression because they have yet to come to the full revelation of what it means when God's Word says, *Greater is He who is in you than he who is in the world.* Many beloved Christians have yet to receive the complete revelation of the triumph we have inherited through the Son of God. Bible teacher and author Derek Prince is credited with saying, *"A triumph is not actually the winning of the victory; it is the celebration and demonstration of a victory that has already been won. Jesus, through His death and the cross, demonstrated to the whole universe His victory over the entire satanic kingdom."*[249]

God has called us to be "more than conquerors" through Him who loved us.[250] The Christian faith is to live out and experience the inheritance of being more than a conqueror. We are to exercise victory and triumph through Jesus Christ in all we do. We are more than conquerors because Jesus has already defeated the enemy of the soul by disarming him, stripping him of all authority, and making a show of him openly on our behalf.[251]

Now thanks be to God who always leads us in triumph in Christ, and through us diffuses the fragrance of His knowledge in every place.[252] Powerful and poetic, they are words that should move us to act for Christ. The words "always" and "in every place" suggests there is no time or place when we cannot visibly share the triumph of Christ over satan's kingdom. Indeed, the aroma of our authority pours from our very being, awakening the atmospheres as we enter as ambassadors for Christ. We've been sealed with God's power to change the atmosphere in which we live, demonstrating unequivocally to the world the power and love of the Throne of God.

---

[248] Matthew 11:24

[249] Derek Prince, *On Experiencing God's Power*, Whitaker House, New Kensington, PA, page 473.

[250] Romans 8:37

[251] Colossians 2:15

[252] 2 Corinthians 2:14

Greater is He who is in us than he who is in the world is a foundational truth of the Holy Spirit of God, and it applies to each and every believer. We are more than overcomers not because of anything we have done, but because of the indwelling presence of God in us. By opening our hearts to the truth of the conquering power of the Holy Spirit in us, we will see great and awesome miracles of God moving throughout today's Church. As we latch onto the heart of the Holy Spirit, we will see God's glory manifested through the outpouring of His Spirit, possessing man's soul and transforming lives as His presence washes over the lost and the broken. The Holy Spirit, His power, and the miraculous are real indeed. We have His power to heal the sick, raise the dead, and break free those held captive by the chains of deceit.

Brothers and sisters in Christ, we cannot keep the God of this universe in a box and expect great and miraculous things to occur. *Greater is He who is in you than he who is this world* is a truth that must be expressed in every thought, word, and deed by breaking down the boundaries of our intellect and stepping into the realm of faith in the supernatural. We have been created in God's own image. God has humbled Himself to dwell in every believer that His Holy Spirit may catapult us into a realm of power, authority, and the miraculous. He is calling all Christians to be a representative of His Kingdom in this world.

Holy Spirit Power

I was in India in February 2003 as part of a ministry team from Liberating Ministries for Christ International. My dear friend and Indian brother, Pastor Jacob Christy, invited me to his cousin's house where I was asked to pray for his cousin who was dying from a cancerous tumor in his throat. We jumped in a cab and traveled about an hour to this man's house, only to learn that he had been admitted into the hospital that morning for radiation and chemotherapy.

I suggested we go to the hospital to pray for him, but was informed that Hindu law prohibited public prayer. So we stayed at the house and interceded on his cousin's behalf. As we prayed, the Holy Spirit began to move, and it was more than obvious to those in the room that the Kingdom of Heaven had opened. I was moved to pray also for the man's wife, son, and twin daughters, and as I finished praying for the family the Holy Spirit brought to my remembrance the Apostle Paul and his anointing of handkerchiefs for the sick. Asking the sick man's wife for a handkerchief, I anointed it with oil and prayed over it. Prophetically, I was led to speak life into the family and to leave instructions for the man's wife to follow upon his return from the hospital.

Once released by the Holy Spirit, we finished praying and said our goodbyes. Pastor Jacob, his wife Blessi, and I hailed a cab and made our way back to the hotel. I was scheduled to return home to the United States the next day. In all the anticipation and busyness of preparing for the flight, the prophetic prayers I'd offered to the needy family the night before had escaped my thoughts and mind.

The email I received two months later assured me of the wonderful and glorious power of God that works through each one of us. After all, I had followed God's lead and adhered to His instructions in praying for that family. God's work there, through me, had been completed. Pastor Jacob wrote:

> *Dear Brother David ~ I hope you remember going to my cousin's house, who was suffering from throat cancer. You prayed over a handkerchief and gave it to his wife. She did exactly what you said, and glory to God, he got completely healed, and he is now back to work. I am writing this letter from Sharjah, because I took the responsibility to escort him there. He has gained a lot of strength, and is a living witness to God's grace and healing power. He and his wife wanted me to share this with you and wanted you to rejoice with them. I do want to take this opportunity to thank you for coming and praying for my cousin. I want to assure you of all our love and continuous prayers for you, your wife Julie, your kids, and for your ministry. Closing with much love and prayers. ~ Jacob*

God is faithful in fulfilling His promises! The glory and power of God's Throne is available on a daily basis for all Christians willing to step into and experience God's presence. Similar to the healing of Pastor Jacob's cousin, supernatural power is available for all who believe that Jesus Christ is the Son of God. The testimony above is an example of the power of the Holy Spirit dwelling in each of us, desiring to work with us to manifest the Kingdom of Heaven in this world.

Jesus has positioned us to be one with the Father empowering us to release the Kingdom of God in this world and destroy all the works of the devil.[253] The only way we are able to fulfill this call of God's anointing is by submitting to and following the Holy Spirit of God inside us. The Word commands each believer to be filled with the Holy Spirit[254] that we may be empowered to live the Christian life as it was designed to be lived with dominion and authority over all the works of the devil.

---

[253] 1 John 3:8; Romans 16:20
[254] Ephesians 5:18

Acts 10:38 reveals how *"God anointed Jesus of Nazareth with the Holy Spirit and with power, who went about doing good and healing all who were oppressed by the devil, for God was with Him."* The power and authority Jesus demonstrated, and indeed lived, was a result of the Holy Spirit coming upon Him and anointing Him. It was impossible for Jesus to minister through His deity while on this earth, because He had given up His Godly inheritance and position to live as Son of Man. It was the only way He could overcome the temptations of man in order to position Himself as our High Priest in the Heavenly realm.[255]

John the Baptist saw the Holy Spirit descending upon Jesus like a dove.[256] It was then, and not before, that Jesus' ministry of power and authority began. God had anointed Jesus of Nazareth with His Spirit and power so that Jesus could destroy the works of the devil and demonstrate the Word made flesh for mankind. Jesus Himself said , *"Do you not believe that I am in the Father, and the Father in Me? The words that I speak to you I do not speak on My own authority; but the Father who dwells in Me does the works. Believe Me that I am in the Father and the Father in Me, or else believe Me for the sake of the works themselves."*[257] We, too, have been commissioned and empowered to go throughout the world doing good and healing all who are oppressed by the devil.[258] *For he who is joined to the Lord is one spirit with Him.*[259] God's Holy Spirit, dwelling in each believer, has empowered us to be like Christ in this world. We are full of the power, glory, peace, and love of Christ in us fulfilling the New Covenant promise of health and prosperity.[260]

The Key to Receiving God's Power

One of the secrets to stepping into the glory and releasing God's manifested power rests in our relationship with the Holy Spirit. Many Christians today have yet to receive the baptism of the Holy Spirit because they lack accurate teaching on the Holy Spirit and His purpose. In other words, while many have received Jesus Christ as Lord and Savior, allowing the Holy Spirit to dwell within them, they have yet to receive the baptism, the full immersion, of God's Holy Spirit. As a result, they have yet to acquire the power to release the manifestation of the Holy Spirit that transforms and empowers lives.

---

[255] Hebrews 2:16-18
[256] John 1:32
[257] John 14:10-11
[258] Matthew 28:18-20; Mark 16:15-20
[259] 1 Corinthians 6:17
[260] 1 John 4:17

Yet, there are also those Christians who have been baptized in the Holy Spirit who still struggle because they do not understand how to release the power God bestowed upon them. The fact that we can supernaturally bring Heaven to earth in all we think, say, and do has eluded them. As a result, many Christians are beaten down, sick, oppressed, and struggling with life, even though the greatest power known to man dwells within them. Misappropriating the Holy Spirit in the body of Christ has limited our ability to live in His supernatural presence.

To be sure, there is far more to the Holy Spirit than just His filling and residing presence within us. He is our guarantee of an inheritance of divine power in all things that pertain to life and godliness.[261] The Holy Spirit of God has sealed us with the divine Promise and forever marked us as children of the Living God. Yet His power is not being demonstrated, because through our lack of faith and understanding we have inhibited the Spirit of God from flowing through us.

Christians have been marked, called and appointed to live in the power of the Holy Spirit. Accordingly, everything we say and do has the power to transform lives. The Holy Spirit awaits its entrance into the world, through us, to save the lost and heal the sick and tormented. We can do nothing apart from God's Spirit.

Sadly, though, a very prominent bible teacher erroneously and publicly announced that Holy Spirit power was only for the dispensation of the early Church for the purpose of beginning the Christian movement. The same power today, he continued, simply is not needed.

I disagree. The Book of Acts is the Father's picture album of the Church in its infancy. His baby book, if you will. We have been called to grow up in God, to demonstrate more power, more glory, and more of HIM! Acts records not the acts of the apostles, but the acts of the Holy Spirit working through believers. Scripture clearly points out that Ananias and Stephen were not apostles, but that by the Holy Spirit they were made to perform miraculous works following their baptism in the Holy Spirit. The Book of Acts clearly spells out what is available to today's Christian believer when performed with faith and trust in the New Covenant promise.

Judging from today's headlines, we need God's Holy Spirit power more today than even in the early Church. We have wrongs to undo, holy ground to reclaim, false teachings to uncover. We must recover God's land and establish His Kingdom on earth as it has already been done in Heaven. To say that the Holy Spirit today is not the same as in the early Church is a misunderstanding of Who

---

[261] Ephesians 2:13; 4:30

the Holy Spirit is and what His purpose is for us today. It is a misguided, blatant falsehood and one that has successfully established harmful limits on our ability to truly experience God's awesome power.

The Holy Spirit of Acts is the same today as He was then. Yet many Christians take the intellectual sidestep, denying that the Spirit in us possesses the same power today through us. It's far easier for us to hold onto fear, doubt, and worry failing to exercise faith in the New Covenant promise established by the blood of Jesus than it is to boldly step out against human reasoning and understanding by trusting that God's Word will not fail.

The Holy Spirit Provides Understanding

Let's look for a moment at the actions of Jesus' disciples following His crucifixion. Here was a group of men who had personally traveled with Jesus throughout His earthly ministry. They had spent morning, noon and night with the Lord, observing His power and righteousness. Yet, after Jesus was crucified and buried, the very disciples who experienced the power of the Holy Spirit in this world hid in a room, fearful of the persecution awaiting them.[262]

As they congregated together in a single room and mourned the death of Jesus, confused about their future and curious about their past, they received word that Jesus had risen from the dead. Despite the fact that they had been the fortunate few to witness firsthand their Lord's miraculous powers, they rebuked the words and did not believe them.[263] Mark 16:14 states, *"Afterward He (Jesus) appeared to the eleven as they sat at the table; and He rebuked their unbelief and hardness of heart, because they did not believe those who had seen Him after He had risen."*

How could it be that they did not believe Jesus was truly the Son of God, the Messiah, the living Christ? Truthfully, they had yet to receive the Holy Spirit through Whom all faith and understanding are revealed. After Jesus rebuked His followers, He said, *"Peace to you! As the Father has sent Me, I also send you." And when He had said this, He breathed on them, and said to them, "Receive the Holy Spirit."*[264] Jesus breathed on the disciples and imparted the Holy Spirit of God in them, that their eyes of understanding were opened and they saw and believed that Jesus was the Christ.

---

[262] John 20:19
[263] Mark 16:14
[264] John 20:21

As it is so clearly rendered in 1 Corinthians 12:3, *"No one can say that Jesus is Lord except by the Holy Spirit."* This truth is confirmed in Matthew 16:13 where Jesus asked His disciples who He was. When Peter responded, "You are the Christ," Jesus said, *"Blessed are you, Simon Bar-Jonah, for flesh and blood has not revealed this to you, but My Father who is in heaven."* The Holy Spirit of God had fallen upon Peter to give him the revelation of who Jesus was, but at this point the Holy Spirit did not reside in him. We know from Scripture that the Holy Spirit was not released to all who believe until Jesus ascended to the right hand of the Father where He was given the precious Holy Spirit of God to pour freely into all who believe.[265]

No one can confess that Jesus is the Christ, the Messiah, the Son of God without the faith and the revelation imparted through the Holy Spirit. When Jesus breathed upon the disciples, He imparted a filling of the Holy Spirit that opened their eyes of understanding. The breath Jesus imparted upon them was not baptism of Holy Spirit power, but a filling of the Holy Spirit that opened their hearts to the truth of who Jesus was, is, and always will be. Therefore, even though the disciples received the impartation of the Holy Spirit when Jesus breathed on them, they were not yet baptized in the Holy Spirit of God. Therefore, the only thing they lacked was to be charged with God's power in order to transform lives.

The Baptism of the Holy Spirit

The greater revelation here is that a filling of the Holy Spirit gives us faith to be born again, but there is also a baptism of the Holy Spirit, an immersion in God's glory, that supplies the power to fulfill God's heart in this world. Many have received Jesus Christ as their Lord and Savior and have been filled with the Holy Spirit and become born again. What they're missing, though, is the outpouring of the Holy Spirit by baptism.

The word "baptism" derives from the Greek word *baptizo*, which means to be submerged, to wash, and to be overwhelmed.[266] Baptism of the Holy Spirit, then, is a submerging, washing, and overwhelming immersion into God's glory and presence. Much like a glass of water filled to the top, the more water added, the more it will spill over, touching everything in its path. The baptism of the Holy Spirit energizes the soul to an overflowing capacity, spilling into the lives of others.

---

[265] Acts 2:33
[266] Strong's Concordance Dictionary

Acts 5:14-15 provides an account of the overflowing capacity of the Holy Spirit in the Apostle Peter: *And believers were increasingly added to the Lord, multitudes of both men and women, so that they brought the sick out into the streets and laid them on beds and couches, that at least the shadow of Peter passing by might fall on some of them.* Peter's shadow is not what healed the multitudes; rather, the actual runoff of the Holy Spirit of God from his presence. This, my brothers and sisters, is available today to all Christians who desire to be immersed in His presence.

Holy Spirit baptism is a Christian's privilege and duty to obtain. It is only through the baptism of the Holy Spirit that we are able to truly step into the power and authority that God has called each Christian to fulfill. John the Baptist knew this truth when he said, *"I indeed baptize you with water unto repentance, but He who is coming after me is mightier than I, whose sandals I am not worthy to carry. He will baptize you with the Holy Spirit and fire."*[267]

Jesus Christ, the Son of God, was commissioned to baptize in the Holy Spirit. His role was to ignite fire in our souls with a passion and thirst to know the Father and experience His power and glory. Jesus commanded the disciples not to depart from Jerusalem, but to wait for the Promise of the Father. He said, *"For John truly baptized with water, but you shall be baptized with the Holy Spirit not many days from now."*[268] Baptism of the Holy Spirit changed the apostles' lives, enriching them with a boldness and wisdom to speak to the multitudes. Through the power of the Holy Spirit, they performed signs, wonders, and miracles. The Holy Spirit had energized their faith to stand in the midst of persecution and uphold the Gospel Truth. No longer were the disciples hiding in a small room from persecution, but with the Holy Spirit power they went out and proclaimed the truth of the Gospel of Jesus Christ! The body of Christ can do nothing without first being baptized in the Holy Spirit. We must cry out from the depths of our souls to be immersed into God's glory and presence.

I have discovered that one of the limitations to baptism of the Holy Spirit for many Christians is their struggle with fear and doubt. Lives have been destroyed and lost due to fear and the perverted, twisted powers of darkness of this world. The good news lies in the testimonies of the baptism of the Holy Spirit. There is an explosion in the soul of man that drives out darkness and fear and anchors man's hope to the truth of the New Covenant promise.

---

[267] Matthew 3:11
[268] Acts 1:4-5

Always remember, *Where the Spirit of the Lord is, there is liberty. But we all, with unveiled face, beholding as in a mirror the glory of the Lord, are being transformed into the same image from glory to glory, just as by the Spirit of the Lord.*[269] The baptism of the Holy Spirit provides not only freedom and liberty, but also the power to be transformed, from glory to glory, into the very image of our Lord and Savior.

As the body of Christ, we fail to grasp the power of God dwelling within us. We must trust our common-sense reasoning that if the Holy Spirit of God indeed has come down from heaven to reside in us, then God certainly has made us master over the powers of this dark world. *Greater is He who is in us than he who is in the world*! And if we exercise the faith to believe that the "He who is Greater" is in us, we could not help but step out in boldness and majesty.

John G. Lake adequately summed it up: "*There is not a devil or demon that comes within a hundred feet of a real God-anointed Christian!*"[270] If we are walking and living an anointed life, we are not waiting for the enemy to attack, but we are attacking the enemy. We are going forth in boldness and confidence, reclaiming and restoring God's people and His land. We become an open heaven from which God's entire Kingdom is released on the darkness of this world, and victory and triumph become our signature. The devil is terrified of this truth. There is nothing the devil can do to a Christian who is living the God-anointed life, because he no longer possesses the power or the authority over that life! He is a defeated foe, judged and sentenced to a life of eternity in hell. We, on the other hand, hold claim to a mantle of authority through the mighty name of Jesus Christ. Please make these words your own: The devil and his kingdom are terrified and will run when they see a God-anointed Christian walk into a room. You have the power to be that God-anointed Christian.

Recognize the Holy Spirit

What are we missing to manifest God's promise for our health and prosperity, to be that God-anointed Christian in this world? As I look around the Body of Christ I see children of God suffering from sin, sickness, torment, poverty, and premature death. I see Christians on their knees crying out to the throne of God for forgiveness, but living in guilt and shame; crying to the Lord for healing, deliverance, or financial blessing only to live in continual lack and despair. Christians are wrestling with the trials and tribulations of this world becoming

---

[269] 2 Corinthians 3:17,18
[270] John G. Lake, *His Life, His Sermons, His Boldness of Faith*, Kenneth Copeland Publications, Fort Worth Texas, 1994.

discouraged and loosing their hope in all that God has promised. I ask again, what are we missing to manifest God's promise of the New Covenant in our lives?

The answer lies in the revelation of "Who is the Holy Spirit." The truth of Who the Holy Spirit is in our lives is a revelation that will liberate and set God's people free! It will break the yoke of oppression that smothers the life of God's Spirit in our lives and prohibits the manifestation of His Kingdom promise. There is great hope in the gift of the Holy Spirit for He is everything that we have ever cried out to God to obtain. He is our promise of eternal life, a God kind-of-life, now and forever.[271] He is the very Kingdom of God dwelling in us!

Jesus states, *"The kingdom of God does not come with observation; nor will they say, 'See here!' or 'See there!' for indeed, the Kingdom of God is **within** you."*[272] The presence of the Holy Spirit of God in us brings with Him all of the resources available within the Kingdom of God. This is the revelation that Jesus was communicating when He stated, *"But seek first the Kingdom of God and His righteousness, and all these things shall be added to you. Do not fear, little flock, for it is your Father's good pleasure to give you the Kingdom."*[273] Jesus did not say seek God first, but the Kingdom of God. He then gave the Kingdom the pronoun "He." Jesus was talking about the Holy Spirit, the very breath and life of God in us!

Jesus was clear when He said, *"Nevertheless I tell you the truth. It is to your advantage that I go away; for if I do not go away, the Helper will not come to you; but if I depart, I will send Him to you."* When Jesus released the Holy Spirit into our lives He released the very nature of the Kingdom of God. The Kingdom of God dwells in you, because it is the Father's good pleasure to give you His Kingdom.

This truth is so powerful that it will transform all of your prayers! *Christ in you, the hope of the glory* is the promise of the *"anointed and His anointing"* dwelling in us. The anointed is the Holy Spirit and His anointing is the very power of God given to us, to dwell in us, that God's glory, His Kingdom be experienced through us. This revelation then clarifies the truth of what God's will is for our lives. *Thy Kingdom come, Thy will be done on earth as it is in Heaven* is a declaration from the Father that if it does not exist in Heaven then it should not exist in the Christian life! This declaration and the promise of the New Covenant will only occur when we receive the truth of Who the Holy Spirit is in our life.

---

[271] Luke 24:49: 1 John 2:25
[272] Luke 17:20-21
[273] Luke 12:31,31: Matthew 6:33

He is the very essence of God, therefore, the Kingdom of God. Jesus stated, "*But if I cast out demons by the Spirit of God, surely the Kingdom of God has come upon you.*"[274] Receive, today, the revelation of Who dwells in you, for if God is for us who can be against us?

Read the various names by which the Holy Spirit is known throughout Scripture (see below). Each name is a spiritual reality and a perfect answer to the cries of our hearts. You will notice that each name of the Holy Spirit represents the very essence of the Kingdom of God and all of its resources and spiritual blessings that are already yours.

The Holy Spirit is called:[275]

the Spirit of God	the Spirit of the Living God
the Spirit of Life	
the Spirit of Truth	the Spirit of Holiness
the Spirit of Glory	the Spirit of Mercy
the Spirit of Christ	Spirit of Counsel
the Spirit of Grace	the Spirit of Joy
the Spirit of Wisdom	the Spirit of Love
the Spirit of Knowledge	the Spirit of Power
the Spirit of Understanding	the Spirit of Might
the Spirit of Revelation	the Spirit of Self-Control
the Spirit of Promise & Prosperity	the Spirit of Gentleness
the Spirit of Praise	the Spirit of Patience
the Spirit of Peace	the Spirit of Goodness
Spirit of Reverence	the Spirit of the Father
the Spirit of the Son	the Holy Ghost
the Spirit of the Lord	and the Comforter

It is interesting to note that the name "Comforter" derives from the Greek word *parakletos*, which means "to be called alongside, to help, to aid or to support." A sobering truth is realized when we recognize that God has humbled Himself to come alongside man to be his helper and support. The depth of this understanding will liberate anyone from the bondage of this world. In all His splendor and Awesome glory, God humbled Himself and released His Spirit, His Kingdom, to dwell in us that we may have dominion and power. He has given us Kingdom authority to exercise His will and truth on earth. The kingdom of hell

---

[274] Matthew 12:28
[275] This is not a comprehensive list.

does not stand a chance! Dear believer, you possess the very traits of the Father because you are His child. Look inside yourself and see the forces ready to be called into action. They are the Spirit of Peace, Prosperity, Power and Might. Even the Spirit of Revelation has made His dwelling in your heart.

The Person of the Holy Spirit represents the entire essence of the Christian life. He is the Kingdom of God - God, Himself - dwelling in us to empower us in this world. Our greatest gift came at the great cost of Jesus' suffering, death, resurrection, and ascension. The Father has made His entire Kingdom available to all those who believe.

Rev. Dr. Dale Sides summed it all up in profound fashion when he made the statement, "Prosperity does not come to us; it comes out of us." That same truth can also be applied to anything that our hearts are crying out to the Lord to experience. Health, peace, joy, prosperity – they do not come to us, they are waiting to be birthed from within us. Colossian 3:3 states, *"your life is hidden with Christ in God."* The very essence and presence of the Great I AM dwells within us, in that hidden place waiting for us to search it out through our hunger for the promised Divine Life. If you listen, you will hear His still small voice as it whispers the reminder, "Here I am." It is time we learn to share the blessings God has stored inside us for His use, work, and glory.

The Kingdom of Heaven Is NOW At Hand

Elijah was a prophet. Exhorting the children of God to stop wavering in their faith and to choose either to follow Baal or the Great I AM,[276] Elijah implored the children of Israel, *"How long will you falter between two opinions? If the Lord is God, follow Him; but if Baal, follow him."* When they failed to answer,[277] Elijah presented a challenge to the false prophets: *"You call on the name of your gods, and I will call on the name of the Lord; and the God who answers by fire, He is God."* They accepted the challenge, and 450 prophets of Baal and 400 prophets of Asherah called upon their gods to ignite a fire under their prepared sacrifice.

The 850 prophets did everything according to their custom to call upon their god Baal, but nothing happened. From morning until evening, they cut themselves, threw themselves on the ground, and cried out "O, Baal, hear us," but there was no response. No fire, not even a spark.

---

[276] 1 Kings 18:17-41
[277] 1 Kings 18:21

Then Elijah stepped forward and said to the people, "Come near me." So the people came, anticipating that something great was about to happen. The fragrance of the knowledge of God was in that place, and all those who were near understood that something miraculous, something powerful, something awesome was about to take place. Through faith in God, Elijah changed the atmosphere created by the satanic kingdom of idolatry and released the Kingdom of Heaven upon that place.

Elijah took his time to repair the altar of the Lord that was destroyed by the pagan worshippers, and carefully he reestablished a place of worship and honor to the Lord according to the Laws of Moses. Positioning the wood, Elijah laid down the sacrificed meat of the bull, presenting it as ready to the Lord. He dug a deep trench all the way around the altar and ordered that four large water pots be filled and poured over the entire offering until the deep trench around the altar of the Lord was full.

When the wood, meat, and altar were saturated with water, Elijah began to pray, *"LORD God of Abraham, Isaac, and Israel, let it be known this day that You are God in Israel, and that I am Your servant, and that I have done all these things at Your word. Hear me, O LORD, hear me, that this people may know that You are the LORD God, and that You have turned their hearts back to You again."* Then the fire of the LORD fell and consumed the burnt sacrifice, the wood, the stones, the dust, licking up even the water in the trench. The people saw it, and they fell on their faces, saying, *"The LORD, He is God! The LORD, He is God!"* And Elijah said to them, *"Seize the prophets of Baal! Do not let one of them escape!"* So they seized them; and Elijah brought them down to the Brook Kishon and executed them there. [278]

This account of Elijah and the prophets of Baal is a testimony of how the Kingdom of God can penetrate this reality we call life. Through faith, Elijah called down the fire of God, and God responded by destroying, in one single act, all strongholds of fear, doubt, and idolatry in the hearts of His children. Elijah demonstrated that God is the Great I AM – meaning God is the "present future," right now. How does this affect us today? God's timing to release His glory through those who believe is RIGHT NOW – *the present future*. He desires right now to heal His people, to set us free from the strongholds of satan, and draw our hearts back to His truth and presence. God is the God of "right now." He is waiting for you and me to understand that we, too, can be servants like Elijah and call down His purifying fire.

---

[278] 1 King 18:36-40

Understand, however, that the battles will be many, perhaps even daily. The Word of God is clear that *we do not wrestle against flesh and blood, but against principalities, against powers, against the rulers of the darkness of this age, against spiritual hosts of wickedness in the heavenly places.*[279] So often I minister to loving, moral Christians who are under attack from the kingdom of hell, wondering why these things are happening to them. People struggling with illness, disease, mental and emotional problems, family division, and financial instability come to me for prayer, and each time I strive to help them understand the truth of their position and life within the New Covenant. It is satan's primary objective to undermine man's faith and life in God's promises, thereby, trying to kill, steal, and destroy God's children.

Matthew 12:22-29 holds our proof. Jesus had healed a demonized man who was mute and blind. But the people had begun to question whether Jesus really was the Messiah, the Christ. The Pharisees were the ruling religious leaders at the time, after all, and they proclaimed that Jesus healed through the chief of the demons.

Thankfully, Jesus perceived their hearts and stated, *"But if I cast out demons by the Spirit of God, surely the kingdom of God has come upon you. Or else how can one enter a strong man's house and plunder his goods, unless he first binds the strong man? And then he will plunder his house."*[280] Jesus illustrated that when we exercise the mantle of authority through our faith and release the power of God through the Spirit of God, we commission God's angelic army to engage the kingdom of hell, at which point a collision between two kingdoms is experienced. Jesus taught and demonstrated that when we call upon the Spirit of God, surely the Kingdom of God will come upon us and the strong man and his stronghold shall be bound and plundered!

The Kingdom of God responds to a faith that is uncompromised. When we exercise our faith in the authority of The Blood, we call down the Kingdom of Heaven and the power of the Throne of God is released to liberate us into the victory that has already been won! Jesus made it very clear; if it does not exist in Heaven then it should not exist in the Christian life. The power of the Throne of God is available to you today to live in the victory and triumph that Jesus provided for all of God's people! Call down, today, the Kingdom of God by the Spirit of God and experience God's divine promise in your life.

---

[279] Ephesians 6:12
[280] Matthew 12:28-29

Reflection Verse: *1 John 4:4*

> *You are of God, little children, and have overcome them,*
> *because He Who is in you is greater than he who is in the world.*

Thought for Reflection:

What does this verse say to you? Jesus gave us the greatest gift – eternal life. This eternal life is a mantle of authority we are expected to exercise. "Eternal" means NOW and forever, and "Life" means a God kind of life, full of abundance and blessings. Therefore, you are an overcomer because greater is He who is in you than he who is in the world! You have the Holy Spirit of God dwelling in you empowering you to be an overcomer in all areas of your life. The Holy Spirit is your Comforter, Truth, your Life. Does the Holy Spirit possess you? Allow Him to possess your soul and He will transform your life!

Daily Confession:

I am an overcomer, because greater is the Holy Spirit in me than he who is in the world. I have the mantle, the blood of Jesus Christ, covering me, empowering me to be all that I can be. I have the power and authority to heal the sick, raise the dead, and cast out demons, because the very essence of God, the Kingdom of Heaven, dwells in me. By faith today I exercise my spiritual authority over the kingdom of darkness and oppression in my life and declare by faith that God's Word is true and unfailing. I am free, prosperous, and healthy, because I know the Father loves me and it is His will for me. For where the Spirit of the Lord is there is liberty!

10

Releasing the Power of God

Without faith it is impossible to please Him, for he who comes to God must believe that He is, and that He is a rewarder of those who diligently seek Him.

Hebrews 11:6

Great Faith

On a hill overlooking the river outside my mother-in-law's cabin, I found myself swept away by the peace that surrounded me. Soon rain began to fall. I watched the raindrops fall ever so softly upon the calm surface of the water, and praying in the Spirit, I heard the Lord speak to me very clearly. "David, my son, walk on the water."

My first thought was *"What?,"* but God responded immediately: *"It's that seed of doubt that initially keeps My children from experiencing My miraculous power. The seed of doubt is what My children must overcome in order to receive My blessings of healing and miracles in their lives."*

Jesus made it abundantly clear in the Word when He stated, *"I say to you, if you have faith as a mustard seed, you will say to this mountain, 'Move from here to there,' and it will move; and nothing will be impossible for you."*[281] What a wonderful and faithful God we serve! Jesus Himself has assured us that nothing is impossible for us if we have faith the size of a mustard seed!

The truth of this statement, on the other hand, suggests that the opposite is also true. If we have <u>doubt</u> the size of a mustard seed, then the mountains in our lives will remain. God has given us the responsibility to exercise our faith and to release His power in and through us. The mountains that appear so ominous and unmovable become nothing when faith in God's promises is activated and His power is released. Laying hold of the truth that our faith releases the power of God allows us to step into a consciousness of power, confidence, and peace that comes from knowing that with God all things are possible.

---

[281] Matthew 17:20

Elisha's servant learned this truth in the midst of what could have been a terrifying experience. Waking early one morning to prepare the day for his master, he noticed the Syrian army surrounding the city of Dothan and positioning itself to destroy Elisha.[282] Chariots and horses were coming upon the city, the servant ran to Elisha, saying, *"Alas, my master! What shall we do?"* Anxiety and fear gripped his heart as he cried out to his master.

Elisha, however, met his servant's fears with faith-filled words: *"Do not fear, for those who are with us are more than those who are with them."*

He spoke with a confidence quite foreign to his servant. We can almost imagine the servant looking at Elisha, perplexed, his heart beating fiercely against his chest in terror. Elisha looked upon his servant and saw his fear and confusion. Laying his hands upon the servant, Elisha prayed, *"Lord, I pray, open my friend's eyes that he may see."*

And see he did! The servant's eyes were opened to mountains full of horses and chariots of fire, all at Elisha's service. All fear and doubt disappeared the moment he took his eyes off the world and his circumstances and allowed God to open his spirit to see what was *really* happening. God calls us today to the same kind of great faith – a knowing belief that allows us to activate His truth and power.

We are reminded also of the occasion when Jesus and his disciples had gathered together beneath a tree to keep cool in the heat of the day. A Centurion soldier approached Jesus, pleading with Him, *"Lord, my servant is lying at home paralyzed, dreadfully tormented."*[283] And Jesus said to him, *"I will come and heal him."* Jesus' response to the Centurion must have shocked the disciples who were gathered around Him, because they knew the soldier was of Roman descent and not a Hebrew. They also knew Jesus had been called not to the Gentiles, but to the children of Israel.[284]

Jesus had perceived through revelation from His Father, however, that the Gentile's faith would set an example for the children of Israel to follow. For as soon as Jesus responded, *"I will come and heal him,"* the Centurion answered, *"Lord, I am not worthy that You should come under my roof. But only speak a word, and my servant will be healed. For I also am a man under authority, having soldiers under me. And I say to this one, 'Go,' and he goes; and to*

---

[282] 2 Kings 6:15-17
[283] Matthew 8:5-13
[284] Matthew 15:21-28

another, '*Come,*' *and he comes; and to my servant, '*Do this,*' and he does it.*" Jesus marveled at the Centurion's faith, saying to His disciples around Him, "*Assuredly, I say to you, I have not found such great faith, not even in Israel!*"

Then Jesus began to teach and prophesy that the Gentiles would be brought into the Father's Kingdom, instructing the Centurion, "*Go your way; and as you have believed, so let it be done for you.*" The Centurion's great faith had released God's power to heal his servant many miles away! This measure of faith, which is strong enough to move the mightiest of mountains, is available to each and every Christian today.

A Canaanite woman had cried out to Jesus, "*Have mercy on me, O Lord, Son of David! My daughter is severely demon-possessed.*"[285] But Jesus chose not to respond. His disciples urged Him to "*Send her away, for she cries out after us,*" and yet Jesus' initial reaction was, "*I was not sent except to the lost sheep of the house of Israel. It is not good to take the children's bread and throw it to the little dogs.*" Much like the Centurion soldier, the Gentile woman persisted, demonstrating a faith great enough to release the Kingdom of Heaven upon her daughter. The women responded, "*True, Lord, yet even the little dogs eat the crumbs which fall from their masters' table.*" Jesus' response to her was immediate and true, "*O woman, great is your faith! Let it be to you as you desire.*" Her daughter was healed that very hour.[286]

The power of God's Holy Spirit and the promise of His covenant dwells within us as believers. Unlocking that power requires only that we exercise our faith. Great faith releases the Kingdom of Heaven to set people free. We must activate the faith locked deep within our hearts if we hope to release God's glory and power.

At a time before seat belts became law, a young father was making a left-hand turn through an intersection when the back door flew open and his daughter was flung from the car.

Hearing her scream, the father looked just in time to notice a large semi-truck heading straight for his daughter. Responding according to his faith, the man cried out *Jesus, Jesus, Jesus*! When he brought his car to a stop, he ran to the front of the semi, where he found his little girl curled up in the fetal position, terrified, crying, and just inches from the front bumper.

---

[285] Matthew 15:22
[286] Matthew 15:28

Scooping his daughter up in his arms and comforting her, the father went to the driver of the truck to thank him for reacting so quickly. The driver, however, was found slumped over, heaving and gasping for air. Putting his hand on the truck driver's back, the father thanked him for saving his daughter's life. In obvious bewilderment, the driver straightened up, looked the father in the eyes, and said, "Mister, I never took my foot off the gas pedal. Something else stopped this truck!"

The father had reacted in great faith. He could have reacted in fear, expressing useless screams and expletives. Instead, he called upon the Name above all names, upon Jesus the Christ, to save his daughter. He was a man of faith, one who knew Jesus as His Lord and Savior, because he never hesitated to trust in Jesus Christ. At a time when he needed Jesus most, when every second counted, the father reacted from his heart, in faith. The father had put all his trust in the power and saving grace of our Redeemer and his great faith saved his daughter's life. Praise God!

Establishing "Great Faith"

Perhaps you are wondering whether you could ever exercise "great faith." The act of "great faith" does not stem from our thoughts or our intellect, but from a conviction, a "knowing," and a confidence that resonates deep from within our hearts. Great faith is activated when our complete consciousness is possessed by the very Spirit of God and we "know that we know" that our Father is faithful in all that He has promised. This type of "great faith" destroys fear, doubt, and worry and produces an atmosphere in which the Kingdom of God is produced.

There is a revelation within the Word of God that needs to be revealed about our faith in God's promises. Hebrews 10:23 states, *"Let us hold fast the confession of our hope without wavering, for He Who has promised is faithful."* The word "confession" derives from the Greek word *homologeo*, which means to covenant, promise, and commit.[287] This same word has been translated into the words profession or proclamation found throughout the New Testament. The truth to our confession or profession of the Gospel of Jesus Christ is a faith that is anchored upon our commitment to the promises found in the Spirit of God within us. We have been exhorted not to grieve the Holy Spirit[288] by our lack of faith and commitment to the New Covenant promise. Our confessions are not just the "act" of repeating God's Word, but it is an "act" that is committed to the truth of God's promises and fulfilling His will. We are instructed to fight the good fight

---

[287] Strong's Concordance Dictionary
[288] Ephesians 4:30

of faith, trusting God with a full commitment to Him that *all* things are possible to him who believes.

There is a level of faith that is connected to our commitment that transcends the faith found through our intellect and emotions. As stated earlier in Chapter Five, the soul is the place where our intellect, emotions, imaginations, and free will are created. When we try to master our faith by our intellect and rely solely on how our five senses perceive a situation, then we are limiting the truth of God's Spirit dwelling in us. *Holding fast to our confessions of hope* suggests that we must stand with an anticipation, joy, and confidence that rests upon our commitment to God's faithfulness in all that He has promised. This type of faith can only be found in our unshakable commitment to the victory we have through the blood of Jesus Christ.

There is a transition that must occur throughout our relationship with the Father where we develop a conviction in the consciousness of our souls where we are fully convinced that God is able to perform all that He has promised.[289] When our souls submit and become committed to the Spirit within us we then begin to confess the truth of God's Word. When this oneness occurs between the Spirit and soul all doubt and wavering is destroyed. We develop a confidence that is founded upon our commitment of *Christ in us, the hope of the glory*. We then begin to live from a Kingdom perspective, confessing words of life and experiencing the fulfillment of His divine promise.

This is the mustard seed of faith that Jesus spoke of in His proclamation of moving mountains through our faith.[290] 3 John 1:2 refers to this "great faith" as a "prospering soul." The Word of God states, *"that you will prosper in all things and be in health, just as your soul prospers."* The prosperity of our souls influences the prosperity of our lives. This truth is established upon our souls becoming one with the Spirit of God in us. Our souls cannot prosper if we rely on our intellect and emotions for our faith. God has never called us to stand on our own faith, but to be one with His faith from His Kingdom. We must harness this truth and link our souls with the faith of our hearts releasing the manifested glory of His promise and presence.

We are told to *"draw near with a true heart in full assurance of faith, having our hearts sprinkled from an evil conscience and our bodies washed with pure water."*[291] The concept of an evil conscience is defined when Jesus rebuked Peter

---

[289] Romans 4:21
[290] Matthew 17:20
[291] Hebrews 10:22

for being mindful of the things of man and not the things of God.[292] A faith that moves mountains is released when our souls become aligned with the Spirit dwelling in us. When we draw near with a true heart in full assurance of faith we are in a place of "great faith" where soul and spirit are working together to fulfill the will of God. The manifestation of this revelation truth lies in the ability of our spirits, souls, and bodies to be fully *committed* to the promise of the New Covenant. "Great faith" is released when we are continually immersed in God's Holy Word allowing His Holy Spirit to consume our thoughts, transforming our souls and bodies to release His glory.

Many struggling Christians find a Bible verse and confess it over and over again regarding their healing or deliverance *expecting* it to produce a miracle in their lives. Yet, they continue to harbor a faith based on their own intellect and knowledge holding on to the mustard seeds of fear and doubt. There commitment to the New Covenant promise wavers when "bad news" is experienced and they become mindful of the things of man and not of God. When the results are not immediate they began to lose hope and their faith is undermined, limiting their experience of God's promise and power. However, those who stay diligent and committed, "knowing" that God's Truth and Word are unbreakable began to experience deep within their hearts a fire that is unquenchable. This fire consumes their hearts and souls and they begin to act and respond to the undefiled Truth of the New Covenant promise.

Confessing God's Truth, therefore, requires us to allow the Scripture to take root in our hearts to transform our very soul, igniting a confidence that releases God's promises. When that unquenchable fire possesses our souls, we come to a place of rest and conviction where God's Awesome Spirit and power are experienced. The seed of doubt must be removed from our consciousness. A person can have all the head faith in the world for Jesus to restore them, but if a tiny seed of doubt enters one's consciousness, faith is lost! We need a faith so convicted, so firm, so unshakable that no amount of doubt or fear could ever remove it. This "great faith" is found when the Spirit and soul become one and our commitment to God's promises is the "rock" from which we stand.

More than a few people have considered me out of my mind for believing in miracles as I do. However, my response is always the same, "*I am not out of my mind. I'm out of your mind.*" As Christians, we are expected to achieve a level of faith that falls far outside any intellectual understanding. We are told to set our minds on the things of above, not on the things of the earth,[293] to walk in the

---

[292] Matthew 16:23
[293] Colossians 3:2

Spirit and not in the flesh,[294] and the only way that is possible is through unwavering faith in God's promises. God requires our faith to be unmovable, unshakeable, because it is our hearts' faith that moves mountains, stops storms, and releases miracles.

Just ask the woman with the issue of blood.[295] Here is a woman who had a flow of blood for twelve years, suffering at the hands of many physicians and spending all she owned, and yet only got worse. She had heard about the man called Jesus and was determined to touch Him and be healed. The woman believed that, "*If only I may touch the hem of His clothes, I would be made well.*" Crawling on the ground, being kicked, stepped on, and cursed she pressed in and laid hold of His garment. Immediately the fountain of her blood was dried up. She knew she had been healed, and Jesus knew power had gone out of Him, having turned to the crowd and asked, "*Who touched My clothes?*"

But His disciples said to Him, "*You see the multitude thronging You, and You say, 'Who touched Me?'*" "And He looked around to see her who had done this thing. But the woman, fearful and trembling, knowing what had happened to her, fell down before Jesus and told Him the whole truth. And He said to her, "*Daughter, your faith has made you well. Go in peace, and be healed of your affliction.*"

It is interesting to note that there were many people reaching out to Jesus at the same time. The difference is that her faith released God's healing power. We know from Scripture that God is not a respecter of persons;[296] therefore, He did not single out this woman to be healed over anyone else. She had the faith and the ability to pull the virtue and power of God from Jesus. *How was this possible?* There are two reasons:

First, our introduction to this woman occurs when she is at the depths of her desperation. She was an outcast, untouchable because of the flow of blood, and for twelve years she had suffered isolation and condemnation as she spent all her money trying to find a cure to her ailment. She was destitute. She had heard that Jesus, the miracle-worker, was passing through her city and that great healings followed Him everywhere. Her great desperation ignited a fire of faith deep within her heart that rested upon her conviction that if she could just touch the hem of His garment she would be healed.

---

[294] Romans 8:1
[295] Mark 5:21-34
[296] Acts 10:34

Second, she acted on her newfound faith. Lacking doubt and fear, she knew if she simply touched Jesus' garment she would be healed. So she crawled on the ground, being kicked and pushed as she pressed toward her prize. When finally she was near Jesus, she reached through a jungle of legs and sandals to touch His hem. Holy Spirit power flowed from Jesus into the woman, and instantly she was healed. Fueled by desperation, she acted on her faith and pulled the restorative power of God into her life.

I had asked a pastor from India once why there are more miracles and healings experienced in services in India than in the United States, and his response was profound. "In India, all we have is our faith in God and His miraculous power to heal and set us free. In America, you have a hospital or clinic on every corner. For us," he said," it's a matter of faith and desperation."

For some people, hearing the Word of God for the first time is enough. Many times, they are in a state of deep desperation, and the purifying fire of God was easily able to enter and heal their souls and bodies. The measure of desperation one experiences has a profound effect on the level of faith one is ready to act upon. Many Christians today have faith to believe that Jesus is Lord, but they doubt healing and deliverance is for today. Our worldly circumstances cannot prohibit His supernatural abilities.

The power to release God's miracle and healing blessing in the Christian life is found at the place of great faith, where we become unshakable in the promises of God's New Covenant in our lives. We must get to a place deep in our souls, in our conscious awareness, where we desire, hunger and thirst for more of His presence, more of Him, where we can boldly stand before our accuser and confess the words of the Apostle Paul: *"To live is Christ, but to die is gain."* We need a faith rooted in the deep desires of our hearts to live and be like Christ in all we think, say, and do. We must get to place where our lives are marked by Christ in us.

I ministered to a young man who was struggling with Paranoid Schizophrenia, a mental illness the world defines as incurable and one by which people so oppressed hear voices and hallucinate. This young man was certain that the condition that tormented him would extend his entire life, because this is what he was told by all those closest to him. It is this type of thinking that keeps Christians in bondage. Even after we had spent an abundance of time in prayer, and in the presence of the Almighty God, he kept saying he "hoped" he would be healed, he "hoped" he would experience a day without voices, a day without hallucinations.

Of all the words misapplied and understated in the English language, "hope" certainly ranks near the top. The "hope" found in Scripture is defined as a waiting period of joy that produces a full confidence in anticipation for something good to be experienced. The worldly definition of "hope" today contains massive elements of doubt and a chronic lack of joy. It was the latter "hope" this young man expressed. I asked him where his faith was and whether he believed with total conviction that Jesus had already set him free. He responded, "Yes, I believe that Jesus *can* set me free, *but* I think I will have this illness until the day I die because the doctors, my mom, and everyone else says this illness is a life-long battle."

Certainly, he had the head faith that God had the power to heal him, but he questioned whether he would receive the blessing of God's healing. Seeds of doubt grow like thorns in our hearts, choking out the truth of God's Word and keeping us in bondage *until* the day we act on our faith with full assurance and confidence that God's promises of divine health are available. Until we act in faith with resolve and desperation committed to the indwelling Spirit of health and prosperity, we will remain in bondage limiting the magnificent power of God in our lives.

Is it possible, brothers and sisters, for us to experience the Word of God in such a way that we know, with great faith, that each word holds the power to transform our lives? How many of us today suffer in bondage to sickness, strife, emotional or mental illness, torment, affliction, or oppression because we are listening to what the world says and not to what the Word of God promises? Where is our commitment to the New Covenant established through the blood of Jesus Christ and sealed by the Holy Spirit of God? Only through our commitment and unwavering faith can we stand and experience the fullness of God's promise in our lives.

Faith Is the Substance of Things Hoped For

Faith was not designed to be complex in our understanding and operation to the Christian life. Faith is, however, above the realm of our physical understanding of mind and body. We must be able to know without evidence from our physical senses that the Word of God is truth. Only then will the truth and faithfulness of God's Word be manifested. By definition, "faith" is *the substance of things hoped for, the evidence of things not seen.*[297]

---

[297] Hebrews 11:1

By faith alone we are able to reach into the future and lay hold of that which we believe to receive. Accordingly, faith enables us to see the unseen, knowing and waiting with joy and full confidence that it shall come to full and complete manifestation. The Word of God is clear that we cannot please God without faith, for he who comes to God must believe that He is, and that He is a rewarder of those who diligently seek Him.[298] Living a Christian life full of power, dominion, and triumph over the works of the devil requires a strong measure of faith. It is impossible to please the Father otherwise. Believe, in full confidence, that His promise and truth will be experienced. Faith is not an entity too difficult to understand. The proof rests in the truth that God is faithful in all He has promised.

Take note of the words exchanged between Jesus and "Doubting Thomas": *Reach your finger here, and look at My hands; and reach your hand here, and put it into My side. Do not be unbelieving, but believing. And Thomas answered and said to Him, My Lord and my God! Jesus said to him, "Thomas, because you have seen Me, you have believed. Blessed are those who have not seen and yet have believed."*[299] Believing without seeing is fundamental to our walk with Jesus Christ. All the healings and miracles sprinkled throughout God's Word, as well as those in our present-day Church, rest on faith.

Simply, without faith we will not receive what we desire. The Word of God is clear when it says, *But let him ask in faith, with no doubting, for he who doubts is like a wave of the sea driven and tossed by the wind. For let not that man suppose that he will receive anything from the Lord; he is a double-minded man, unstable in all his ways.*[300]

Which of us is capable of possessing great faith? According to the Gospel of Jesus Christ, God has dealt to <u>each</u> a measure of faith.[301] Each of us has been given a responsibility to grow in faith, *that the righteousness of God is revealed from faith to faith*[302] that we may move from a faith rooted in our intellectualism to faith connected to our commitment to God's promises. We must be moved from the place of simply believing to the place where we know God's Word to be true. Understand that true faith must grow, be nurtured, and continually be sustained. Reaching the level of authority God designed for each believer in Christ requires progression and experience. *Faith comes by hearing, and hearing*

---

[298] Hebrews 11:6

[299] John 20:27-29

[300] James 1:6-8

[301] Romans 12:3

[302] Romans 1:17

by the word of God.[303] The more we hear the Word of God, the greater our faith will develop and become unshakeable. It does not have to take a lifetime to develop great faith. Our souls are transformed to receive the truth when we trust and submit to God's Word. Come to the Father as children, open, innocent, and completely dependent on Him for everything.

Jesus made it possible that great faith would not take a lifetime to develop. It is God's desire that we grow from faith to faith by dedicating our time to study His Word, resting in His presence, and listening to His direction. I once asked Rev. Dr. Dale Sides, my spiritual father, what I had to do to demonstrate more of God's power through me. His response was simple, "pray." Spending more time with the Father, seeking His heart, and being filled with His presence empowered me to be in tune with what God desired to accomplish through me in every situation. It was becoming increasingly clear to me that if I wanted more of God's power to flow through me, I needed to develop a hunger and thirst for more of Him and His Kingdom. As I sought for more of Him I began to develop deep within my soul a conviction and commitment to the New Covenant established for all of God's people. I began to develop a burning passion, rooted in desperation to see God's people set free. Through this commitment and fire deep in my soul I began to see the manifestation of God's power and presence.

Faithfulness Is Great Faith

Generating great faith is accomplished when we hear the Word of God. It is a truth proven by believers worldwide, from every generation. When man puts his trust and understanding in the Father and rests in Him for his every need, faith works. Maturity in Christ brings the believer to a level of faithfulness that allows God's glory to be released into the physical realm that the full manifestation of God may be fully experienced. When Jesus asked the question, *"Nevertheless, when the Son of Man comes, will He really find faith on the earth?,"*[304] He wondered whether His body, the children of God, you and me, would stand on our faith, firm, steadfast, and committed to Him. It is essential for us to contemplate where we are at any given moment. Should Jesus return right now, would He find us truly faithful in everything?

The Hebrew term for "faith" is *emuwnah,* and it means firmness, fidelity, and steadiness. In Hebraic thinking, the very core of faith is by definition

---

[303] Romans 10:17
[304] Luke 18:8b

faithfulness, which is linked to the Hebrew root *emet* for truth. [305] The heart of faith, then, is best depicted by a faithfulness, firmness, steadfastness, commitment, and confidence in the *truth* of God and His promises. The pinnacle of the Christian faith we are called to achieve and experience is to be *faithful* to God's Word. We are to live a life *committed* to the fulfillment of God's word in our lives. We are to be full of confidence and joy, knowing the Kingdom of Heaven is at hand, indeed dwelling in our very being, waiting to be released. Great faithfulness is unmovable. It emits the aroma of authority and power that proclaims triumph and victory everywhere. A deep level of faithfulness changes the atmosphere around us and allows the Kingdom of Heaven to enter the physical realm, raining down the very presence of God.

How often have we prayed for healing or restoration only to try to do it ourselves man's way? Where is our faithfulness, the great faith that is unmovable in God's New Covenant promise of health and prosperity?

One of my favorite demonstrations of the faithfulness in the Word of God is that of the blind Bartimaeus near Jericho.[306] Bartimaeus heard that Jesus was walking by and he began to cry out "*Jesus, Son of David, have mercy on me!*" The crowd chastened Bartimaeus and warned him to be quiet, but he cried out all the more, "*Son of David, have mercy on me!*"

Jesus stood still and commanded the crowd to bring forth the blind man. Throwing aside his garment, Bartimaeus rose and came to Jesus. Understand that Hebrew custom of that time rendered blind persons as outcasts. They were required to wear special garments to alert everyone to the fact that they were without sight and outside the "accepted" – cursed. But Bartimaeus was a man of faith. At the moment he heard Jesus call him, he threw off the cursed garment and arose, going to Jesus knowing he would be healed.

Jesus said to him, "*What do you want Me to do for you?*" The blind man said to Him, "*Rabboni, that I may receive my sight.*" Then Jesus said to him, "*Go your way; your faith has made you well.*" Immediately, Bartimaeus received his sight and followed Jesus down the road. It was Bartimaeus' faith, his ability to believe that Jesus had the power and authority to heal his blind eyes that brought about his healing. Bartimaeus demonstrated faithfulness to God's truth by not being hindered or changed by what other people said. He stood firm, steady, and full of

[305] Dr. Dale Sides, *Exercising Spiritual Authority*, Liberating Ministries For Christ International, Bedford, VA.
[306] Mark 10:46

confidence that Jesus, the Son of David, would have mercy on him and heal his eyes.

Faith is the substance of things hoped for, and the evidence of things not seen![307] We are called to live faithful to God's promise and to His Word. Bartimaeus had it right. Why is it we are unable to see the truth so plainly laid before us in the Bible? Our faith does not need to be elaborate or religious, but just a simple faith in our Father's Word and belief in His promises will release the supernatural power into our very being.

Hope Deferred Makes the Heart Sick

There is a truth tucked in the Word of God that reveals why so many people struggle on their path to a faithful life. In the pages of Proverbs, the book of wisdom and instruction, we learn that *"hope deferred makes the heart sick."*[308] The journey of faith may have bumps and roadblocks, but crossing over holds the key to releasing God's power in one's life.[309]

"Hope deferred" seems to sum up our everyday disappointments. We have all heard the old adage that "life is full of disappointments." Unfortunately, for some the disappointments result from traumatic events such as abuse, loss, or divorce. For others, disappointment followed on the heels of what appears to be an unsuccessful period of prayer and fasting, where tragedy occurred despite the amount of time spent on their knees. Whatever the situation, and regardless of the magnitude of the disappointment, when the power of disappointment is experienced, the result often leads to a sick and hopeless heart.

When disappointment invades our own life, hope is compromised and faith is attacked. Allowing disappointment, then, to take root in our souls paves the way for it to fester and poison our faith. We begin to question God's goodness and promises. Lies latch onto our hearts and minds, taking over our emotions and eventually escalating to a supernatural level of bondage. Any area of life not permanently attached to the influence of Hope falls under the influence of the enemy's lies. The disastrous result eventually leads to bondage, affliction, and torment.

Many have yet to allow Jesus' blood to cover the disappointments eating away at their souls. Disappointment in itself will affect individuals differently as they

---

[307] Hebrews 11:1
[308] Proverbs 13:12
[309] James 1:2

grow and mature, but for each person disappointment will begin to corrode, eat away, and destroy the very essence of a person's faith. *Hope deferred makes the heart sick* is a truth that adequately illustrates how sickness, disease, and even death await people who fall into disappointment. Disappointment is a faith issue, and for many of us it has become the barrier preventing us from releasing the power of God in our lives.

To overlook the truth that *Hope deferred makes the heart sick* is serious. Falling out of faith and questioning God because of past disappointments leaves us vulnerable to attack. In my experience, I have witnessed a pattern develop within people's souls as they struggle with disappointment. If the disappointment is not dealt with through the Spirit and the Word then it will lead to discouragement, discouragement will lead to despair, and despair will lead to death. *Hope deferred makes the heart sick* is crucial to our life as Christians. Once the soul is infested with the power of disappointment then the body becomes jeopardized through sickness and disease, which is poised to kill, steal, and destroy the Christian life.

Each one of us needs a childlike faith and dependence on the Father for all things. Jesus made it very clear that *whoever does not receive the Kingdom of God as a little child will by no means enter it.*[310] We have a responsibility to humble ourselves and become completely dependent upon God and His residing presence in our hearts, souls, and bodies. In order for us to enter the Kingdom of God we must resume our childlike faith, humbling ourselves to God's influence and Word. Disappointment keeps us fixed in a useless state of knowledge-based faith that serves as fertile soil to seeds of doubt. As a result, we deny ourselves an intimate, knowing, believing relationship with the Father.

My four-year-old son Joshua had asked me for something once and my response was an uncommitted, "We'll see." Joshua was quick to ask, "Dad, does that mean yes or no?" He wanted to know exactly what to expect. When Jesus exhorted us to be as little children, he instructed us to reclaim our childlike faith and hope in the promise of the New Covenant. We are to be childlike with a deep commitment and resolve that anticipates the fulfillment of the Father's goodness and favor. God's Word is a firm foundation from which we can stand and build our lives, abide in Him, and expect the extraordinary to be fulfilled.

We can not help but marvel at the innocence, purity, trust, and love so characteristic of young children, an outlook so simple and so uniquely profound. Children trust and love all whom they come in contact with and they are

---

[310] Mark 10:15

completely dependent upon their caretakers. As adults, many of us have lost that loving feeling. Disappointments have left scars and hardened hearts. We fail to remember who we are in God's sight. We have been separated from Him far too long because our hearts have hardened and our faith has become unstable.[311] We have traded Truth for lies simply because at some point we were disappointed. At what point do we put disappointment under the blood of Jesus Christ and begin to trust God completely? When do we reclaim our childlike faith and stand faithful, committed, to God's Word, allowing His glory to be released through us?

Reclaiming the Childlike Faith

God has given us the answer to overcome disappointment, discouragement, and despair in our lives. Proverb 13:12 states, *"Hope deferred makes the heart sick, but when the desire comes, it is a tree of life."* We have seen that "hope deferred" is referring to the power of disappointment and "heart sick" refers to our faith being undermined and destroyed. However, at the end of this verse God provides revelation to the power that overcomes disappointment in the Christian life.

When the desire comes, it is a tree of life, is an illustration and promise that disappointment can be destroyed. This statement suggests there is a desire when realized and fulfilled that will manifest the tree of life. The phrase "tree of life" is used in three places throughout the Word of God. We find this phrase used in Genesis, Proverbs, and Revelations. In each instance, it refers to a life of abundance, a God kind of life, wanting and desiring absolutely nothing. This is the life that God has promised all those who believe in Jesus Christ the Son of God. This is eternal life, a God kind of life, NOW and forever. Jesus declared that, *"I have come that you may have life (Zoë life), and that you may have it more abundantly."*[312] Jesus secured the promise of a God kind of life, NOW and forever, however, it is up to us to live in this promise.

The realization of the "tree of life" for the Christian is contingent upon *the desire. When the desire comes, it is a tree of life* is a truth that must be captured within the Christian faith. This desire is a revelation that will change the circumstances of God's people liberating all those who suffer under the power of disappointment and sickness in this world. The desire, simply stated, is the commitment and faithfulness we demonstrate in the New Covenant promise. There must be a desire, a burning resolve within our consciousness that will not accept anything less than what our Father has promised. We are taught that

---

[311] Ephesians 4:18
[312] John 10:10 (emphasis added)

> *We are all sons of God through faith in Christ Jesus. For as many of you as were baptized into Christ have put on Christ. There is neither Jew nor Greek, there is neither slave nor free, there is neither male nor female; for you are all one in Christ Jesus. And if you are Christ's, then you are Abraham's seed, and heirs according to the promise.*[313]

Jesus the Christ has positioned us to receive the blessing of Abraham, which is the inheritance of a Promised Land full of abundance, prosperity, and health. We find in Deuteronomy 28:1-15 the listing of God's provision and blessing for those in covenant with Him. These blessing and provisions are the promises for Abraham's seed.

In Deuteronomy 28:15-68 we find the curses put on man when he is not in covenant with God. All poverty, sickness, disease, torment, division, and oppression are a result of the curse, of being out of covenant with the Father. When man is out of covenant with God, then satan and his kingdom have the "legal" right to kill, steal, and destroy God's people. History demonstrates all throughout the Word of God that every time man stepped outside of God's covenant the curse(s) came upon him.

The Christian faith, however, proclaims that *Christ has redeemed us from the curse of the law, having become a curse for us that the blessing of Abraham might come upon the Gentiles in Christ Jesus, that we might receive the promise of the Spirit through faith.*[314] We must return to the childlike faith that is committed, expectant, and resolved to experience the abundance promised to us by our Father. Faithfulness to the Spirit within us is the key to releasing a desire that pulls the Kingdom of Heaven into our life, releasing the tree of life through us. We must stand in times of trial proclaiming with a deep commitment and understanding that Christ in us, is the hope of His glory. *All* things have been established for you and me to experience His Glory and Kingdom now in our lives. Let us arise in faith, nothing wavering, to demonstrate a great desire to experience the fullness of God's word and promise in all that we do. Reclaim your childlike faithfulness that is committed to the truth of God's Word and not to the religions of man. God is alive! He is the Great I AM, the present future, that we may experience His truth NOW and forever.

---

[313] Galatians 3:26-29
[314] Galatians 3:13,14

The Kingdom of Heaven IS NOW at Hand

Faithfulness is the ability to act without doubt, knowing that the Holy Spirit of God will assist us in all we do. A preacher once said, "If you are not out on the farthest reaches of a branch, without any safety net below you, you are not living a life of true biblical faith." The power of faith is found in our reliance on God for our every need. We are not living in faithfulness if we are not actively demonstrating the truth of God's Word in all we do and say. Faithfulness requires action. It demands that we take a risk and trust that the Holy Spirit will be released through us.

When Jesus proclaimed that the Kingdom of Heaven is at hand, He was referring to the power of God, the Holy Spirit, being released through man to demonstrate the miraculous, supernatural power of God in this world. Throughout history, when the Holy Spirit came upon man, the only way for the power to be released was for man to respond to the leading of the Holy Spirit. The same is true today. The Gospel of Jesus Christ is not only for teaching, but is to be confirmed with signs following.[315] The Apostle Paul said that his preaching was not just with persuasive words of man's wisdom, but in demonstration of the Spirit of power.[316] He also said that the gospel did not come in word only, but in power and in the Holy Spirit.[317] Luke was referring to all Jesus had begun both to "do" and to "teach."[318]

The Word of God is clear that as Christians our lives should be a continual demonstration of the truth of the power of the Holy Spirit in us. We are to have both the Word and the demonstration of the Word in our lives. The parable of the Good Samaritan is a demonstration of a man acting with faithfulness to assist another person.[319] It was a prophetic word for the Church today, this generation, that to exercise the miraculous power of Christ Jesus today, we must be faithful to act in love by applying the "wine" – the Word of God – and the "oil" – the Spirit of God.[320] If you or I were to find a cure for cancer, would we hide it and keep it from the sick? If your answer is pure of heart and full of compassion, then how is the Gospel of Jesus Christ any different? We must act upon that which we have learned, upon that which we have heard. We must act upon our faith to release the greatest power known to mankind.

---

[315] Mark 16:20
[316] 1 Corinthians 2:4
[317] 1 Thessalonians 1:5
[318] Acts 1:1
[319] Luke 10:34
[320] Luke 10:34

The Apostle Paul stated in 2 Timothy 4:7-8, *I have fought the good fight, I have finished the race, I have kept the faith. Finally, there is laid up for me the crown of righteousness, which the Lord, the righteous Judge, will give to me on that Day, and not to me only but also to all who have loved His appearing.* Keeping the Christian faith means we are willing to fight for it. Simple believing is not good enough. We must be willing to exercise our faith and make it work for God's Kingdom. A crown awaits all who believe in Jesus Christ and act in faith. Many good, honest, moral Christians suffer at the hands of sickness, disease, or oppression not because they do not have faith, but because they fail to act on their faith. Releasing the power of God, the Holy Spirit within us, is only accomplished by our faithfulness to act on that which God has promised.

> *What does it profit, my brethren, if someone says he has faith but does not have works? Can faith save him? Faith by itself, if it does not have works, is dead. But someone will say, "You have faith, and I have works." Show me your faith without your works, and I will show you my faith by my works. You believe that there is one God. You do well. Even the demons believe - and tremble! But do you want to know, O foolish man, that faith without works is dead?*[321]

How much clearer must it be? Without action, faith is dead. The Holy Spirit of God will not move without our faith and action. In essence, then, faith is action, and it is this truth that terrifies the demonic kingdom. When we act, we proclaim that we trust in all that God promised, indeed fulfilled, through His Mighty Son Jesus Christ. Every account in the Word of God that demonstrates supernatural, miraculous power was released by an act of faith. Someone had to believe first and then act.

God has provided us with a faith barometer that we may know whether we are living our lives faithful and committed to His promise. Ask yourself are you confident and willing to act upon your faith? Are you willing to lay your hands on the sick in the middle of the grocery store or at the movie theater to release the power of God through you? Are you willing to walk into a hospital and begin to pour out the Holy Spirit of God on every sick or injured person? Are you willing to cast out demons and heal the oppressed? Will you step out in faith and raise the dead?

Check your faith meter. If you hesitated while reading the above, you need more of the Word, for faith comes by hearing, and hearing by the Word of God. You need to open up your soul and allow it to become one with the Holy Spirit of God

---

[321] James 2:14-20

within you. In doing so, you will develop a commitment, a resolve, a desire that will confess and proclaim the promises of God through your words and actions. We have the ability to release the Kingdom of Heaven in all we do *if* we will act upon our faith.

The action of our faith is a demonstration, a witness, to the truth of Jesus Christ's resurrection. *And if Christ is not risen, your faith is futile; you are still in your sins! Then also those who have fallen asleep in Christ have perished. If in this life only we have hope in Christ, we are of all men the most pitiable.*[322] Christ **is** risen and the demonstration to this truth, this triumphant victory over satan and his entire kingdom, is demonstrated through the experience and manifestation of His healing and miraculous power. The power of that verse is found in the statement, *"If in this life only we have hope in Christ, we are all of men the most pitiable."*[323] If we only have hope in Christ and not a conviction of faith, a burning fire of desire to experience His truth and divine presence then where is the power of His resurrection? If our hope is only in Jesus Christ's glorious return for our healing and deliverance, we are not faithful to what He accomplished on the Cross. Faithfulness is an act, a demonstration that Christ is alive and that through Him we are one spirit in Him.

But if the Spirit of Him who raised Jesus from the dead dwells in you, He who raised Christ from the dead will also give life to your mortal bodies through His Spirit who dwells in you.[324] The power of Christ's resurrection is in the truth that the same Holy Spirit of God that raised Jesus Christ from the dead dwells in us and He quickens, heals, and restores our mortal bodies. When we deny the power of the Holy Spirit and fail to act upon it, we deny the resurrection of our Lord Jesus Christ.

The truth will never change. The Kingdom of Heaven is at hand, and it is up to each of us to appropriate and release this truth through our faithfulness and commitment to our Father. When we act according to His Word, by faith and without wavering, the Holy Spirit responds, the glory of God is released, and all spiritual blessings are manifested for His glory and establishment of Heaven on earth. We are His chosen people, a people called to a high level of faith through the demonstration of His promise. We are His children who, through our unshakable faith in the Gospel of Jesus Christ, have the ability to move mountains and release His Kingdom for all to experience.

---

[322] 1 Corinthians 15:17-19
[323] 1 Corinthians 15:19
[324] Romans 8:11

Reflection Verse: *Hebrews 11:6*

Without faith it is impossible to please Him, for he who comes to God must believe that He is, and that He is a rewarder of those who diligently seek Him.

Thoughts for Reflection:

Jesus asked the question, "Nevertheless, when the Son of Man comes, will He really find faith on the earth?" At what point do we, as Christians, embrace the New Covenant promise of divine Life <u>now</u>? Faith is expressed only through our actions. Exercise your faith today, through your faithfulness to God's Word.

Daily Confession:

Father, You are faithful in what you have promised, You cannot lie. I seek the Kingdom of God and Your righteousness in all that I do. I proclaim today that I stand unshakable in my faith toward Your Word. Thank you for the Holy Spirit and the Promise of Divine Life. I praise You, Father, from the depths of my heart.

Spiritual Weapons for the Advancement of the Kingdom of God

Spiritual Weapons for the Advancement of the Kingdom of God

I.   WEAPONS OF DEFENSE

He has delivered us from the power of darkness and translated us into the kingdom of the Son of His love.

Colossians 1:13

When Two Kingdoms Collide

In the following five chapters, I will endeavor to unveil a truth in God's Word that will prove valuable in defeating and overcoming satan's kingdom. It is a truth that, once revealed, will equip us with the spiritual weapons necessary to tear down the demonic strongholds that inhibit God's children from developing an intimate, personal relationship with the Father and from living a true biblical life of faith. God is operating against satan's army through the body of His Son, the Church, and we have been empowered and equipped with spiritual weapons that, when used correctly, disarm and destroy the works of the devil.

I have had the privilege of ministering to many people and experiencing the mighty presence of God as demonic strongholds are destroyed. I have witnessed people transformed upon receiving the truth of who they are through Jesus Christ and exercising their God-given authority and power to change the atmosphere in which they live. Once the truth of who we are in Christ Jesus becomes a living, breathing life force, there is nothing in this world to prevent us from releasing the power of God to transform our sphere of influence.

As believers in Jesus, stepping into a conscious awareness of our authority creates an atmosphere of God's Kingdom all around us. We are heirs to the Kingdom of God, yet most of us have not effectively exercised that dominion in this world. We have failed to appropriate the spiritual weapons bestowed on us by God's Spirit. We have not understood that we already have at our disposal every spiritual blessing necessary to conquer the kingdom of hell. The heavenly hosts wait patiently, diligently, for us to release them into battle so they may exercise holy judgment against the defeated foe.

A fierce and deadly battle is raging in the spirit realm, and it is a fight for our souls and bodies. The devil and his kingdom are out to kill, steal, and destroy all that God has created. The enemy of our Father, the accuser of our brethren, has tormented God's children from the beginning of time, and he will continue as long as we are blinded to his schemes and to the blatant lie that we are mere lambs being led to the slaughter.

What we fail to fully comprehend is that satan is desperate. He knows the time is near when the judgment of eternal hell will be executed. He seeks now to persecute and torment all whom God holds dear. *He roams about as a roaring lion, seeking whom he may devour,*[325] making a lot of noise in an effort both to frighten us and to cover up the truth of his defeat. He is testing the faithfulness of God's people.

Those who live in fear tremble at the enemy's roars. Unfortunately, they have opened a door and given satan a place in their lives through their lack of trust and faith in God's Word. Jesus made it clear that we are to be violent against satan's kingdom, rising above it in love, power, and authority, destroying its perversion and the twistedness that grips the soul of man.

We are called to be violent against satan's kingdom, for God has said *you that love the LORD, hate evil; The fear of the LORD is to hate evil: pride, arrogance, and the evil way.*[326] The only way we can become violent against satan's kingdom is to develop an attitude that hates evil. We must hold the conviction deep within our souls that *"Enough is Enough,"* that through the power of the Holy Spirit we will overcome and defeat all the works of satan and his evil horde. We are called to be warriors, determined and armed with God's truth, loving not our lives unto death but standing firm, without wavering, proclaiming the good news of our Redeemer, Jesus Christ. We must resolve to fully comprehend the truth of the triumph and victory we, as children of God, hold over satan's kingdom. Once we know the truth, the truth will set us free and we will be free indeed.

A young woman was busy studying for final exams in her college dorm room when a man in a ski mask burst into her room, locking the door behind him. Spinning around in her chair, instantly she sensed that the intruder's intentions were to gag, bind, and probably rape her. In a remarkable defiance of fear, the woman stood up and faced the man in her room, renouncing the perverse spirit and proclaiming her heritage as a daughter of God. She took authority over the

---

[325] 1 Peter 5:8
[326] Psalm 97:10; Proverbs 8:13

demonic presence controlling this man, and through the power of the Word of God and the blood of Jesus Christ she drove the demon out of the man. The man left her room in a hurry. She called Campus Security and the man was caught fleeing the women's dorm in an obvious state of confusion.

This young lady understood who she was in Christ Jesus and she exercised her God-given authority over the demonic influence that sought to harm her. She understood that the battle is not against flesh and blood, but against the hosts of satan's kingdom. She demonstrated that the Kingdom of Heaven is at hand and that all of God's resources, weapons, and power are at our disposal to destroy and reclaim the victory and triumph that our Redeemer died to restore. We too must arise each day and affix our armor, taking on the attitude of a warrior willing to stand against the roar of the lion and plunge the sword of the spirit under the enemy's fifth rib, driving it through our enemy and destroying his demonic presence in our lives.

A stage performance being rehearsed in the church sanctuary was about to be disrupted. The gunman had just shot several people in the church lobby, and he was headed to the sanctuary. They had heard the gunshots from the lobby, and immediately, fearful and confused, the parishioners took refuge beneath the pews. Because the lights were down and the spotlights on, the gunman had to walk to the front of the sanctuary, turn and begin to walk back in order to focus his eyes on his next targets. But a funny thing happened on the way to the altar.

As the gunman reached the front near the altar, a young man who had been overcome by the Spirit of God bravely rose up and confronted the man. With the gun pointed in his face, he said, "You can shoot me, but I know that I will go to heaven when I die. Do you know where you will go when you die?" The Kingdom of God had been released on the gunman. The spirit of murder was driven off and the gunman lowered his gun. A child of God had exercised his spiritual authority, and his faithfulness at the moment of greatest fear silenced the devil's roar. Boldly he had stood face to face with the demonic kingdom, and faithfully he had destroyed the kingdom of hell by releasing the Kingdom of God upon it.

The courageous young man was only sixteen years old. Even more amazing, he had given his life to Jesus Christ only two weeks before the incident. As a new Christian this young man did not understand what deliverance or spiritual warfare was all about, but he knew enough to trust God. He knew he had been saved and that his eternal home was with the Father in heaven. And when he stood up in faith, not loving his life unto death, saying the only "spiritual" thing he knew at that point to be true, he released the Kingdom of Heaven upon the demonized man and the kingdom of darkness was destroyed. How similar are we to this young man who had the faith to trust that God's Kingdom is greater than the devil's? Has our resolve softened over the years since we first came to trust our King?

A young nursing assistant working the evening shift at a psychiatric facility utilized the spiritual weapons at his disposal as well. A demonized man had begun manifesting great strength, nearly destroying a community area within the ward. The doctors and nurses had run for safety, but the nursing assistant stayed to wage war against what he recognized was a demonic presence. The crazed man picked up a very large end table, a table too heavy to lift on his own, and he hoisted it over his head and threw across the room at the nursing assistant.

The nursing assistant was a child of God, and he exercised his birthright authority. With doctors and nurses observing a spiritual battle right before their eyes, the nursing assistant pointed his finger at the end table hurling toward him in the air and commanded it to stop and fall in the name of Jesus Christ. And with these words the end table stopped in mid air and fell straight to the ground as if it had hit a solid wall. Pointing his finger at the demonized man, then, in the name of Jesus Christ, he proceeded to cast the demon out of the man, setting him free. Faithful to his inheritance of authority and power, this child of God had pulled the Kingdom of Heaven down upon the kingdom of hell and there was a collision between two kingdoms. Victory and freedom were restored.

We are called to be violent against the kingdom of hell and to restore the victory and triumph of our Lord and Savior Jesus Christ in all we do. As the sons and daughters of God, we are to be living examples of the victorious, triumphant Jesus Christ in this world.

Jesus provided us with an important revelation in relation to spiritual warfare. He demonstrated that, through the power of the Holy Spirit, the Kingdom of God is released to destroy both the strongman and the stronghold that supernaturally keep people in bondage to sin, sickness, and death. [327] That is, through the Holy Spirit there is a collision between the Kingdom of God and the kingdom of hell, and victory and triumph will always be restored because the Spirit of God released by faith is greater than any demonic strongman.

Take, for instance, the seven sons of the Jewish chief priest Sceva.[328] They were Jewish exorcists who took it upon themselves to call on the name of the Lord

---

[327] Matthew 12:28,29
[328] Acts 19:13-16

Jesus to cast an evil spirit out of a man by saying, "*We adjure you by the Jesus whom Paul preaches.*" These were words that indicated the men did not know or even have faith in Jesus the Christ, let alone embody the power of God's Spirit to overpower the stronghold in the man's life.

The evil spirit answered, "*Jesus I know, and Paul I know; but who are you?*" Then the man in whom the evil spirit dwelt leaped on them, overpowered them, and prevailed against them, so that they fled out of that house naked and wounded. Satan's kingdom knows whether or not we possess the faith, birthed out of our relationship with Jesus the Christ, to overpower them with the Holy Spirit of God. An aroma is released that the spirit realm easily detects. It can be an aroma of faith, of doubt, or of fear.[329]

The aroma of God's Kingdom is released when we stand in faith with the attitude of a warrior, completely dependent upon the Holy Spirit of God, convinced without a doubt that God always leads us in triumph through Christ. This is a fragrance of God's own presence. This fragrance is one of victory, power, and triumph that terrifies and drives out the presence of satan's kingdom. Evil spirits respond according to the fragrance of God's authority and power within us.

We are in a spiritual battle, and the Word reveals the weapons made available for us to defend ourselves. We are to fight to reclaim the victory that Jesus provided for all of us. Every chapter of this book leads to this point of truth in the revelation of who we are in Jesus Christ. Faith, the Holy Spirit, the mantle of authority, God's love, God's holiness, God's will, and the New Covenant sealed by the blood of Jesus Christ can do nothing for any of us if we lack the commitment and attitude of a warrior. How willing are we to truly put on the armor of God and yield the sword of the spirit to defend, reclaim, restore, subdue, and replenish this earth with the truth of God's Kingdom?

The battleground of this spiritual battle is in our minds and bodies. When we are born again, the Holy Spirit possesses our spirits, and the battle fought between the two kingdoms is one for our souls and bodies. God desires to have our whole being, spirit, soul, and body, that we may be perfected in His image and one with Him. Satan has a different plan, and in the sphere of influence given to him by man, he will continue using deception and lies to kill, steal, and destroy everything he can. The entirety of man's trials, temptations, struggles, and afflictions are a result from the kingdom of darkness trying to disarm our faith.[330]

---

[329] 2 Corinthians 2:14 (emphasis added)
[330] James 1:13-17: James 1:2,3

We must be ready to defend ourselves with the armor of God, the defensive posture that protects our whole being by placing us under the sovereign care and protection of the Father and His Spirit. Through the armor of God we have the ability to go forth and release the weapons of offense that destroy the works of the devil. Without the sovereign protection of God's armor, we leave ourselves vulnerable to satan's counterattack. We need the armor of God to defend and protect us in this spiritual battle.

Prepare yourself now to put on the full armor of God that you may be protected from the schemes of the devil. Release the Kingdom of God upon the kingdom of hell and bring victory and triumph through Jesus Christ. The Kingdom of Heaven is at hand!

11

The Armor of God

For we do not wrestle against flesh and blood, but against principalities, against powers, against the rulers of the darkness of this age, against spiritual hosts of wickedness in the heavenly places. Therefore take up the whole armor of God, that you may be able to withstand in the evil day, and having done all, to stand.

Ephesians 6:12-13

Put on the Armor

The book of Ephesians packs one of the most powerful truths in God's Word. With poetic word pictures of God's people, the body of Christ is depicted as a legislative assembly, a family, a temple, and as the bride of Christ wrapped in the love and security of God the Father. And in the last chapter of Ephesians we find the body of Christ depicted as an army.

As representatives of God's Kingdom, we are expected to confront the highly organized opposing kingdom. Each piece of the armor defends something significant in the Christian's life, and overlooking or downplaying any of the defensive weapons at our disposal results in the believer experiencing serious, sometimes deadly, consequences.

The armor in Ephesians Chapter Six is not intended to be offensive in nature, but defensive, to keep the warrior safe from the counterattack of the enemy. We are not required to "hold down the fort," but instructed to aggressively attack. Many of those I have assisted in ministry and prayer have been in a position of defense most of their lives. They find themselves continually putting out the fires of their life, always contending with the demonic kingdom and being distracted, rather than developing a strong personal relationship with God and advancing His Kingdom daily. We are to engage the enemy, to attack and destroy his strongholds, not sit passively by and hope somehow the demonic kingdom will overlook us.

King David was a young boy, only sixteen or seventeen years old, and he was equipped with a warrior's attitude. Having trusted completely that God would lead him into victory over the giant heathen who cursed the God of Israel, David did not need a spear or sword, because he knew God had already provided his spiritual weapons. David did not wait for Goliath to attack first, but ran at Goliath, attacking the giant with a sling and killed him.[331]

Notably, it was neither the sling nor the sword was the greatest weapon at David's disposal. An angelic host had been released the moment David uttered words of faith. He spoke with boldness and courage against the giant of Gath. Our words and testimony of the truth of God's Word will destroy any giant we face, because by our confessions, our proclamations of God's Word, we release God's angels to carry out His divine plan to restore His Kingdom on earth.

Another example of the importance of our attitude toward an offensive spiritual posture is found when Jesus learned that his cousin and good friend John the Baptist had been beheaded by King Herod. Jesus had tried to depart to a deserted place to mourn his friend's death, but a great multitude followed Him.[332] Instead of mourning and getting caught up in His own personal anguish, He made the decision to attack the devil's kingdom.

Jesus set a precedent for all Christians to follow. When the devil and his kingdom counterattacked Jesus by working through man to kill his beloved cousin, He immediately attacked the devil's kingdom again. He did not hide behind the armor of God, but made a decision to attack and tear down the kingdom of hell using God's armor to defend Him as He destroyed strongholds. The Bible says Jesus was moved by compassion for the multitude and He healed their sick. Then he took five loaves of bread and two fish and created a miracle that fed five thousand.

They were acts of faith that released Holy Spirit power and defeated the works of the devil. In so doing, God the Father got all the glory! The people marveled at the authority and power of God in Jesus and worshiped God from the depths of their hearts. Worship and praise destroyed the deception and tormenting sicknesses that infected God's people. What was revealed when Jesus finished ministering was the Father's love and compassion for mankind. Jesus always stayed on the offensive, never letting the power of disappointment steal His faith in the Almighty God.

The defensive armor of God is ours to put on and wear with confidence. Understand, fellow believer, that the armor of God is only effective when we are moving forward, attacking and defeating the enemy's strongholds. We are not called to sit still and wait for the enemy to attack us, but we are called to attack.

---

[331] 1 Samuel 17:20-54
[332] Matthew 14:13-21

Interestingly, God has not instructed us to put on any armor for the back. Instead, He has promised to watch our backs when we are in His will, defeating the works of the devil. When we are living in God's will we are running *after* the enemy, not *from* him. We will be the one attacking. The armor of God is designed that we may stand against the schemes of the devil and advance His Kingdom and His will.[333]

The Girdle of Truth

Among the pieces of defensive armor available to us, the girdle of truth tops the list. The girdle used in the Roman Empire, particularly the Roman legionary, was important in keeping soldiers' outerwear from inhibiting tactical movements and weapons use during battle. The clothing worn at the time was usually a loose garment that came at least to the knees. In the case of the Roman legionary, it was a kind of tunic. When a Roman legionary was required to do something active, such as fight or use his weapons, he would need to take care of that loose garment. The first thing he had to do was to tie his girdle tightly around his waist to prevent the tunic from flapping free. Absolutely essential, it was the basis for everything else the soldier performed.[334] As such, it has a significant purpose in our ability to apply and keep the rest of our armor intact that we may be poised for battle.

The importance of the girdle of truth in the Christian life takes its cue from the same reasoning associated with the Roman soldiers. It is the first thing that must be applied to allow us to effectively use the rest of our spiritual weapons.

Truth is a weapon of defense for our effectiveness as Christians. The girdle of truth represents not abstract theological truth, but everyday-life truth. It is the very integrity by which we live. We are to be honest, sincere, open, and frank. If we struggle with integrity, a very vital piece of our armor is missing and we are left wide open for attack.

There is no compromising this piece of armor. Little white lies, fibs, or manipulation undermine and destroy the armor's ability to protect us from the enemy's efforts to destroy our peace and joy. We need the girdle of truth – honor, integrity, sincerity, and openness – in order to release the true power of God. The girdle of truth will release us to be more effective as Christians, because it will protect our character, reputation, and validity as ministers and children of God.

---

[333] Ephesians 6:11,13
[334] Derek Prince, *On Exercising God's Power*, p. 482

Looking back at more recent Church history, how many of the generals and soldiers of God's army had been attacked because they failed to gird up the girdle of truth and live a life of sincerity? How many Christians have only haphazardly applied the girdle, resulting in an attack on their validity and supposed God-like character? The literal meaning of "Christian" is "Little Christ," to be Christ-like. We must uphold a Christ-like character demonstrating honor, respect, and importance in all that we perform.

Authenticity of God's Holy Word has been compromised by man's manipulation of the truth in general. Christians are stepping out of their faith in God and stepping into practices of witchcraft or "New Age" spiritualism because they have not found the instant-fix power they desire of Christianity. All this is a result of not putting on the girdle of truth with honor and dignity. If the devil gets his way, prisoners will not be taken – they'll be destroyed, and all in an attempt to discredit our Loving God. It is vital, therefore, that we put on the girdle of truth and live honest, God-fearing lives. It is within our reach to truly be instruments of righteousness for God and His Kingdom.

The Breastplate of Righteousness

Roman legend holds that the breastplate was used to protect the torso of the body from fatal blows. God's breastplate was designed to protect our hearts -- the innermost recess of our being where the life of God resides. From the beginning of time we have been reminded to *keep our heart with all diligence, for out of it springs the issues of life.*[335] The breastplate of righteousness is God's unique gift to us to guard and protect the "wellspring of life."

What does this breastplate look like? Quite simply, it takes the form of faith and love working together, bringing us to a place of oneness with Father, Son, and Holy Spirit. Faith, we all know, is essential to the Christian life, because without it we would not be able to believe the supernatural truth of God. Righteousness itself is not something we can achieve on our own, but only through faith in Jesus Christ.[336] That is, our faith in Jesus Christ brings us to the place of God's grace where we are given, by the blood of Jesus, the ability to be made right before God, perfected, that we may fellowship, commune, and be one with Him. Faith guards the heart and keeps it in God's divine presence and protection.

---

[335] Proverbs 4:23
[336] Philippians 3:9

Paul wrote to the church of Thessalonica to encourage them to stay clear in thought and protected by the body armor, the breastplate, of faith and love.[337] His instructions ring true even today: *Through the Spirit we eagerly wait for the hope of righteousness by faith. For in Christ Jesus neither circumcision nor uncircumcision avails anything, but faith working through love.*[338] Faith works through love, Paul wrote, because without love we cannot have faith in God's promises. This is why Jesus gave us one critical command – to love, which is the Law of Christ!

We are warned to be cautious when it comes to the futility of our minds, not to allow our understanding to be darkened or to be alienated from the life of God because of our ignorance and the hardening of our hearts.[339] Only *agape* love allows the heart to be open to the life of God and the promises of His New Covenant. A love perfectly patient and kind, the love God requires does not envy, is not prideful, and does not behave rudely. God's perfect love *rejoices in truth, bears all things, believes all things, hopes all things, and endures all things. His love never fails.*[340]

The armor required for the protection of our hearts is the breastplate of faith and love. Love, after all, always protects, trusts, hopes, perseveres, and never fails. When we have on the breastplate of faith that works through love, we are always protected.

As we learned in the last chapter, hope deferred makes the heart sick. We also know it is our responsibility, by the breastplate of righteousness, to overcome the disappointment, shame, rejection, fear, and guilt used by the enemy to destroy our faith in God. We must put on the breastplate of righteousness and faith, the heavy armor that works through love to protect our hearts from enemy wiles. *God made Jesus who knew no sin to be sin on our behalf, that we might become the righteousness of God in Christ.*[341] Be convinced by the Word that by God's divine love for us we have become His righteousness through faith. Only the breastplate can adequately protect our hearts, and therefore, our lives.

---

[337] 1 Thessalonians 5:8
[338] Galatians 5:6
[339] Ephesians 4:17-19
[340] 1 Corinthians 13:4-8
[341] 2 Corinthians 5:21

Feet Shod With the Preparation of the Gospel of Peace

The third defensive armor listed in Ephesians 6 has to do with our feet, that they be shod with the preparation of the Gospel of Peace. The Word of God is perfectly precise, praise the Lord! Each word in this description bears a weight of importance.

First we find a description of our feet being shod, or undergirded, with the preparation of the Gospel of Peace. We have been given a visual image of what we are to expect in the spirit realm as we put on this piece of our Commander's armor. The feet of the Roman legionaries were shod with strong, heavy, thronged sandals that were usually laced at least halfway up the calf with leather straps that held the entire sandal tightly in place. The sandals were a very important part of the warrior's equipment because they enabled him to march long distances at great speed. This gave the soldiers mobility and enabled them to engage in battle at any time and any place needed.[342]

We are to be prepared to provide the Gospel of Peace in every situation we encounter. To wear this piece of armor effectively, we must know the Word of God by memorizing Scripture and allowing God's truth to penetrate deep inside our hearts. Only then will we stand faithful to the promises of God at the time they are needed.

Jesus illustrated this truth with His disciples when He answered their question of why they could not cast a deaf and dumb spirit out of an epileptic boy.[343] Jesus said, *This kind can come out by nothing but prayer and fasting.* We cannot postpone praying and fasting, preparing our hearts against an attack of the enemy or to assist a brother or sister in Christ who is in need. We must prepare ourselves daily – in advance. Prayer and fasting are the disciplines which we should regularly practice in order to ensure we are prepared for battle.

The Gospel of Peace is the Gospel of Jesus Christ. It releases a peace, the baptism of the Holy Spirit, to those who are willing to receive it. Jesus said, *Peace I leave with you, My peace I give to you; not as the world gives do I give to you. Let not your heart be troubled, neither let it be afraid.*[344] Jesus encourages us: *Come to Me, all you who labor and are heavy laden, and I will give you rest. Take My yoke upon you and learn from Me, for I am gentle and lowly in heart, and you will find rest for your souls. For My yoke is easy and My burden is*

---

[342] Derek Prince, *On Experiencing God's Power*, p. 488
[343] Mark 9:28-29
[344] John 14:27

light.[345] Jesus was clear when he told us not to worry, but to *seek first the kingdom of God and His righteousness, and all these things shall be added to you. Therefore, do not worry about tomorrow, for tomorrow will worry about its own things.*[346]

We are called to live in God's peace, a tranquility that surpasses all understanding and keeps our hearts and minds on Christ Jesus![347] The Gospel of Peace serves as our covering in times of enemy attack. When we are prepared with the Word of God, we have a peace that goes beyond our understanding and we rest in His truth and power. When we are prepared in God's peace, there is no worry, discouragement, anxiety, or doubt, because we have made our habitation in Him. The peace of God provides a confidence in God's Word and presence that cannot be overturned.

To shod our feet with the preparation of the Gospel of Peace, then, literally means that we are to be undergirded by preparing ourselves with the Word of God, prayer, fasting, and communion with the Holy Spirit. We must be ready, available, and mobile when the time is needed to respond to battle. Again, this is not to be taken lightly. Satan and his kingdom are not playing games! This is life and death. Be prepared now that you may defend yourself from the counterattacks of a defeated foe.

The Shield of Faith

The fourth weapon of defense or armor of God listed in Ephesians Chapter Six is the shield of faith. In the Greek New Testament, there are two different meanings for the word *shield*. One is a small, circular shield, shaped similar to a large, round, flat wicker basket. The other is long and rectangular, somewhat like a door. It is the latter shield spoken of in Ephesians 6:16. A properly trained Roman legionary would use his shield to protect his entire body from enemy missiles. It protected him completely. This is the kind of faith Paul spoke of when he referred to the shield.[348]

The Christian faith as a whole is an interesting phenomenon. A believer's faith is able to release God's power and provide protection from satan's attacks. Faith is both defensive and offensive, and it is the focus – the battleground – where satan makes his attacks. Over the years, I have found that a faith under attack is one in

---

[345] Matthew 11:29-30
[346] Matthew 6:33-34
[347] Philippians 4:6
[348] Derek Prince, *On Experiencing God's Power*, p. 491

which the power of God is not being manifested. The Christian faith must be able to shout in assurance that the indwelling Christ is greater than anything in this world. Mind you, the enemy is not picky about whom he attacks. He will not hesitate to go after those closest to you until your faith wavers so he may strike at you. He will go after your marriage, finances, health, time, anything that will destroy your faith, and if he cannot get you there, he will look to your family or friends.

It is imperative, then, that our shield of faith completely covers not only ourselves, but also those closest to us. It is our responsibility to teach and edify those around us that they, too, have a shield of faith that will quench all the fiery darts of the wicked. This is why it is important to be in fellowship with like-minded believers, attending a faith-based church that provides a family of faith where all shields may be linked together to cover those under attack. Spiritual covering is an important issue in the battle for our souls. The shield of faith is vital to our success.

My ministry trip to India was a huge success as a direct result of Reverend Sides providing round-the-clock prayer coverage for attendees and their families. Unity of the body of Christ is a uniting of the shields of faith that creates a spiritual hedge of protection to destroy the fiery darts aimed at God's sons and daughters. Without unity with our brothers and sisters in the Lord, we are isolated targets who stand an excellent chance at being hit by enemy fire. We need to be united in faith, connecting our shields that we may move forward covered in protection and confidence, destroying the enemy's strongholds even as we advance.

An obviously intoxicated person once staggered into my office early in my ministry. As soon as he sat down, my spiritual eyes were opened to the fiery darts coming at me from every direction. Demons were cursing me and hurling insults of my "unworthiness," something that earlier in my life would have undermined my faith in God's Spirit within me. My faith in Christ and the baptism of His Holy Spirit enabled me to confidently press on.

I locked eyes with the soul across from me, and purposely I sought after the attention of the demons, speaking in faith, "In the past those words would have hurt me. But not today, because I know who I am in Christ Jesus!" With that, the man's mouth dropped open, and he stood and ran out of my office. Later that evening in prayer, the Holy Spirit allowed me a glimpse of the shield of faith that had protected me from the arrows of destruction that were launched to destroy my faith.

In the course of my ministry, I have counseled individuals whose shields of faith were too small or even nonexistent. In every instance, they had been bombarded with demonic devices that effectively destroyed their faith in God. Until they were able to rebuild their faith and get behind their shield for complete protection, they were sitting targets for satan's kingdom. Remember, *faith comes by hearing, and hearing by the word of God.*[349] Therefore, get into the Word of God today and begin strengthening your shield of faith. Before long, you will notice those pathetic evil attempts are crumbling beneath your feet.

The Helmet of Salvation

Quite similar to the breastplate, the helmet was divinely designed to protect the head from fatal blows. The helmet of salvation protects not the physical brain, but the soul, the mind, the very place where the enemy launches deceptive lies and twisted thoughts in an effort to disarm man's faith. The helmet of salvation is important to our biblical lives of faith and our opportunity to live in God's supernatural power. Without it, our souls are wide open for the enemy's shrewd schemes and strongholds. The helmet is our hope, the joyful anticipation for something good and the confidence we have in God.

Hope also is continual optimism, which is a quiet, steady expectation of good based on the promises of God's Word. Hope is anchored on God's promise with the oath given to those who believe in Jesus Christ.[350] We have been secured, anchored to the Rock of Salvation. The storms of life cannot sway us or change our course.

Where faith and love are protection for our hearts, hope is the protection for our minds. It is absolutely essential for our salvation experience. The helmet of hope, firmly affixed, protects our faith and optimism in God's Word by blocking out the doubt, worry, self-pity, mistrust, discouragement, and fear that confuses and disarms our faith in the New Covenant. We are to hold to the hope we profess.[351] Put on the helmet of salvation, the helmet of hope and optimism, and protect your mind from the counterattacks of the enemy!

---

[349] Romans 10:17
[350] Hebrews 6:19
[351] Hebrews 10:23

The Kingdom of Heaven **Is** at Hand

God's Word has provided us with five essential weapons of defense to enable us to link directly with the Kingdom of Heaven. I find it interesting that there are five, because the number five in Scripture is symbolic of God's grace. We are to put on these weapons without complaining, because it was by God's grace and the blood of Jesus that they have been given to us. We must be willing to submit. We must obey the Almighty and, like Jesus and King David, continually attack the devil and defeat his work.

We have been given the responsibility to fulfill God's Word in this world releasing the New Covenant promise in our lives. When our spirits, souls, and bodies are aligned with God's will and the presence of His Holy Spirit in us, then great blessing and favor will follow. We have the responsibility to act upon God's Word, to fulfill, through faith and action, the will of God in this world. We are God's Kingdom enforcers and we are to be the aggressors. You and I are armed with the spiritual weapons necessary to take down the lies that torment God's people. The Body of Christ must receive the revelation that we are to be the ones tormenting satan's kingdom, not the ones being tormented! We are the victorious ones!

We are God's chosen people to enforce His truth, His power, and His love in all that we do. It is imperative we put on the armor of God, for it is our responsibility to live in the New Covenant anchored upon the blood of Jesus the Christ, our true Redeemer. We have the ability to appropriate all power and blessings of the Kingdom of God through His promise and oath in the New Covenant!

Let us adhere to His Word and Spirit and stand with an attitude of a warrior poised for battle always resting in His protection and divine will. Do not be deceived, the armor of God is not designed to protect anyone who is unwilling to stand! The armor is not designed to protect as we sit back and let someone else attack the kingdom of hell, but it is designed to protect as we step out in faith exercising our Kingdom authority and destroy the works of the devil. It is time to put on the armor of God and stand, for the Kingdom of Heaven is at hand.

Reflection Verse: *Ephesians 6:12-13*

For we do not wrestle against flesh and blood, but against principalities, against powers, against the rulers of the darkness of this age, against spiritual hosts of wickedness in the heavenly places. Therefore, take up the whole armor of God, that you may be able to withstand in the evil day, and having done all, to stand.

Thoughts for Reflection*:*

Jesus, the perfect Lamb of God, has empowered us to be more than conquerors through His perfect sacrifice and the gift of the Holy Spirit dwelling in all believers. We have been given the armor of God to protect us as we advance the Kingdom of God in this world. Keep this in mind: We are to be tormenting the kingdom of darkness, not the kingdom of darkness tormenting us. Stand and exercise your faith in the blood of Jesus Christ and the power of the Holy Spirit within you! In Jesus' Name be free to exercise your Kingdom birthright by fulfilling the primary mission of Jesus Christ: destroying all the works of the devil!

Daily Confession:

I am protected by the armor of God; therefore, I put on the girdle of truth, the breastplate of righteousness. I shod my feet with the Gospel of Truth. I put on the helmet of salvation and carry a shield of faith that will quench all the fiery darts of the wicked. By faith, I proclaim that I have the power of the Holy Spirit to torment all the works of the devil and advance the Truth of God's Kingdom in all that I do.

Spiritual Weapons for the Advancement of the Kingdom of God

II.   WEAPONS OF OFFENSE

*For the weapons of our warfare are not carnal
but mighty in God for pulling down strongholds.*

2 Corinthians 10:4

The Attitude of a Warrior

In the last chapter we looked at the weapons of defense (the armor of God) and the importance of Christians putting on the armor to acquire God's divine protection. We also determined that the armor of God is be used to "*stand against the wiles of the devil*" as we attack the enemy, instead of waiting for the enemy to attack us. We have been exhorted that our attitude must be one of hatred toward evil, thus fueling our desires to attack and destroy, by God's power, the devil's work in our lives and the lives around us. We must be willing to stand and proclaim, "*Enough is Enough!*" Thereby, putting on the girdle of truth, the breastplate of righteousness, shod the feet with the preparation of the Gospel of Peace, take up the shield of faith, and secure the helmet of salvation that we may go into battle equipped and protected to defend ourselves and those around us with the grace of God.

However, as is the case with any physical battle, we cannot simply utilize defensive armor. We should be armed with the weapons of offense necessary to destroy what the enemy possesses. Praise be to God for the weapons of offense He has given every believer in Jesus Christ! We are equipped to destroy all evil works and establish the Kingdom of God here on earth. We have the responsibility to understand what weapons have been given to us and how to use them effectively to ensure that the victory of our Lord and Savior Jesus Christ is restored to all God's people.

Jesus commanded His disciples, *Go and preach, saying, 'The kingdom of heaven is at hand.' Heal the sick, cleanse the lepers, raise the dead, and cast out demons. Freely you have received, freely give.*[352] As a prophetic impartation of

---

[352] Matthew 10:7

God's power, Jesus' disciples today – all of us – are equipped with the spiritual resources of Heaven.

Jesus' command flows in natural progression. First, He instructs the disciples "Go!" Without our faith, Holy Spirit power is not released; without our works, according to Scripture, faith is dead. We are to go forth releasing the supernatural power of the Holy Spirit everywhere. When Jesus first called His disciples He said, "Follow Me," and when He released His disciples, He said, "Go and preach that My Kingdom is now at hand!" The only way we can "go" and "preach" is if we follow the Great Teacher and do as He did. Preaching and teaching still is not enough; we are instructed also to demonstrate that the Kingdom of Heaven is at hand by healing the sick, raising the dead, and casting out demons.

Studying the thirty-five specific miracles and healings Jesus performed (not including the accounts when He healed "them all," but the specific accounts of miracles and healings), you will find Jesus always used action and teaching to reveal that the Kingdom of Heaven is at hand. We are to do the same thing today! The only way we can fulfill this call effectively is by going forth, in faith, preaching the Kingdom of Heaven and demonstrating God's love and power. We are on a mission to set the captives free and destroy the forces of darkness that inhabit this world just as our Great Teacher had done before us.

Jesus said, *Peace to you! As the Father has sent Me, I also send you.*[353] Jesus released all disciples to finish His purpose and ministry here on earth. In order for this statement to be true, our primary purpose as Christians must be in line with the true purpose of Jesus. The Word of God states, *The Son of God was manifested, that He might destroy the works of the devil.*[354] Our role is to take up the primary mission of Jesus Christ and finish what He started. We are expected to go and preach that the Kingdom of Heaven is at hand, healing the sick, cleansing the lepers, raising the dead, and casting out demons. Jesus sent us with the same purpose with which the Father sent Him. It is time we take up the mighty weapons of warfare to pull down demonic strongholds – saving, delivering, and healing all of God's people!

The next four chapters look at the four primary weapons at our disposal, ready to be released in any situation. God has promised us *that the man of God (or woman) may be complete, thoroughly equipped for every good work.*[355] Hence, God has provided powerful weapons with the potential to transform not only our

---

[353] John 20:21
[354] 1 John 3:8
[355] 2 Timothy 3:17

lives, but also our entire atmosphere. When we appropriate these weapons effectively, we will experience the power of the Kingdom of Heaven in this world.

Bear in mind, though, that these powerful weapons can only be released – and used – when we are faithful. As discussed in chapter ten, a great faith is necessary to operate and use any one of the weapons of offense. An intellectual, knowledge-based faith that comes from the head will struggle with the faith necessary to recognize and operate these special and very powerful weapons of God. We must have a faith that comes from the heart, one that burns in our consciousness with an absolute assuredness of the truth of God's Word for His children. Great faith is required for each and every one of these weapons to be effective in the life of a Christian.

12

Weapon of Offense #1: Baptism of the Holy Spirit

For the weapons of our warfare are not carnal
but mighty in God for pulling down strongholds.

2 Corinthians 10:4

Holy Spirit Power

We learned in chapter nine about the power of the Holy Spirit and the importance behind believers being baptized in the Holy Spirit. The Word of God says that Jesus Himself will baptize us with the Holy Spirit and with fire.[356] It is the will of the Father that we are filled with His fullness, His very Life and Spirit, that we may be one with Him. *Baptizo* of the Holy Spirit is a submerging, a cleansing, an overwhelming immersion into God's glory and presence.

We are to desire and pursue this immersion with a passion that hungers for more of the Father's presence in our lives. Jesus declared, *It is to your advantage that I go away; for if I do not go away, the Helper will not come to you; but if I depart, I will send Him to you.*[357] It was necessary that Jesus ascend to the right hand of the Father to assure the sons and daughters of God that they would be able to live in the same power and authority Jesus exercised on earth. He was clear when He said, *"But you shall receive power when the Holy Spirit has come upon you."*[358] The baptism in the Holy Spirit grants us a divine power that, through our faith will allow miracles, signs, wonders, and healings. The manifestation of this power enables us to be witnesses to the true and living God.

Power Gifts

Baptism of the Holy Spirit provides us with nine "power" gifts, each of which we are instructed to release by virtue of our relationships with the Holy Spirit. We are not to be ignorant about the purpose and function of these gifts.[359] Each gift is immediate and available upon the baptism of the Holy Spirit in order to profit the

---

[356] Luke 3:16
[357] John 16:7
[358] Acts 1:8
[359] 1 Corinthians 12:1

body of Christ. Unfortunately, it is here that great confusion surfaces regarding the gifts of the Holy Spirit.

Many Christians have been misled to believe only one gift of the Spirit has been given to him for application within the body of Christ. Great misunderstanding has arisen from the words of 1st Corinthians 12: 7-11:

> *But the manifestation of the Spirit is given to each one for the profit of all: for to one is given the word of wisdom through the Spirit, to another the word of knowledge through the same Spirit, to another faith by the same Spirit, to another gifts of healings by the same Spirit, to another the working of miracles, to another prophecy, to another discerning of spirits, to another different kinds of tongues, to another the interpretation of tongues. But one and the same Spirit works all these things, distributing to each one individually as He wills.*[360]

The result of misunderstanding our spiritual gifts has disarmed many Christians from operating in Holy Spirit power. A thorough study of the Scriptures presents clear evidence that every one of the nine gifts of the Spirit are available to *every believer,* distributed to each one as the Spirit wills for the profit of all.

The greatest misunderstanding of the truth of the nine power gifts is found in the phrase "for to one," which derives from the Greek phrase *"ho men gar."* It's a phrase that refers to the particular profit or benefit each gift produces. The Greek word *ho* in this phrase is a demonstrative pronoun linking the phrase to the closest associated noun. The phrase "for to one," then, is a transitional conjunction connecting the closest noun to the current sentence. [361] Much more than a grammar lesson, this revelation is important.

Look at the verse once again. *But the manifestation of the Spirit is given to each one for the profit of all: for to one is given...*

We have been taught to believe that the phrase "for to one" refers to the phrase "each one" in the previous verse, completely altering the verse to mean one person will receive one gift while another receives his or her own unique gift. This is incorrect, however, as proven by the principle established by the Greek pronoun *ho*. The pronoun *ho* refers to its most closely associated antecedent or noun, which is the word "profit," not the word "one."

---

[360] 1 Corinthians 12:7-11
[361] Dr. Dale Sides, *Flowing in all Nine Gifts of the Holy Spirit*, Liberating Ministries for Christ International, Bedford, VA, p. 10

The power of this truth produces a completely different understanding of the nine gifts of the Holy Spirit. The phrase "for to one" and the eight uses of the word "another" found to describe the nine gifts of the Holy Spirit do not refer to a man, but to the profit for all. The word "profit" means to help be profitable, be expedient to collect or contribute in order to help.[362] Recall that the Holy Spirit is the Comforter, the Helper, the One called to come alongside all believers to support and help. The Holy Spirit provides the power gifts. It stands to reason, then, that the noun "profit" is the noun used to introduce the nine power gifts of the Holy Spirit. The use of the noun "profit" now aligns the section as a whole to the gifts of the Spirit with the truth of the Gospel of Jesus Christ, which simply states, *Christ in you, the hope of the glory!*[363] All nine of the power gifts together enable the Holy Spirit to help us become profitable and expedient in releasing the Kingdom of Heaven in this world.

Read 1 Corinthians 12:7-10 again in light of the above revelation: *But the manifestation of the Spirit is given to each one for the profit of all: specifically, for to that one (profit) is given the word of wisdom through the Spirit, to another (profit) the word of knowledge through the same Spirit, to another (profit) faith by the same Spirit, to another (profit) the gifts of healings by the same Spirit, to another (profit) the working of miracles, to another (profit) prophecy, to another (profit) discerning of spirits, to another (profit) different kinds of tongues, to another (profit) the interpretation of tongues.*

To fully grasp the functions of the nine gifts of the Holy Spirit, let's go back to verse seven once again. *But the manifestation of the Spirit is given to each one for the profit of all.* Look at the beginning of this verse, "the manifestation of the Spirit." The whole truth of the power gifts is that each gift has a unique profit and, when worked together in combination, they produce a particular manifestation of the Spirit in our lives. "Each one" means "each man," that is, you and me. The Word is clear that God desires to manifest His glory in each of our lives for the profit of all.

By God's divine love and mercy, manifestation of the Spirit is "given" to each believer that the Father's glory may be revealed. Likewise, manifestation of the Spirit extends for the profit of all men. Please understand this revelation: *the manifestation of the Spirit has been given to all those who believe in Jesus Christ for the profit of all.* It is God's will that all men see and experience His promise and glory. The entire verse is the will of God! He has given every believer the ability to offer His manifestation in order that all men may experience His love

---

[362] Strong's Concordance Dictionary
[363] Colossians 1:27

and faithfulness. Manifestation of His Spirit draws man closer to Him, to reclaim this world and create Heaven on earth. And it is a manifestation given to each of us for the profit of the whole Church.

Take, for example, Philip, who went down to Samaria to preach the Gospel of Jesus Christ. *And the multitudes with one accord heeded the things spoken by Philip, hearing and seeing the miracles, which he did. For unclean spirits, crying with a loud voice came out of many who were possessed; and many who were paralyzed and lame were healed. And there was great joy in that city.*[364] By operating the gifts of the Holy Spirit, Philip produced in Samaria a manifestation of the Spirit through miracles, deliverances, and healings. And there was great joy in the city! Christians are called to manifest the Spirit of God by being in the will of God at all times. We must position ourselves to release the gifts of the Holy Spirit by faith in order to reconcile the heart of man back to the heart of the Father.

First Corinthians 12:27-30 helps to clarify the truth of the Holy Spirit's gifts available to all believers:

> *Now you are the body of Christ, and members individually. And God has appointed these in the church: first apostles, second prophets, third teachers, after that miracles, then gifts of healings, helps, administrations, varieties of tongues. Are all apostles? Are all prophets? Are all teachers? Are all workers of miracles? Do all have gifts of healings? Do all speak with tongues? Do all interpret?*[365]

Remember, many Christians have been taught, and thereby believe, that this list of questions is directed toward the gifts of the Holy Spirit. Again, that is incorrect. The list actually reveals the ministries members of the body of Christ are called to fulfill. God's will for our personal lives is directly related to the ministry we were designed and predestined to fulfill, whether we are apostles, prophets, evangelists, pastors, teachers, or helpers, administrators and those of intercession. The question asked in these verses is whether we all have the same ministry. The answer, clearly, is no, we do not. That is not to say we are limited to one function. Indeed, each of us is expected to incorporate all nine gifts of the Spirit in order to fulfill our personal ministries. God has very specific reasons for equipping the Church with each of the ministries, and the nine "power gifts" of

---

[364] Acts 8:5-8
[365] 1 Corinthians 12:27-30

the Holy Spirit are given to every believer for the fulfillment of each and every ministry in the body of Christ.

The purpose of the spiritual gifts, then, is to bring profit to the body of Christ, and our role is to successfully work to that end. Scripture is clear that every baptized, energized, and equipped believer filled with the Holy Spirit has the ability to operate the gifts and manifest the Spirit. The only prerequisite to the operation of the nine gifts is the baptism of the Holy Spirit that Jesus promised. Holy Spirit baptism provides us with a power greater than man could ever imagine. We have the power potential to reach the lost through healing the sick and delivering the oppressed. Praise God for this powerful offensive weapon!

Functions of the Nine Gifts of the Spirit

Now that we understand the purpose of the nine gifts of the Holy Spirit, let's look at their functions so we may recognize and release them as needed. The gifts are categorized here for better understanding.

The three categories are:

A. Inspirational, Worship, or Utterance Gifts
1. The gift of tongues.
2. The gift of interpretation of tongues.
3. The gift of prophecy.
B. Revelation, Instructional, or Knowledge Gifts

1. The gift of the word of knowledge.
2. The gift of the word of wisdom.
3. The gift of the discerning of spirits.

C. Power or Impartation Gifts

1. The gift of faith.
2. The gift of healing.
3. The gift of the working of miracles.

As we will see, the secret to releasing God's power and manifesting the Spirit in our lives is to work these gifts in combination with one another. When the gift of prophecy is used with the gifts of a word of knowledge and of faith, healing is released and manifestation of the Holy Spirit is produced. Linking these categories, we see the following truth emerge:

Spiritual Utterance + Spiritual Knowledge + Spiritual Faith = Spiritual Power.[366]

Before we look at biblical examples of this truth, let's consider the differences in gifts and how they function.

Inspirational, Worship, or Utterance Gifts

The Gift of Tongues

The gift of tongues, also known as speaking in tongues, is energized by the Holy Spirit and used primarily in worship and intercession. It is also a gift that receives great criticism. Many Christians do not believe they need to speak in tongues to be a "good and faithful" Christian. There is a belief that speaking in tongues is something only "the other group" does.

At one point early in my faith, I too entertained similar thoughts. Until, that is, I was baptized in the Holy Spirit and began to speak in tongues. I found my relationship with the Father became more intimate and intense the more time I spent praying in the Spirit. My faith increased beyond my limited understanding, and the power of God began to be released through me. Speaking in tongues (or praying in the Spirit) edifies the regenerated spirit of man to strengthen the indwelling Holy Spirit for a more powerful base of operating all nine gifts of the Holy Spirit.[367]

I believe speaking in tongues and the necessity to do so is similar to the importance of food to our physical bodies. There simply is no way for a Christian to operate the gifts of the Spirit, the weapons of power, without edifying and strengthening the Spirit inside. We can be "good," moral Christians, but without Holy Spirit baptism and the ability to strengthen our Spirit by speaking in tongues, we will not be faithful to the Gospel of Jesus Christ and our designed purpose as Christians in this dark world. The gift of tongues is precisely that important to the Christian heritage.

That said, we should know that there are two basic kinds of tongues. We will start with the one most helpful to one's individual prayer life.

---

[366] Dr. Dale Sides, Flowing in the Nine Gifts of the Holy Spirit, Liberating Ministries for Christ International, pg. 21
[367] Titus 3:5; Ephesians 3:16; 1 Corinthians 14:4

Praying in the Spirit, or *praise tongue*, is the language of angels given to us by the Holy Spirit.[368] Praying in the Spirit is divinely inspired to provide us with spiritual words for perfect prayer and thanksgiving, words that otherwise mere humans would be incapable of expressing.[369] It enables us to give God the glory He deserves, a splendor and majesty we are not able to express with our human understanding. The praise tongue is our prayer language, initiated by the Spirit within us, and a direct line to the throne of God. Great peace rests in this tongue, enabling a more in-depth sense of understanding and a greater revelation of the Kingdom of Heaven.

When we pray, worship and praise "in the Spirit" the Holy Spirit in us is connected to the throne of God. In doing so, the Spirit in us is strengthened and nourished to provide power and understanding. Praying in the Spirit is the type of prayer the apostle Paul exhorted us to perform often, because it positions us spiritually to exercise more effectively the authority and power given us by the Holy Spirit.

The second form of the gift of tongues is *diverse kinds of tongue*.[370] This is different than the praise tongue (or praying in the Spirit) in that the unction to speak the unknown language comes <u>from</u> the throne of God <u>to</u> the Spirit within us. It is also different in dialect and force, and quite often an interpretation will follow.

An example of a diverse kind of tongue occurred on the day of Pentecost.[371] The disciples had been baptized in the Holy Spirit and began to speak in an unknown language. The rushing sound of the Holy Spirit brought together the vast number of men in the temple to determine what was happening. When they came upon the disciples speaking in tongues, they were confused and fascinated, because they heard the disciples speaking in the language of their own countries. The disciples were speaking in diverse languages that men from various countries could understand! I have heard people say, "I understand the disciples spoke in a foreign language, but that was then, and this is now." The truth is, this same gift, this same power, is available still today by the same Spirit!

A pastor friend of mine was in a prayer meeting with a number of denominations. They had gathered to pray for their community. My friend felt led by God to speak in tongues while the group prayed on their own before uniting. When they

---

[368] 1 Corinthians 13:1
[369] Romans 8:26; 1 Corinthians 14:14; Ephesians 6:18; Jude 20
[370] Acts 2:1-12; 1 Corinthians 12:10; 12:28; 13:1
[371] Acts 2:1

finished, a Catholic priest looked over at my friend and said, "I didn't realize you spoke Latin."

"I don't," my friend responded.

"Well, I do," the priest said, "and every word you just spoke was Latin. This is what you said," and he proceeded to interpret what God obviously intended the priest to hear.

The diverse kinds of tongue comes from the throne of God to us that we may speak forth, through the gift of utterance, what He desires to communicate. The use of diverse kinds of tongue on a repetitive basis, and being open and sensitive to the change in tongue during praise and worship, is vital in our intercession and ministry of tongues. Scripture is clear that God desires to commune with us that we may receive His spoken Word and direction. It is vital that we learn the power of speaking in tongues and how it can and will change not only our own personal prayer life, but also that of the whole body, to edify and direct others through God's spoken Word.

A dear friend of mine was experiencing very uncomfortable pain in his mid-section. He began to exercise his faith by confessing healing, and one day he took the day off from work to get into the Word and presence of God to destroy the affliction. As he began to praise God and pray in the Spirit (in tongues), his hands began to rise toward the ceiling. The dialect and force of his tongue began to change. And with a sudden "blast," his back arched and his head was thrown back so that he was looking straight up to the Heavens.

He prayed that way for quite a while, until he felt he had been released. When he regained his composure, my friend stood up and knew the pain was gone – for good.

In another instance, a young woman was witnessing to a person on the street who did not understand English. Putting her hands on the woman's shoulder, she began to pray in the Spirit. When she finished, the woman for whom she had prayed was weeping, so the young woman stopped a gentleman walking by to see if he could help bridge the communication barrier. He obliged, and the young lady learned that as she was praying in the Spirit, the woman being ministered to had understood every word, and she understood that it could only have come from God!

The woman on the street was healed, delivered, and saved by a faithful young lady praying in the Spirit, with a diverse kind of tongue, the direct communication in the spirit realm that uses the voice of man to issue the commands of God into our senses.[372] We must be open to the manifestation of the Spirit in our lives through the gift of tongues.

The Gift of Interpretation of Tongues

The gift of the interpretation of tongues is used often, as led by the Holy Spirit, whether in private worship, public worship, or public ministry. In many cases, ministers of intercession find they have an ability to exercise speaking in tongues and interpretation of tongues readily throughout their activities.[373] However, please realize that the other seven gifts are also vital to their success in fulfilling the whole ministry God has called them to perform.

Interpreting tongues can also be experienced in our own personal prayer and worship time. God is always communicating what He desires for us in order to bring our souls into alignment with His Spirit. It may be edification, reproof, or just a desire to talk to us and connect with us. Whatever the situation, God gives us the diversity of tongues and the interpretation of tongues for our understanding and growth in Him.

God also uses interpretation of tongues in public ministry to bring the corporate body of Christ into the flow of His Spirit so that believers may experience His presence.[374] I ministered once to a man who had understood every word uttered by the person who prayed in the Spirit during praise and worship at their church. He had received the gift of interpretation and it was his responsibility to communicate to the congregation what God was saying. As a result, everyone was able to profit and draw closer to God's divine presence.

Interpreting tongues requires sensitivity to the Holy Spirit and to the heart of the Father. Our hearts must be open to the opportunity and to the will of the Spirit to communicate the spoken Word of God in order to release the presence of God.

The Gift of Prophecy

Prophecy is the ability of man, through the Holy Spirit, to bring forth in the language of our understanding a message directly from the heart of God to His people. We are told, therefore, that it must first be judged to be a true word from

---

[372] Psalm 103:19-21
[373] 1 Corinthians 12:29,30
[374] 1 Corinthians 14:25

God and not from man.[375] We are told to judge prophecy by the content of the message, the spirit from whence it came, whether or not it comes to pass, and the reliability of the individual who brought it forth.[376]

Prophecy is energized by the Holy Spirit to bring edification, exhortation, and comfort.[377] What it is not is a premeditated message. Prophecy that originates from the heart of God will always agree with the Word of God, and many times will consist of, in whole or in part, portions of Scripture. It is not a revelation. However, when prophecy is used in combination with a revelation, an individual may speak specific information to an individual or an entire church. Many times the gift of prophecy is used to communicate a message from God directly to those to whom we are ministering. Energized and equipped by the Spirit of God Himself, the gift of prophecy brings revelation to reality.

Utterance, Inspirational, and/or Worship gifts are important to our relationships with the Holy Spirit. And when used in conjunction with other gifts, speaking in tongues, interpretation of tongues, and prophecy provide powerful weapons of offense for building confidence in the presence of God and the release of the manifestation of His Spirit in our lives and in the lives of those around us.

Revelation or Instructional Gifts

The Gift of the Word of Knowledge

Revelation gained through *the gift of the word of knowledge* may come in the form of pictures,[378] an audible word,[379] a smell or scent,[380] or through a feeling.[381] It is a revelation gift that enables a person to receive foreknowledge of facts concerning something, anything, otherwise humanly impossible to know. It is a gift of information received in the realm of our senses.

Oftentimes when ministering to a person, my spiritual father will receive a word of knowledge regarding an area in need of the gift of healing. He begins to experience pain in his own body, in the same location where the person being

---

[375] 1 Corinthians 14:29
[376] Dr. Dale Sides, *Flowing in the Nine Gifts of the Holy Spirit*, Liberating Ministries for Christ International, p 16
[377] 1 Corinthians 14:3
[378] Jeremiah 1:11,13
[379] Revelation 1:10
[380] Mark 9:25
[381] Mark 5:30

ministered to has pain or sickness. When it happens, he speaks forth the word of knowledge and proceeds to minister to that afflicted area, releasing the gift of healing, manifesting the Spirit for the benefit of all. I, too, often receive an audible word or a visual picture that reveals the word of knowledge I am to convey as I minister to someone's needs. Once the word is spoken to the intended recipient, manifestation of the Spirit begins to occur. As a result, recipients of the word of knowledge are made to understand and receive the blessing of God.

All revelation is accessed through the Spirit, but in order to understand it we must process it through our senses. The revelation we gain through the gift of the word of knowledge may not comprise the entire, complete understanding at first, but when we begin to speak it forth (to prophesy) more understanding is released.

As an example, early in my ministry I ministered to a young girl who was dealing with a spirit of fear. As we prayed, I saw the image of a bicycle, but because I was not sensitive enough to the spirit, I dismissed it. Later investigation revealed the root, the stronghold gripping the young girl's life. The Holy Spirit brought back to her remembrance a bicycle accident she had when she was very young. She had fallen into a deep ditch and could not get up. She remembered being terrified and screaming at the top of her voice for someone's attention. Panic and anxiety overcame her, and she was never able to break the hold they had on her. Once she shared the memory with me, I shared the word of knowledge I had received, and we prayed in faith against her fear.

How I wished I had acted in faith at the moment I received God's word on her condition, trusting the gift of the word of knowledge and sharing it with the young woman. The Lord revealed to me in prayer that night that my doing so would have led to the development of her great faith and that her fear would instantly and permanently have been cast aside.

We all have the ability to receive a revelation word of knowledge. And when we do, the Lord is certain to unlock the faith of those to whom we are ministering, releasing the power of the Holy Spirit to destroy the strongman and the stronghold for their goodwill and profit.

I heard of a group of teenagers who would sit around a table praying and writing down on a piece of paper the word of knowledge they would receive. Once they were released from prayer, they would take their different pieces of information and minister according to what God had given them.

In one instance, a person received a street name, one received a "right" or "left," another received a house number, another received the name of the man who would answer the door, and the other received the medical condition for which he needed healing. Armed with the information, they jumped into a car, located the house, walked up to the door, and rang the doorbell. When a man answered, they asked if his name was Larry and if he had the specific medical condition.

Dumbfounded, and no doubt a little scared and confused, he answered quietly, "Yes." The teens ministered to him, and he was completely healed right there on the spot!

When we use the gift of the word of knowledge in combination with other gifts, such as the gift of prophecy to impart the knowledge to individuals or to a whole congregation, a strong and life-changing manifestation of the Spirit brings profit.

The Gift of the Word of Wisdom

The *gift of the word of wisdom* is revelation about how to perform what God shows you, either from a word of knowledge, the discerning of spirits, the instruction of someone speaking by revelation, or from the written Word of God. Simply put, the *gift of the word of wisdom* is the application of the knowledge received from above.[382]

It is a powerful tool when used to empower individuals, families, or congregations to accomplish God's will. The *wisdom* gift specifically provides God's solution to the problem, either present or future, in order that certain actions may be accomplished.

When people are diligent to heed the word of wisdom received through counsel and revelation, the power of God is released and lives are restored! Sadly, I have ministered to people through the gift of the word of wisdom and they have chosen not to receive the knowledge from above and failed to implement the solutions. In doing so, their lives continued to be chaotic and miserable. The gift of wisdom brings God's solution to the situation, and when received and implemented, will change circumstances in a person's life. However, like any of the nine gifts of the Holy Spirit, sensitivity to the Spirit and obedience to God's Word are required.

---

[382] James 3:17

The Gift of Discerning Spirits

The *gift of discerning spirits* is a revelation necessary for spiritual warfare. The information gained through the gift of discerning spirits is knowledge in the spirit realm, insight to the evil spirits inhabiting someone's body,[383] and/or knowing the presence and stronghold of principalities and dominions in a certain geographical area.[384] It is a gift mandatory for subduing the spiritual kingdom,[385] enabling us to detect the presence and identity of spirits, and to cast out evil presences that seek to do us harm.

Walking through New York City's Time Square years ago, an overwhelming spiritual sense of despair came over me. A feeling so heavy, it was almost physical. My spirit sensed the lusts and brokenness of a great number of lost and lonely people, and I could feel the demonic presence and strongholds keeping them in spiritual bondage. When our hearts are open to receive such vital information, we will be equipped by God to release His power upon the demonic strongholds.

I was once able to witness a teen-age girl open her heart to receive the Spirit's revelation about an evil spirit strangling another woman. Using her spiritual authority and power, the teen-ager cast the spirit off the woman, and the woman being strangled was healed immediately and completely of a throat ailment. It is mandatory for Christians to come to the place of being able to discern evil spirits. We must be sensitive to what the Holy Spirit is directing us to say and do.

These three "revelation" or instructional gifts provide the direction for God's children to fulfill His will in any given situation. The Holy Spirit of God works right alongside of us, enabling us to serve the Kingdom of God more effectively in all that we do.

---

[383] Acts 16:18
[384] Mark 16:18
[385] Matthew 11:12

Impartation Gifts

The Gift of Faith

The *gift of faith* comes to us as a heavenly faith through the Holy Spirit. It is the gift that allows us to believe for extraordinary and miraculous things. Because we cannot perform the works of the Holy Spirit without faith, faith is essential to draw the power of God that transforms lives. When we study the list of the nine gifts of the Holy Spirit in First Corinthians 12:8-10, we notice the gift of faith is listed third. This is no coincidence. The number three represents spiritual completeness in God's Word. God is demonstrating through His numerical code that faith completes the operation of all the other gifts. Failing to understand this gift has prevented many miracles, signs, wonders, and healings from being consistently produced in Christians' lives.

Brother Kenneth Hagin ministered to woman with a large tumor in her stomach. The Holy Spirit told Brother Hagin to punch the lady in the stomach in order that the healing would be manifested. Certainly not something Pastor Hagin would have done without the Father's prompting, the Holy Spirit provided him with the faith he needed to carry out its fulfillment. Not surprisingly, Pastor Hagin's faith resulted in the woman being healed.

It was by the gift of faith that Brother Smith Wigglesworth threw people out of their wheelchairs or off the platform, knowing that the healing blessing of God would be manifested in their lives when he complied with Holy Spirit revelations.

The gift of faith is distributed to Christians to carry out the revelations given them to perform.[386] God would not send us forth to accomplish His will without injecting the faith to fulfill it. What we must do in operation of this gift, is to trust God, follow the Spirit's lead, and be obedient.

In an effort to break the stronghold of depression in a woman's life, I once relied, disastrously so, on ministerial techniques rather than on the Holy Spirit. Needless to say, nothing worked. Until, that is, the Holy Spirit broke in and asked me, "Did Jesus not cast out a demon with a word?"

I followed the Spirit's lead and immediately turned to Matthew 8:16: "*When evening had come, they brought to Him many who were demon-possessed. And He cast out the spirits with a word, and healed all who were sick.*" Filled with a

---

[386] Mark 11:22; Acts 3:6

new boldness and a strengthened spiritual faith, I looked the woman in the eyes and, with a "word," the spirit of heaviness and depression was cast off. The gift of faith is spiritual. It is the heart faith discussed in chapter ten, a spiritual faith that must be released to exercise the power bestowed upon us through the Holy Spirit.

Gift of Working Miracles

A miracle is defined as a wonder or marvel, a manifestation of the Spirit that happens above or beyond the realm of the laws of nature. The words used to describe this particular gift of the Holy Spirit in First Corinthians 12:10 are transforming and reveal a particular truth that empowers the children of God to utilize this power gift.

First Corinthians 12:10's description does not say a gift of miracles, but a working of miracles. "Working" suggests there are several gifts of the Spirit acting together to produce a desired effect. It is not to say we have to "work" at creating miracles, but we have to be sensitive to the flow of the Spirit, because the Holy Spirit works the different gifts through us in order to bring about miracles. The "working" of a miracle usually utilizes all three categories of Holy Spirit gifts: the gift of revelation (which brings us the desire of the Holy Spirit – usually through a word of knowledge), utilization of the gift of utterance (sometimes the gift of prophecy), and the gift of faith (which is stirred to release Holy Spirit power to manifest a desired miracle). The entire process is called "working of miracles."

The plural form of the word "miracle" is also used in this description, thereby expressing "a working of miracles" not "working of a miracle." The plural form here is based on its Greek origin. The Greek word for "miracles" is the word *dunamis*, which derives only from the plural sense of the word. The word *dunamis* means inherent power, one waiting to be released by some form of action; power for performing miracles.[387] We also find this same Greek word *dunamis* in Acts 1:8 when Jesus instructed the disciples not to leave Jerusalem, but to wait and, *"receive power when the Holy Spirit has come upon you."* "Power" here stems from the same Greek word *dunamis*, an inherent power, one waiting to be released by some form of action! It is clear that we can only receive this *dunamis* power through the Holy Spirit, releasing the ability to perform miracles in the Christian life!

---

[387] Strong's Concordance Dictionary

182

Interestingly enough, we get the word "dynamite" from this same word *dunamis* – a perfect metaphor for the gift of the working of miracles. Manifestation of a miracle is much like the explosion of a stick of dynamite. All the power is found inside us, but there is work involved and an energy that must be released to produce the desired effect. The miracle-waiting power in each of us must be released much like the gunpowder in dynamite. By God's command (or word of revelation), we must act (or speak) to release spiritual faith and produce the desired effect (the miracle of God). Therefore, we release God's power through the *dunamis* stored in us that the Spirit will be manifested.

The Gift of Healings

Both the *gift of healings* and the *gift of working miracles* are effects of a combination of Holy Spirit gifts working together. The gift of healings is supernatural, not a natural process of regeneration of the body to health. It's a gift that goes beyond medical science and the realm of natural laws. The ability to release the *healing* gift results from our sensitivity to the Holy Spirit and allowing the different gifts to work together for the desired manifestation.

A woman who attended one of our Holy Spirit meetings had been experiencing severe pain and discomfort in her left hip joint, resulting in a limp and an inability to be active. She came to me for prayer after a healing meeting and said she was ready to give this tormenting pain and affliction back to the enemy.

Hearing the cry of her heart, I laid my hands on her lower back just over her left hip and received a revelation word of what was happening in her hip. I then began to speak it out through spiritual utterance. The healing manifestation did not occur immediately, so I stepped back and asked the woman to do something she had not been able to do because of the pain. It took an exercise of faith for her to do so, but obediently the woman bent over to touch her toes. Standing, she cried in pure joy and began to dance around the sanctuary giving praise to God.

Through her faith and obedience, the gift of faith given to her by the Holy Spirit broke through the stronghold of affliction controlling her body and released the gift of healing.

The gift of healing was used at the gate of Beautiful when Peter and John healed the lame man. Their word of knowledge (gift of revelation) spoke out, "In the name of Jesus of Nazareth rise up and walk" (gift of utterance), and pulling the man by his arms (gift of faith), faith went through him to manifest complete healing to his body.[388] Peter and John received revelation, spoke it forth, and released the gift of faith to bring about the miracle.

Jesus had instructed His disciples to *Go and preach the Kingdom of Heaven is at hand, heal the sick, cleanse the lepers, raise the dead, and cast out demons, freely you have received, freely give.* In this verse, Jesus' last instruction regarded exercising gifts of the Holy Spirit. Freely we receive the revelation to work a miracle or heal a person, but it is our responsibility to freely give through the gift of utterance and the gift of faith.

I am reminded of a testimony of Brother John G. Lake. He had been walking down a sidewalk discussing the ministry of healing with skeptics in the community. As they considered the possibility of God working through man to produce miracles and healings, a horse fell dead in the road, blocking traffic. The skeptics looked at Brother Lake and said, "If you have the power of God within you to perform miracles, go heal that horse."

Brother Lake stepped into the road, laid his hands on the horse's stomach and immediately received revelation of the problem. Speaking forth the revelation word, he commanded that healing be restored. Brother Lake's bold faith and willingness to minister resulted in a completely healed horse. We have the same miracle-working, healing power at our disposal *if* we are willing to boldly step out in faith and allow the Holy Spirit to work through us.

All nine gifts of the Holy Spirit are designed to work together to produce a powerful result, whether a gift of miracles or of healing. Remaining sensitive to the Holy Spirit's flow allows us the opportunity to release this power in our lives. The power to heal and perform miracles resides in every believer in Jesus Christ. It is our responsibility to release the power by obedience to the revelation word. We are God's instruments for bringing His Kingdom to this world. We are called to speak forth and stand in faith to the revelation word we receive through the Holy Spirit, demonstrating that God's will shall be done on earth as it is already done in Heaven.

New Testament Support for Power Gifts

The truth that power gifts of the Holy Spirit are for all Christ followers is supported throughout the New Testament. We are told that we are to be lacking

---

[388] Acts 3:6, 16

in no gift[389] and to earnestly desire the best gifts (plural).[390] Translation: every one of the nine gifts are available to each believer.

Jesus demonstrated the use of the Holy Spirit gifts in His earthly ministry. Recall that Jesus did not perform the miraculous by being the Son of God, but by being anointed by the Holy Spirit of God.[391] The same Holy Spirit that dwells in us![392] Consider the time Jesus first talked to the disciple Nathanael when Philip told him that Jesus was the "One" the prophets spoke about.[393] Jesus saw Nathanael coming toward Him, and said of him, "*Behold, an Israelite indeed, in whom is no guile!*" Nathanael said to Him, "*How do You know me?*"

Jesus answered, "*Before Philip called you, when you were under the fig tree, I saw you.*"

"*Rabbi, You are the Son of God! You are the King of Israel!*" Nathanael replied.

Jesus replied, "*Because I said to you, 'I saw you under the fig tree,' do you believe? You will see greater things than these. Most assuredly, I say to you, hereafter you shall see heaven open, and the angels of God ascending and descending upon the Son of Man.*"

Jesus was operating the power gifts of revelation and spiritual utterance. He demonstrated the gift of the word of knowledge, the gift of discerning spirits, and the gift of prophecy. By so doing, Jesus produced a sign and wonder that increased not only Nathanael's faith, but also the disciples' faith in the promises of Jesus.

Take another look at Jesus' last statement to Nathanael: "*Most assuredly, I say to you, hereafter you shall see heaven open, and the angels of God ascending and descending upon the Son of Man.*"

Jesus was speaking to the manifestation of the Spirit through Him and the operation of the gifts of the Holy Spirit. As Christians, we too have the potential to accomplish the same thing. We are authorized to call for the heavens to open, for angels of God to ascend and descend upon us, and for the words we speak to release God's manifested power. Praise God that we have been given the power and authority to exercise the power of the Gospel of Jesus Christ today.

---

[389] 1 Corinthians 1:5
[390] 1 Corinthians 12:31
[391] Acts 10:38
[392] Romans 8:11
[393] John 1:45-51

Consider also Jesus' instruction that Peter go to the sea and catch a fish. The first fish Peter would catch, Jesus said, would have a coin in its mouth.[394] Many of you may be thinking right now, *How could Jesus make a coin appear in a fish's mouth if He was not operating in this earth as the Son of God?* Recall, however, the time the prophet Elijah threw a stick on top of the water and an axe head rose to the top. Like Elijah, Jesus was operating power gifts of the Holy Spirit.

> *His disciples had come to Capernaum, those who received the temple tax came to Peter and said, "Does your Teacher not pay the temple tax?" He said, "Yes." And when he had come into the house, Jesus anticipated him, saying, "What do you think, Simon? From whom do the kings of the earth take customs or taxes, from their own sons or from strangers? Peter said to Him, "From strangers." Jesus said to him, "Then the sons are free. "Nevertheless, lest we offend them, go to the sea, cast in a hook, and take the fish that comes up first. And when you have opened its mouth, you will find a piece of money; take that and give it to them for Me and you."[395]*

Notice how the Word of God says Jesus "anticipated" what Peter was going to say. The gifts of the word of knowledge and of discerning spirits provided Jesus with the revelation. The gift of working miracles was produced when Jesus received the revelation from the Holy Spirit of what God was going to do for His Son. Jesus spoke it forth, and by the gift of faith, the coin was manifested in the fish's mouth. Do you suppose the coin could have manifested if Jesus had not spoken the revelation with faith? I wonder how many miracles we have missed because we failed to respond to a revelation with faith and to speak it from our mouths.

The **Kingdom of Heaven** Is at Hand

We have seen that power for the gifts of the Holy Spirit is established when the gifts are used in combination with one another. The Holy Spirit is called our Helper, the Comforter, and the One who comes alongside to assist us. One of His purposes is to provide, when we need them, gifts for the profit of all. Linked with our faith and corresponding action, the Holy Spirit will always respond.

In the accounts above, Jesus spoke the revelation word, then exercised, by faith, the power or impartation gifts, and the gift of working a miracle was produced.

---

[394] Matthew 17:24-27
[395] Matthew 17:24-27

When He spoke the revelation word to Peter regarding the fish and the coin, through His words He released the gift of faith that then released the gift of working miracles. Praise the Living God! You and I have the same ability as Jesus to exercise those power gifts.

Still not convinced? Consider these:

Ananias operated at least five gifts of the Spirit: prophecy, word of knowledge, word of wisdom, the gift of faith, and the gift of healing when he ministered to the Apostle Paul (Acts 9:10-19).

Philip operated at least seven of the gifts of the Holy Spirit: prophecy, word of knowledge, word of wisdom, discerning of spirits, the gift of faith, gifts of healing, and working of miracles.[396] Both the Apostle Peter and the Apostle John spoke in tongues, prophesied, operated with words of knowledge, words of wisdom, discerning of spirits, the gift of faith, the gift of healing, and working of miracles.

Stephen operated the gift of prophecy, word of knowledge, word of wisdom, discerning of spirits, gift of faith, gift of healing and the working of miracles.
The truth is, all believers have the ability to exercise the gifts of the Holy Spirit. If we believe that Jesus Christ is our Lord, then the Holy Spirit dwells in each of us. Yet we must be baptized in the Holy Spirit to be energized and equipped with the power to release the manifestation of the Holy Spirit in our lives and in the lives of those around us.

Take time right now to seek the Father for the baptism of the Holy Spirit. This is an act between you and God. Pray, listen for His guidance, and ask for His Spirit to be your counselor. Then seek His presence and be immersed in His sweet Spirit! When you submit to God, He will possess your very being. This is not a mere religious act, and it is not difficult to achieve, because God wants to possess every part of you. If the act is one performed in humility and with a trust that comes from your heart, God will always respond.

If you have already been baptized in the Spirit, seek Him right now to teach and train you to become more sensitive to His leading and the gifts He provides. I urge you to pray in the Spirit – and often! – that by the Spirit in you He may be so energized that He pours from your very being into the lives of those around you. If you truly desire to be set free from an ailment or sickness, healed or delivered of a tormenting spirit, or you want to release the power of healing and

---

[396] Acts 8:25-40

miracles in your life, the only way to accomplish this is by developing a sensitivity to the Holy Spirit in you.

There must be a fire, a burning desire, to have the fullness of the Father in us, that we, too, may echo the words of Jesus, *"The Father and I are one!"* If we desire to have the full presence of God in our hearts, manifesting His Spirit in our lives, we must acquire a deep cry from our souls that acknowledges we have the Greatest Power dwelling in our very being. We are the sons and daughters of God and He has given us the Promise of a great inheritance and the power to fulfill His will. We have the potential to exercise all nine gifts of the Holy Spirit to release a manifestation of the Spirit for the profit of all in the body of Christ!

Today, right now, take up the weapon of the "power gifts" and be equipped by God's mighty spiritual weapons to pull down strongholds and establish peace, health, and joy in your life.

Reflection Verse: *2 Corinthians 10: 2*

*For the weapons of our warfare are not carnal
but mighty in God for pulling down strongholds.*

Thoughts for Reflection:

Jesus said, "Nevertheless I tell you the truth. It is to your advantage that I go away; for if I do not go away, the Helper will not come to you; but if I depart, I will send Him to you." The Holy Spirit is in every born-again believer in Jesus Christ, and we are told to hunger for the baptism of the Holy Spirit and power that we may be effective in our commission to serve all the world. All Christians have at their disposal the nine gifts of the Holy Spirit for the profit of all. Exercise these gifts through your faith and allow the Holy Spirit to freely flow through you to transform the lives of others. We are children of God, we serve mankind, and we have dominion over the kingdom of hell! Go forth and serve mankind by exercising the power of the Holy Spirit. Greater is He who is in you than He who is in the world.

Daily Confession:

My Father and I are one through the indwelling presence of His Spirit in me. The Heavens are open everywhere my feet tread, because the Spirit of God is flowing through me. I have the mighty weapons of the nine gifts of the Holy Spirit available to me to pull down the strongholds in my life and in the lives of others! I can do all things through Christ who strengthens me, for Christ is in me, the hope of the glory. Come upon me, Holy Spirit, and fill me with your awesome and sweet presence. I hunger and thirst for all of you!

13

Weapons of Offense #2: Power of Prayer

Have faith in God.
For assuredly, I say to you, whoever says to this mountain, 'Be removed and be
cast into the sea,' and does not doubt in his heart, but believes that those things
he says will come to pass, he will have whatever he says. Therefore I say to you,
whatever things you ask when you pray, believe that you receive them, and you
will have them.

Mark 11:22-24

Pray Without Ceasing

The next great weapon of attack we have been given by God to tear down and destroy the strongholds of satan's kingdom is that of prayer. Throughout the Old and New Testaments, prayer was the method God used to communicate to His people. Prayer is vital to the Christian life, because it is through prayer that the supernatural is released.

Jesus continually departed from the great crowds and His disciples to be alone and to pray.[397] He would go into the mountains or the wilderness to isolate Himself and commune with His Father. The personal, intimate time Jesus spent with the Father made Jesus more sensitive to the Holy Spirit's leading and better able to release the power of God through Him. The power of prayer is found in our communication with the Father. God's Word explicitly states that prayer is to be the center of our Christian lives. We are to pray with fervency,[398] confidence,[399] without ceasing,[400] both in the Spirit and in understanding,[401] and continuing steadfastly in prayer, day and night seeking the face of God.[402] The

---

[397] Matthew 14:23; Luke 5:16; Mark 1:35; John 17
[398] James 5:16
[399] 1 John 5:14
[400] 1 Thessalonians 5:17
[401] 1 Corinthians 14:15
[402] Romans 12:12; Jude 1:20

Father's desire is that men and women pray everywhere, lifting up holy hands, without wrath and doubting.[403]

The power to transform this world is released through prayer. We are responsible for taking up this weapon and exercising it. The ability of the Christian faith to reach a level of power and transformation through prayer must become a discipline, a way of life. Abiding in Christ is not an option, it is a command, and the only way we can abide in Him and He in us is if we learn more about Him and spend time with Him in prayer. We must take up this weapon and exercise it effectively to release God's power and might.

A Time to Pray

Despite the fact that prayer is essential, I am amazed at the number of Christians who do not spend time on a daily basis alone communicating with the Father to connect, fellowship, and develop a relationship with Him. I know that my relationship with my wife would fail if the only time I communicated with her is when I needed something from her. As we know, when communication is absent in a relationship, the two parties eventually will grow apart.

The power of prayer is released when we spend quality time communing with the Holy Spirit, seeking the heart of God and becoming one with Him. Prayer must be a hunger and longing from our hearts to be connected to our Father, understanding that we can do nothing without His presence in our lives. We are predestined to be in contact with our Father continually, trusting in Him and making Him our habitation.

The apostle of faith Smith Wigglesworth once said, "I do not spend ten minutes a day praying and do not go ten minutes without praying." We are to be continually in prayer, seeking the face of the Father, desiring His fullness in every facet of life. We are spiritual beings, and as such it is a part of our heritage, our spiritual DNA, to be in fellowship with the Spirit as often as we possibly can throughout the course of the day. Prayer's power is released when we grasp its importance and put it into constant practice.

Many people come to the place in their struggles where only God can intervene in their life, and more than once I have heard, "All I can do now is pray." Unfortunately, those words are usually laced with connotations so negative that the faith necessary for manifestation of the Spirit has been destroyed by disbelief.

---

[403] 1 Timothy 2:8

We should be rejoicing to be able to pray, when it is time to finally give it all over to the Father for His divine power and presence to change the whole situation. Prayer is not something we should feel we have to do or fall back on as a last resort. Prayer is something every Christian should desire to do. It's all about a relationship, an intimate love with the complete Godhead. Without prayer, we are alone and isolated in a world intent on destroying God's children. Prayer is vital for the survival of the Christian faith! Prayer full of power can pull down every demonic stronghold. It is a useless weapon, however, unless and until a relationship, firmly grounded in faith, is established. We have to learn to pray from our hearts and not our minds.

Prayer From the Heart

Jesus rebuked the Pharisees for the formality, repetition, and the religion behind their prayers. *But when you pray, do not use vain repetitions as the heathen do. For they think that they will be heard for their many words. Therefore do not be like them.* [404] Likewise, Jesus warns us not to use in our prayers the vain repetitions that destroy intimacy with the Father. God is not looking for us to methodically worship Him with our mouths or to merely go through the motions we perform in church. He is looking for a people willing to give Him full attention, praising Him from the love and passion of the heart. Our Father is looking for individuals willing to walk with Him in the garden and interact with Him on a personal level. Jesus said, *"These people draw near to Me with their mouth, and honor Me with their lips, but their heart is far from Me, and in vain they worship Me, teaching as doctrine the commandments of men."*[405] Prayer is a heart issue developed and shaped by a hunger and thirst for personal interaction with the Father.

Brother Derek Prince once said, "If we are praying for ten minutes, then nine of those minutes should be in praise and adoration to the Father, connecting His heart to ours, and the last minute seeking that which we desire." He had it right – when we are truly connected to the Father's heart, when we are truly conscious of the power of the Holy Spirit in us, our prayer lives change. We begin to spend more time drawing closer to God and allowing Him to draw closer to us.[406]

The Father knows everything we are going to pray before we pray it, and yet He desires to witness our vulnerability and the trust and love in our expressions.

---

[404] Matthew 6:7,8
[405] Matthew 15:8-9
[406] James 4:7

Prayer does not have to be eloquent to be effective and powerful. It does, however, need to come from the heart.

Have you noticed that the simple prayers of a child are almost always answered? It is not because God loves them more than us or that their needs are greater, but because their hearts are innocent and full of faith, uncorrupted by lies, pride or fear. We, too, have a responsibility to pray from the heart and not from our experiences or intellectual understanding. Our hearts are able to release a desire our minds could never understand. We must learn to shut off our minds when we pray and allow our prayers to come from the heart.

The Established Principle of Prayer

True prayer, from the heart, is a principle God established. It is necessary that we obey His wishes if we hope to pray effectively and with power. In God's own words: "*If My people who are called by My name will humble themselves, and pray and seek My face, and turn from their wicked ways, then I will hear from heaven, and will forgive their sin and heal their land. Now My eyes will be open and My ears attentive to prayer made in this place. For now I have chosen and sanctified this house, that My name may be there forever; and My eyes and My heart will be there perpetually.*"[407]

If we are willing to humble ourselves and submit to Him and His ways completely – spirit, soul, and body – consecrating ourselves to His truth, repenting and turning from our wicked ways, our hearts will be ready to seek His face and enter into communion with Him through prayer. We are instructed, therefore, to humble ourselves under the mighty hand of God, that He may exalt us in due time, casting all our cares upon Him, for He cares for us.[408]

When Daniel understood the number of years specified by the word of the Lord (that God would accomplish seventy years in the desolations of Jerusalem), as given through Jeremiah the prophet, he set his face toward the Lord God to make his request by prayer.[409] Daniel repented, through sackcloth and ashes; he fasted and then made supplications through his prayer. He cleansed his heart and humbly approached the throne of God through prayer, seeking justice and restoration for the people of God. Daniel prayed for twenty-one days, humbly, steadfastly seeking the face of the Lord.

---

[407] 2 Chronicles 7:14-16
[408] 1 Peter 5:6
[409] Daniel 9:2-3

On the twenty-first day, an angel appeared and informed Daniel that from the time he had begun praying, God heard his prayer, but God's response was detained due to the battle in the heavenlies. God is faithful to His Word! When we humble ourselves before Him, He will lift us up, hear us, and respond to our prayers![410]

God said that *if we pray from our hearts, He will hear from heaven, forgive our sins, and heal our land*! God will hear our prayers when they come from the heart. Vain repetitions are not prayers from the heart; they are prayers that come from the soul to soothe a person's conscience and allow him to think he has made an effort to touch God. It's deception! God desires so much more of us; He desires all of us. He desires us to repent from a humble heart and be willing to open our hearts and be joined with Him forever.

Prayer is taking the time to commune with the Father heart to heart. The Father's eyes will be open, His ears attentive, and His eyes and heart will be with us perpetually, without end! Praise the Living God!

A great model of prayer from the heart is found in the 17th Chapter of John, where Jesus intercedes for His disciples. He is praying from His heart, not a repetitious prayer, but one connected to the will of the Father for the advancement of His Kingdom on earth. Failing to connect in prayer with our Father results in unmoved mountains. The only time prayers have power – whether prayers of intercession, supplication, praise, worship, confession, proclamation, or thanksgiving – are when the prayers are connected through our hearts by faith to the will of the Father!

Prayer Is Listening

The power found in the weapon of prayer is established through our ability to hear and listen to what the Father is communicating. Gloria Copeland wrote, "If you are not manifesting the power of God in your life, you do not need more of God, He needs more of you! If you keep Him shut out of your thoughts, then you will live a mere natural life. God wants your undivided attention so that you will learn to hear His voice. When you hear His voice and obey His promptings, you will be sustained daily by the resurrection life that is in you through the Holy Spirit. What many do not realize is that you cannot fill your words with faith. Union with God through His Word fills your words with faith."[411]

---

[410] James 4:10
[411] G.Copeland, *The Power to Live a New Life*, Kenneth Copeland Publications: Fort Worth TX. p. 7

God is calling us to partner with Him, to become His voice in this world, and we can only fulfill this call when we stop and listen to what He is telling us. Oftentimes in prayer, we do all the talking, all the "praying," never really taking the time to hear what the Father is saying. Communication with the Father is a dialogue, not a monologue.

Have you ever wondered why the Word of God informs us to pray without ceasing? [412] It is because God is continually talking to us. It is because we must be in a position to hear from God in order to do His will. The only way it is possible to hear His voice is to spend time with Him, fellowshipping with Him, loving Him and letting Him love us. God has said, *"Trust in the LORD with all your heart, and lean not on your own understanding; in all your ways acknowledge Him, and He shall direct your paths."* [413] He is unable to direct our paths if we are not willing to take the time to communicate and listen to Him. The Lord says, *"Hear and obey My voice for I love you and I desire to be with you. Seek My presence and I will be there for I have promised that I will never leave you nor forsake you."* The purest form of worship is found in our obedience to God's Word. Whether that word is *logos* (written) or *rhema* (spoken), we must be willing to submit and obey what God is instructing us to fulfill. We are called to develop sensitivity to His leading as He enables us to be instruments of His righteousness, voice, and love in this world.

Many people ask me how they can develop a sensitivity to His leading, and my response is simple: *Just spend time with Him.* As with any other relationship, the more time you spend with a person, the more you become sensitive to their issues, desires, and leadings. Please understand that the act of prayer has become a "religious thing," preventing God's children from taking the time to enter into His presence. The Father desires that we spend time with Him – with no expectations or strings attached. He just wants to love on you. Make the time to just sit and listen to Him. He is that still small voice in your heart speaking Life into your very soul! He is the one touching your heart and establishing the peace you experience. Brothers and sisters in Christ, prayer is essential to our Christian lives!

The Kingdom of Heaven Is at Hand

"Most assuredly, I say to you, hereafter you shall see heaven open, and the angels of God ascending and descending upon the Son of Man." [414] We saw

---

[412] Prophetic Word spoken in prayer
[413] Proverbs 3:5-6
[414] John 1:51

earlier that Jesus was speaking to Nathanael in response to Nathanael's faith in the power of God through Jesus. Jesus revealed that the heavens would open and angels would ascend and descend upon Him and upon every word He would speak.

What may not be so clear is the fact that it was Jesus' prayers that opened the heavens and poised the angels to be ready to respond to His command. The heavens were open because Jesus spent time with His Father, seeking the face of God, fellowshipping with Him, listening to God's direction.

Jesus was one with the Father, not because He was the Son of God, but because He was faithful to seek the heart of God and establish a relationship with the Father founded on reverence and humility. Jesus obeyed everything the Father asked Him to do, He was faithful, and as a result, He exercised great power in His prayers to release the supernatural, the angelic forces of God in the heavens.

The angels of God are ready and waiting for you to take up your weapons of prayer and release them into battle against the enemy. *"And I will give you the keys of the kingdom of heaven, and whatever you bind on earth will be bound in heaven, and whatever you loose on earth will be loosed in heaven."*[415] When we exercise the authority bestowed on us by the keys of the Kingdom of Heaven, we release an angelic army to either bind up or loose in accordance with our words. We are God's voice in this world.[416]

The weapon of prayer derives from the sword of the Spirit, which is the Word of God. We are exhorted and commanded to *"pray always with all prayer and supplication in the Spirit, being watchful to this end with all perseverance and supplication for all the saints."*[417] We are responsible for releasing the angelic forces of God in this world through prayer. If we are not praying, the angels are not being released. We are the body of Christ, and the head can do nothing if the body is unwilling to move and fulfill its purpose. Likewise, the body cannot move if it is not attached to the head.

The Word of God states, *"But God shall shoot at them with an arrow; suddenly they shall be wounded. So He will make them stumble over their own tongue; all who see them shall flee away. All men shall fear, and shall declare the work of God; for they shall wisely consider His doing."*[418] God will shoot at the workers of iniquity and destroy their plots against the children of God. The "arrows" here

---

[415] Matthew 16:19
[416] Psalm 103:20-23
[417] Ephesians 6:17,18
[418] Psalm 64:7-9

are our spoken words. Please understand, the very words we speak in prayer are the arrows that God will shoot at the demonic kingdom.

"It is written, 'My house shall be called a house of prayer,' but you have made it a 'den of thieves.'"[419] Jesus was angry. We are the temples of the Holy Spirit, the "house of God." We are called to be a praying Church, not a den of thieves. It is time we take up the weapon of prayer and engage the heavenlies with the Word of God, releasing His power and His angelic army against the kingdom of satan.

Jesus said to the crowd when He was about to release the miracle-working power of God to raise Lazarus from the dead, *"Father, I thank You that You have heard Me. And I know that You always hear Me, but because of the people who are standing by I said this, that they may believe that You sent Me."*[420] He had spent so much time with the Father that Jesus knew the Father heard His every prayer. The power of prayer is established when we can reach this same faith, this same place of consciousness that we know with confidence that the Father hears and answers our prayers. *Now the confidence that we have in Him, that if we ask anything according to His will, He hears us.*[421] We must believe in what we pray![422]

When we are in relationship with the Father, abiding in Him and He in us, then we will know that He hears us, because we will only be praying according to His will. The Kingdom of Heaven is at hand when we can take up the weapon of prayer for all men – whether a prayer of faith, confession, proclamation, supplication, thanksgiving, or intercession – and heed the will of God to be fulfilled and to know that God has heard our prayers. Prayer is a powerful weapon, one to be utilized often, from the heart and with love, always confident, knowing that the extraordinary will happen because the Father is listening!

---

[419] Matthew 21:13
[420] John 11:41,42
[421] 1 John 5:14
[422] Mark 11:22-24

Reflection Verse: 1 John 5:14

> *Now the confidence that we have in Him, that if we ask anything*
> *according to His will, He hears us.*

Thoughts for Reflection:

Prayer is essential to the Christian life. God is calling us to communion with Him through His Holy Spirit. Have confidence in your prayers and know that He hears you! Our Father just wants to spend time with us, to love on us and bless us. Are we that busy that we cannot make the time to develop a relationship with Him?

Daily Confession:

I know that if I just believe I will see the glory of God. I believe Jesus' words that whatever things I ask for when I pray, if I believe, I will receive them. In your name, Lord Jesus, I pray and I stand upon your promise that whatever I ask for in your name I will receive! My prayers are heard and I know that I have the petitions I have asked of You. Thank you, Father!

14

Weapons of Offense #3: Power of Praise

Bless the LORD, O my soul; And all that is within me, bless His holy name!
Bless the LORD, O my soul, and forget not all His benefits: Who forgives all
your iniquities and Who heals all your diseases!

Psalm 103: 1-2

Praise ~ An Act of Faith

The next great weapon of attack given to us to tear down and destroy satan's strongholds is the weapon of praise. *"These things I have spoken to you, that in Me you may have peace. In the world you will have tribulation; but be of good cheer, I have overcome the world."*[423] There is great revelation in this profound little statement by Jesus. He is telling us that when the storms of life are set against us, we are to elevate ourselves above the storm by resting in the truth that we are God's children and we live a victorious life.

Jesus said, *"Be of good cheer, I have overcome the world."* He is telling us to live a life of praise in times of trouble, tribulation, and struggle, because He has already overcome the world. This act of praise is an act of faithfulness to God's promise and to the New Covenant established through the blood of Jesus Christ. Satan's kingdom has no defense against it! When we enter into a position of praise and worship in the midst of a storm, we are demonstrating our trust in the faithfulness of our Father and His unconditional love for us. This type of faith and trust in God destroys any form of demonic stronghold in our lives.

Paul wrote to the church of Philippi, *"Rejoice in the Lord always. Again I will say, rejoice! Let your gentleness be known to all men. The Lord is at hand."*[424] Those were the words written by the Apostle Paul as he lay in the middle of a deep and dark prison cell where he was chained, unclothed, cold, and bleeding. He was being tortured and persecuted for the name of Jesus Christ, and yet he was able to rejoice and praise the Lord.

---

[423] John 16:33
[424] Philippians 4:4

Paul understood that if *God is for us, who can be against us!*[425] Satan could not steal Paul's joy or peace, because the Spirit in him was greater than anything in this world. We, too, can enter into this place of rest and confidence, knowing that the overcoming Christ dwells in us through the very presence of the Holy Spirit of God. We, too, can come to the revelation understanding that the Kingdom of Heaven truly is at hand!

There comes a time in our understanding of the Word of God that rises above all the circumstances of life, that offers us the strength and courage to boldly stand upon what God the Father has promised, and once there, to shout with praise. When we reach that place, we are able to stand in the midst of hell on earth and rejoice – for God is faithful in what He has promised!

Receive the revelation: We are more than conquerors through Jesus the Christ! We are triumphant, victorious, and there is nothing satan's kingdom can do to steal this truth except to deceive us into believing that we are hopeless and helpless. Our acts of praise demonstrate a faith and trust in the delivering power and promise of God our Father. Only through our revelation of the Spirit of God in us can we rise to a level of trust and faith that the victory is won even before the battle begins. Praise the Lord today for He is worthy to be praised!

The Word of God clearly states, *"Not by might nor by power, but by My Spirit, says the LORD of hosts."*[426] We are to rejoice in the Lord for our God and Father will always lead us into triumph through the victory of Jesus the Christ. The power of praise will destroy any stronghold the enemy might claim. When we enter into a place of pure, heartfelt praise, the peace of God will fall upon us and His anointing will destroy any yoke of oppression in our lives. If we are willing to stand and lift our voices in the highest praise, removing all fear, doubt, and religious doctrine created by man, then the deception and lies of the devil will come crashing down around us.

The Praise Principle

God the Father has established a principle of praise, setting at our disposal a weapon that destroys the influence of the kingdom of darkness in our lives. The principle of praise has tremendous power to destroy fear and doubt, demonstrating victory and triumph in all that we do. The Father gives beauty for ashes, oil of joy for mourning, and a garment of praise that will destroy the spirit

---

[425] Romans 8:31
[426] Zechariah 4:6

of heaviness that undermines the foundation of our faith and hope in God's Word.[427]

King David best portrayed the principle of praise. By his faith in God during even the most tumultuous of his days, he was able to exercise the power of praise through worship and love toward the Father. Playing his harp and praising God with psalms, David was successful in driving out the tormenting demons that bound King Saul and restored Saul's peace of mind.

Likewise, even as Paul and Silas sat chained in a dungeon, they were able to praise the Lord and rejoice in His name and power. The Kingdom of Heaven was released and the chains holding the disciples were broken.

However, the principle of praise was first established when God gave Joshua a simple command: "*See! I have given Jericho into your hand, its king, and the mighty men of valor. You shall march around the city, all you men of war; you shall go all around the city once. This you shall do six days. And seven priests shall bear seven trumpets of rams' horns before the ark. But the seventh day you shall march around the city seven times, and the priests shall blow the trumpets. Then it shall come to pass, when they make a long blast with the ram's horn, and when you hear the sound of the trumpet, that all the people shall shout with a great shout then the wall of the city will fall down flat.*"[428]

Faithful to God's command, Joshua obeyed and a great power was released. When the children of Israel came together and shouted praise and worship to the Great I AM, the mighty, powerful wall of Jericho came crashing down. The children of God acted upon their faith and stood confidently on God's command and the Kingdom of God was released upon Jericho. They marched around the city for six days, and on the seventh they marched seven times, and on the seventh time they praised the Lord with a loud shout and the earth shook, destroying the city.

Seven is the number used throughout Scripture to represent God's covenant. Accordingly, through this act of faith by Joshua and the children of Israel, a covenant was established, a promise that God would respond to the praises of His people. God gave His people the city of Jericho because they were faithful to His Word and because they shouted His praise in the midst of the storm.

---

[427] Isaiah 61:3
[428] Joshua 6:2-5

The same principle applies to our lives today. No matter the size of the wall, when we enter into praise the angelic army of God is released to annihilate the surrounding kingdom of hell. The principle of praise is established when we truly know, with an absolute, concrete consciousness of God in us, that He is faithful to His promise. When our souls know without a doubt that God is for us, we enter into a new realm of revelation and understanding and live a life of triumph that celebrates a victory already won. We begin to experience the New Covenant promise of *Christ in us, the hope of the glory* with a triumphant shout of praise that pours from our very being!

Brothers and sisters in Christ, there is freedom in our praises when we can worship the Father from the heart without any reservations. Completely giving our souls to God, we step into a freedom unavailable through anything else in this world.

A woman I knew had struggled with bipolar condition her entire life, with its continual episodes of mania, hyperactivity, and depression. She had spent all the money she had on doctors, medications, therapy, and treatment trying desperately to defeat the tormenting spirit that was slowly killing her.

Then one day she got saved and baptized with the Holy Spirit, and she turned her lifelong battle with depression and mania over to the Lord. Soon she began to allow her mind to be captive to His Word. But the demons kept coming. They continued tormenting her, and she continued to fight them with the truth of the Word. But despite her "acts of faith," one day a spirit of heaviness came upon her with such a vengeance that she did not feel like moving or even living anymore. She felt defeated, alone, isolated from everyone. She also felt worthless, despised, and rejected. She had gotten to a place where she believed even God could not heal her, and a deep level of despair overcame her.

Suddenly from the depths of her heart came a truth from God's Word that had been planted there so many days before. A fire began to arise in her belly, one of righteous anger, and she forced herself to get out of bed. She literally stood upon her Bible and began to praise God from the depth of her heart for the blood of Jesus Christ. She stood face to face with the depression, the mania, the fear, doubt, worry, self-hatred and rejection, and she praised her Father with everything in her being. She took upon her the garment of praise and tore down the wall of Jericho in her life. She is now completely free from the tormenting demons of the past!

The anointing released through her praise of victory and triumph destroyed the yokes of oppression and depression in her life. We have that power of praise to destroy the supernatural stronghold of bondage in our lives, too. When we exercise our faith by standing in the midst of the storm, praising the Father for His love and faithfulness, the devil is destroyed. Praise comes from a consciousness deep in our souls that knows that God is always with us and that through Jesus we are triumphant, more than conquerors in all that we do.

I heard a preacher give a testimony of praise that had broken satan's hold over his family and ministry. He told of the financial difficulty he and his family had to endure when he entered the ministry. He had received two phone calls from the bank in a single day: the first to inform him that his house would be foreclosed on, and the second to let him know his truck was being repossessed.

As storms go, he was standing in a hurricane, on the very verge of losing all he had. Walking into his den, the preacher fell to his knees and asked the Father why this was happening when all he was doing was obeying God's word and command. As he knelt there on the floor, tears trickling down his cheeks, feeling utterly defeated, a strong witness came over him and the word "rejoice" resonated through his spirit. He sat there for a moment and then he knew.

Jumping to his feet, the preacher ran into the living room where his family was huddled in sorrow and prayer. Grabbing their hands, he pulled each of them to their feet and they followed his lead – dancing around in the middle of the living room, praising and worshipping God. The whole family was of one accord, pouring out their hearts in praise and worship, demonstrating and celebrating a victory that had already been won for them through the blood of Jesus! Before long, the oppression against their family was broken completely. Before the bankers could get to their house, a friend had called and said "I believe God has just told me that I am to give you a check." The amount of the check covered the mortgage of their house and the loan on their truck.

The testimony of God's faithfulness and love did not stop there. Returning home from an evening of worship and celebration with friends, the preacher and his family noticed computer boxes and other packages on their front porch. Everything the family had prayed for over the last year had been delivered to their door. The power of praise had broken through the demonic stronghold and released the glory of God upon this family. There is great power released in our praises.

The Kingdom of Heaven IS NOW AT HAND!

The Lord revealed to me several years ago that many people are very close to receiving their breakthrough, their blessings, their deliverances, and their healing, but because they fail to utilize the weapon of praise, they have been defeated by the kingdom of satan. The demonic kingdom can sense when we are on the verge of a breakthrough in our understanding, and when it does, it will do everything in its power to undermine our newfound faith. It is this desperate effort on behalf of the demonic kingdom that oftentimes is effective at stopping God's people just short of receiving their breakthroughs and promises. There is only one thing powerful enough to defeat the demonic kingdom from destroying our lives of faith with God: *PRAISE!*

The power of praise — our shouts of thanksgiving and our psalms of adoration and exaltation — releases a faith that creates the manifestation of the Spirit. When we enter into praise, we release angelic forces to attack and destroy the kingdom of hell in this world. Praise is faith that the God of hope has filled us with all joy and peace in believing, that we may abound in hope by the power of the Holy Spirit.[429] The very genuineness of our faith is increased when we are able to stand in praise in the midst of the storm and rejoice with joy inexpressible, full of glory, praising, honoring, and glorifying the revelation of Jesus Christ.[430]

We have the power today to rejoice and praise the Father, glorifying Him and proclaiming His victory in us who believe. Stand today and praise the Lord. Allow your praise to destroy the demonic stronghold in your life once and for all.

Reflection Verse: Psalm 103:1

Bless the LORD, O my soul; and all that is within me, bless His holy name!

Thoughts for Reflection:

Praise is a weapon satan cannot defend. Lift up your holy hands and praise the Father!

Daily Confession:

I have victory through Jesus Christ my Lord and Redeemer! I am in Christ, therefore, I praise my Father with all my heart! Bless the Lord, O my soul, bless Your Holy Name!

---

[429] Romans 15:13
[430] 1 Peter 1:7

15

Weapons of Offense #4: Power of the Testimony

And this is the testimony: that God has given us eternal life,
and this life is in His Son.

1 John 5:11

Testimony is a Prophetic Word

Our ability to tear down and destroy the enemy's strongholds would not be possible without also using the weapon of our testimony. *"And they overcame him by the blood of the Lamb and by the word of their testimony, and they did not love their lives to the death."*[431] Each of our individual testimonies, whether of our salvation, a healing, or deliverance, any form of victory experienced through the blood of Jesus Christ becomes our testimony to demonstrate the faithfulness of God's love in our lives. Every testimony that gives God the glory comes equipped with great power, and once released, the testimony becomes a prophetic word that increases the faith and hope of those who hear. Maybe not precisely at the moment, but rest assured that God allows the seed of our testimonies to take root and grow.

The power of our testimonies actually becomes a force to change the surrounding atmosphere. When we hear the testimony of the manifestation of the Spirit of God in man, the faith and hope that God can bring the same blessings to our lives begin to take hold. Healings, deliverances, conversions – they are all testimonies with the power to transform not only a person's life, but even a nation.

> *When Jesus entered the country of the Gaderenes He was immediately encountered by a man with a unclean spirit who had been dwelling among the tombs; and no one could bind him, not even with chains, because he had often been bound with shackles and chains. And the chains had been pulled apart by him, and the shackles broken in pieces; neither could anyone tame him. And always, night and day, he was in the mountains and in the tombs, crying out and cutting himself with stones.*

---

[431] Revelation 12:11

But when he saw Jesus from afar, he ran and worshiped Him. And he cried out with a loud voice and said, "What have I to do with You, Jesus, Son of the Most High God? I implore You by God that You do not torment me." For He said to him, "Come out of the man, unclean spirit!" Then He asked him, "What is your name?" And he answered, saying, "My name is Legion; for we are many." And he begged Him earnestly that He would not send them out of the country. Now a large herd of swine was feeding there near the mountains. And all the demons begged Him, saying, "Send us to the swine, that we may enter them." And at once Jesus gave them permission. Then the unclean spirits went out and entered the swine (there were about two thousand); and the herd ran violently down the steep place into the sea, and drowned in the sea.

Now those who fed the swine fled, and they told it in the city and in the country. And they went out to see what it was that had happened. Then they came to Jesus, and saw the one who had been demon-possessed and had the legion, sitting and clothed and in his right mind. And they were afraid. And those who saw it told them how it happened to him who had been demon-possessed, and about the swine.

Then they began to plead with Him to depart from their region. And when He got into the boat, he who had been demon-possessed begged Him that he might be with Him. However, Jesus did not permit him, but said to him, "Go home to your friends, and tell them what great things the Lord has done for you, and how He has had compassion on you." And he departed and began to proclaim in Decapolis all that Jesus had done for him; and all marveled. [432]

Two very important truths are revealed at the end of the above account. First, when the people heard the great miracle-working power of God, they became afraid. Their fear was a result of the sin running rampant amongst the people of Gadara. Jesus had cast the demons into the swine, because, under Mosaic law, it was against the old covenant of God to eat such meat. He was cleaning house.

The people of Gadara were Hebrews, children of God, and they were living lives that did not adhere to the covenant of God. Jesus cast out the unclean spirits into the swine and all the sin perished. It was a miracle that scared the people,

---

[432] Mark 5:1-20

because they thought God's judgment would come against them for living in sin. So they pleaded with Jesus to depart.

What may not be as noticeable here, though, is the abundance of God's mercy and love for His people and the demonstration of His power through the testimony. The man who received deliverance wanted desperately to travel with Jesus, but Jesus told him to go home to his friends and tell them about the great work God had done for him and of God's compassion. The man was sent back home to testify of the Lord's power, love, and mercy.

Before long, the man's testimony had become a prophetic word spoken across the region, drawing the heart of man back to the heart of God. The words of a single testimony had destroyed demonic strongholds of fear, unbelief, and sin in the region and prepared hearts to receive the word of God.

Once Jesus left Gadara, He traveled to Capernaum, to Nazareth, to Bethsaida to Gennesaret, to the region of Tyre and Sidon, traveling across through Mt. Herman to the Decapolis region where eventually He returned to Gadara. When Jesus entered the Decapolis region once again, the multitude was very great, all seeking Jesus to heal and deliver them.[433] The man Jesus had sent back to give his testimony of God's power and love was instrumental in stirring up the faith of the people in the Decapolis region to seek the very presence of God through Jesus.

There is power in our testimonies to change not only lives around us, but also an entire nation!

I was ministering to a young man once when God, through His Holy Spirit, destroyed the strongholds holding the man in bondage. When God healed his heart, the young man was inspired by the Spirit to begin giving his testimony to others struggling with the same demonic oppression. But fear gripped at him and he chose not to follow through with the plan of his heart.

Not long after the man had been delivered from the strongholds, the enemy resumed attacking him all over again, this time destroying his faith and adding even more strongholds to his life. The young man had removed himself from the offensive line and left himself completely vulnerable to the lies and deception of satan's kingdom.

We must continue to attack the enemy through our testimonies, releasing the prophetic word of God, increasing the faith of man, and drawing the heart of man

---

[433] Mark 7:31-8:26

back to God. We have a responsibility to share our testimonies and to continue our assault against the kingdom of hell.

The Power of Words

The truth that our words are powerful is abundantly clear in God's Word. We have a choice to make every time we speak: Will we use the power to bless or to curse? Every word that comes out of our mouths releases either demons or angels to fulfill the spoken word. When we curse or call someone a name, we release demonic forces against that person. When we speak sickness upon ourselves, take ownership through our words regarding a sickness or oppression, or receive as truth a devastating medical/psychological diagnosis, we allow demonic forces to come against us. The enemy stands at the door, invitation in hand, ready to invade; he is like a roaring lion crouched and ready to devour when our words give him the right.

On the other hand, when we bless or speak words of life and edification into a person's life, we release angels and the Kingdom of Heaven upon them. The proof rests in creation. By the power of God's words, the world came into being. From the moment God "spoke" the existence of creation into being, He developed a principle of power through the spoken word.[434]

From the very words we speak forth, we unleash the power to bless or to curse. God said, "*I call heaven and earth as witnesses today against you, that I have set before you life and death, blessing and cursing; therefore choose life, that both you and your descendants may live; that you may love the LORD your God, that you may obey His voice, and that you may cling to Him, for He is your life and the length of your days.*"[435] We have the power to choose life and blessings from the confession that comes from our mouths. Our testimonies release words of Life that prophetically energize the atmosphere and transform man's heart.

"*Death and life are in the power of the tongue, and those who love it will eat its fruit.*"[436] The tendency to complain will release damning words that often result in corrosion and death of our intimacy with the Father, thereby limiting our ability to experience His presence. However, if our words are full of Life and testimony of God's love and compassion, we produce fruit full of faith, hope, and love. Those who love life will speak from their mouth words of life. They will

---

[434] Genesis 1:3
[435] Deuteronomy 30:19
[436] Proverbs 18:21

partake of and enjoy the fruit it produces and will testify to the truth of God's Living Word.

A reason many people cannot release the miraculous healing blessings already given to us by the Father is because they curse themselves or others by their words. I find that most people give testimony more to their sickness or affliction than they do to God. They speak from their mouth how sick they are, how confused or depressed they are, how life is not worth living, how someone hurt them, how they despise someone for an offense, or how unfair life is to them. These types of words curse and destroy a life of faith.

When we grieve the Holy Spirit through our words of unbelief or fear, we will not be able to appropriate all the fullness of God for our lives. The only way our needs may be fulfilled from the Father is if we speak them forth in humility and reverence. The Holy Spirit will not permit lawlessness to the Word of God! We must get our tongues under control. We must speak God's Word from our mouths in order to release our hearts' desire to transform situations.

Jesus made it clear when He stated, *"For assuredly, I say to you, whoever says to this mountain, 'Be removed and be cast into the sea,' and does not doubt in his heart, but believes that those things he says will come to pass, he will have whatever he says."*[437] The power of our tongues enables us to move mountains. When we humble ourselves before God and give Him the glory for our blessings, our testimonies establish an open door from which Heaven flows. Our testimonies produce a truth that we are victorious through Jesus Christ and that the New Covenant promise is fulfilled through those who believe. Our testimonies are truths that destroy the lies and deception of a defeated foe, thereby establishing God's Kingdom of love and power in this world.

The Greatest of All Testimonies

The Gospel of Jesus Christ is the greatest of all testimonies. The New Testament is packed with evidence of Jesus' signs, wonders, miracles, and healings. Through the testimony of the power of the resurrected Christ, man's faith is increased and God's power released to manifest His Spirit. *"And with great power gave the apostles witness of the resurrection of the Lord Jesus: and great grace was upon them.*[438] *And by the hands of the apostles were many signs and wonders wrought among the people; Insomuch that they brought forth the sick into the streets, and laid them on beds and couches, that at the least the shadow*

---

[437] Mark 11:22
[438] Acts 4:33

of Peter passing by might overshadow some them.[439] *There came also a multitude out of the cities round about unto Jerusalem, bring the sick folks, and them which were vexed with unclean spirits; and they were healed everyone."*[440]

The power of Jesus' testimony opens the heavens and releases the power of God to demonstrate His faithfulness. We are commissioned to serve as witnesses to the literal reality of Christ's resurrection from the dead. We are called to preach that the Kingdom of Heaven is at hand. Jesus said, *"I am He who lives, and was dead, and behold, I am alive forevermore. Amen. And I have the keys of Hades and of Death."*[441]

Jesus the Christ is the Name above all names, and it is His dominion and power to which we must testify. What is Christianity without the supernatural power of the resurrected Christ? The Christian faith is founded upon our testimonies of the greatest truth of all time, that Christ dwells in us and He brings hope and the glory of His Kingdom! Arise, children of God, and give your testimony on how He has healed, delivered, and saved you from the wretchedness of this world. Arise and give your testimony of Christ in you. Arise today, for the Kingdom of Heaven is at hand!

The Kingdom of Heaven Is NOW at Hand

The word of our testimony is a powerful weapon that keeps us on the offensive, attacking and tormenting the kingdom of hell by demonstrating the supremacy and power of the Kingdom of Light. The words we release become Life, proclaiming the promise established through the New Covenant. *"And this is the testimony: that God has given us eternal life, and this life is in His Son."*[442] Please remember that "eternal" is defined as time having no beginning or end, now and forever, and "life" is defined as a God-kind of life, full of abundance, wanting and desiring absolutely nothing. God has given us abundant life NOW and forever through His Son that we may all declare the truth through our testimonies that the Kingdom of Heaven in NOW at hand! Jesus gave us the command, *""Go, preach, saying, 'The kingdom of heaven is at hand.' Heal the sick, cleanse the lepers, raise the dead, cast out demons. Freely you have received, freely give."*[443] Through our testimonies we can be followers of Jesus Christ, proclaiming His Truth, His Light, and His Life in all that we do. Go today

---

[439] Acts 5:12a
[440] Acts 5:15-16
[441] Revelations 1:18
[442] 1 John 5:11
[443] Matthew 10:7,8

and give the testimony of your victory through Jesus Christ, through your word and deed demonstrating to all that Christ dwells in you.

Reflection Verse: 1 John 5:11

And this is the testimony: that God has given us eternal life,
and this life is in His Son.

Thoughts for Reflection:

The power of our testimony is found in the prophetic truth it releases. God is not a respecter of persons; therefore, if we hear one testimony regarding His miraculous touch, we know it can happen again. Testimonies have the power to increase our faith to a level where we can expect God to touch our lives as well.

Daily Confession:

I can overcome anything in my life by the blood of the Lamb, the word of my testimony, and not loving my life unto death. The words I speak are words of Life and power. God has given me an abundant life NOW, today, and forever through His precious Son! I am a child of God, an heir to His Kingdom and an instrument of righteousness used to advance the Kingdom of my Father! I stand today in FAITH, expecting the extraordinary in all that I do!

16

The Weapons of Warfare Unveiled

Now may the God of peace who brought up our Lord Jesus from the dead, that great Shepherd of the sheep, through the blood of the everlasting covenant, make you complete in every good work to do His will, working in you what is well pleasing in His sight, through Jesus Christ.

Hebrews 13:20

The Secret to Unveiling the Weapons of Offense

We are called to a life of faith that we may believe that the Father will fulfill His Word and give to us the mighty weapons necessary to pull down demonic strongholds. The weapons we have discussed thus far are the four primary weapons given to us to offer up an attack against the kingdom of hell. These weapons of offense are ours to take up and exercise that all those in captivity to the lies and deception of the enemy may be liberated by the power and truth of the Word of God.

The secret to unveiling or releasing the weapons of offense is our consciousness of the power of the Holy Spirit within us. When we come to a full understanding of the gifts of the Holy Spirit and our privilege and duty to exercise them, we will notice great miracles and healings being manifested in our lives. Through the gifts of the Holy Spirit and our prayers, praises, and testimonies, we activate the power of God. God has already given us the weapons to use. It is up to us now to use them.

Another important spiritual principle we must understand in order to truly release and unveil the Kingdom of God and allow the weapons of offense to be effective is that of *standing on the truth and power of the blood of Jesus Christ*. The principle is found in the truth that the devil cannot attack or develop a stronghold in our lives without a permit to do so. That is, sickness, disease, strife, poverty, or any other form of oppression cannot latch onto a Christian's life unless it has a legal right to be there. The blood covenant established by Jesus Christ reminds us that we have been bought back and redeemed.

"A person shall be put to death for his own sin."[444] Our Father is a God of love. He is also a God of light, and in Him there is no darkness. God does not chasten or punish us when we sin through sickness, disease, or torment – He cannot, for darkness is not in Him. However, when we are disobedient we grieve the Holy Spirit and God's hand of protection must be lifted, because He cannot be around sin. It is then that the door is open for demonic attack. We have built doorways for the demonic kingdom to enter through our sins and lack of obedience to God's Word. Sin is literally anything outside of faith in God's Word. Whatever is not faith-based is sin. When we are scared, worried, anxious, in doubt, or have unforgiveness or bitterness, we are in sin. And sin creates sickness in us all.

A minister friend of mine shared with me recently the testimony of his wife and her fight for life two years earlier. It was a Friday evening. She had had an appendicitis attack, and her appendix exploded. Because the appendix was wrapped around other organs, the pain was in her lower back, and they did not think it was anything more than a backache. So they postponed going to the doctor until the following Wednesday. Five days later.

When she finally reached the clinic, the doctors were quick to determine it was her appendix and she was immediately rushed into surgery. The prognosis was devastating. My friend's wife had little hope for recovering, because no one had ever lived more than four days with a ruptured, toxic appendix. But my friend looked the doctor in the eye, and said, "I believe that God will take care of her."

The doctor pronounced his Jewish faith, and added "I still want you to know that there is a high probability your wife is going to die."

My friend declared, "I pray that our Boss will guide your hands today in surgery and when you do not know what to do, He will guide you."

When the doctor returned to the surgery, he found the infection so bad that the medical team literally poured antibiotics into the open stomach cavity. The stench of decay was so strong that several nurses had to leave the room. After three hours of surgery, the doctor came back and delivered the same "impending death" report. She was in the recovery room, the doctor told my friend, and they would keep her in the hospital as long as they could.

The prognosis was a battle of words for my friend, because of his faith in God's Word. For twelve days his wife remained at the hospital and he prayed and anointed the hospital room, by faith, to release angels to protect the door so no demonic activity could take place in his wife's room. He prayed over and

---

[444] Deuteronomy 24:16

212

anointed by the blood of Jesus every antibiotic they put into her system. On the twelfth day, she was cleared to go home, the infection still active and alive within her.

The medical appointments that followed were for the purpose of checking the woman's bacterial count, still at an extremely high level. The minister and his wife now were convinced that somewhere a door to the demonic kingdom was still open that allowed the sickness to continue. By prayer and listening to the Holy Spirit, they were led to look at any unforgiveness in the woman's life. However, she struggled recalling any unforgiveness or bitterness that she had not confessed and put under the blood of Jesus Christ.

The Holy Spirit provided the answer when He revealed the grudge she had held against a neighbor several years earlier. Immediately, she sought the Lord for forgiveness and cleansing. Then she picked up the phone, called the former neighbor and asked for her forgiveness for the grudge she had carried. A couple days later, they reunited at dinner and personally restored the relationship. It was then that the truth was revealed. The husband of the woman whom she had never forgiven had brought a curse on the woman's head, compliments of an Eastern religion he practiced.

Prayer, faith, forgiveness, and the application of the blood of Jesus Christ quickly broke the curse. The next morning the women had a blood draw and she was completely healed. There was no trace of bacteria or infection in her body. A number of doctors and nurses met together to concur that the test results were accurate and all three different types of bacteria and infection were gone. A second-opinion blood-draw put all lingering doubts to rest and a miracle was pronounced! The couple had found the open door through which the enemy had the right to attack this daughter of God. In repentance and obedience to God's Word, the curse was broken and the Kingdom of Heaven was released upon her.

Brothers and sisters in Christ, the devil and his kingdom cannot attack us unless we offer him the legal right to do so. This is why Jesus said, "*Repent, for the kingdom of heaven is at hand.*"[445] We must repent daily, allowing the Holy Spirit to reveal in us the areas open to attack through our sins. If you have unforgiveness, bitterness, anger, resentment, doubt, worry, fear, or anything else that falls outside of faith, repent — right now! Lift up to the throne room whatever is keeping your healing or miracle from manifesting. Apply the blood of Jesus Christ to it, cleansing it and removing any rights it has to attack you.

---

[445] Matthew 4:17

Plant deep within your heart the truth that *"we do not wrestle against flesh and blood, but against principalities, against powers, against the rulers of the darkness of this age, against spiritual hosts of wickedness in the heavenly places. Therefore take up the whole armor of God, that you may be able to withstand in that day."*[446] Once we repent, we have an obligation through our words to reverse the curse and send the disease, sickness, or oppression back to the oppressor, the accuser of our brethren, the very enemy of the Father. We have the authority to remove his method of attack when we repent and close the door through which evil entered. This truth is nestled in the security of Galatians 3:13-14, which states, *"Christ has redeemed us from the curse of the law, having become a curse for us (for it is written, "Cursed is everyone who hangs on a tree"), that the blessing of Abraham might come upon the Gentiles in Christ Jesus, that we might receive the promise of the Spirit through faith."*

We have the ability to defeat all the works of the devil when we repent and apply the blood of Jesus Christ, exercising the gifts of the Holy Spirit, praying, praising, and testifying all in the Mighty and all-powerful Name of Jesus the Christ, the Son of God. When we abide in God and He in us, there is no room for oppression. We are victorious, triumphant in the Name of Jesus the Christ!

Arise today, take up your spiritual weapons of offense and attack the devil and his kingdom. Take back your health and your inheritance in God. Remove the legal right the enemy of the Father has to plunder your life. You are a child of the Most High God. Exercise that position today and allow the Holy Spirit of God to work on your behalf – for the Kingdom of Heaven is truly at hand!

---

[446] Ephesians 6:12-13

Enough is Enough!

Reflection Verse: *Hebrews 13:20*

Now may the God of peace who brought up our Lord Jesus from the dead, that great Shepherd of the sheep, through the blood of the everlasting covenant, make you complete in every good work to do His will, working in you what is well pleasing in His sight, through Jesus Christ.

Thoughts for Reflection:

As a Christian, you have been empowered with weapons necessary to be more than a conqueror in this world. Through faith you can change the circumstances of reality in your life by exercising your spiritual authority and trusting in God to fulfill His promise. Get out of God's way and trust His Word and you will experience God's power in your life. The blood of Jesus Christ has brought us closer to the Father. There is great power in the blood of Jesus!

Daily Confession:

I confess that I cannot change the circumstances in my life on my own. I submit to God and draw near to Him, knowing that He will then draw near to me. I resist the devil and His kingdom by exercising the gifts of the Holy Spirit through prayer, praise, and the power of my testimony! I proclaim today that through Jesus Christ my Lord I have authority and dominion over all the works of the devil. And by faith, I rejoice and give thanks to the Father who has qualified me to be a partaker of the inheritance of the saints in the Light and that He has delivered me from the power of darkness and translated me into His Kingdom. The Kingdom of Heaven is at hand to heal, deliver, and save me. Praise the Lord!

17

The Third-Day Church: The Hour Has Come

Come, and let us return to the LORD; for He has (allowed us to be) torn, but He will heal us; He has (allowed us to be) stricken, but He will bind us up. After two days He will revive us; on the third day He will raise us up, that we may live in His sight. Let us know, let us pursue the knowledge of the LORD. His going forth is established as the morning; He will come to us like the rain, like the latter and former rain to the earth.

Hosea 6:2-3

The Power of the Resurrected Christ

The first testimony in the first chapter of this book was my personal testimony. My wife and I, by faith in God's Word and promise, exercised our spiritual authority and raised our son from the dead. Several days later, I was in prayer and the Lord spoke very clearly to my spirit: "If you would have relied on the world's method of reviving your son, today would be a completely different day. Instead of rejoicing and celebrating his life, you would be mourning and saying good-bye to him for now. But because you sought me first and put your trust in me, your son is alive! I will never leave you nor forsake you when you put your trust in me and rely on me for your every need. I will always be there to bless you."

I praise God every day for the knowledge and understanding that He has provided me over the last several years regarding God's authority, power, and love for His people. Dear believers, the power of the resurrected Christ has been given to all believers. It is ours to exercise and to experience on a daily basis. My heart cries out for all Christians to receive the revelation of the true power of God residing in each one of us. We have been given a New Covenant from which to live, a new and living way, established under the promise and oath of the Father. It is a covenant of restoration, healing, and deliverance for all the children of God that we can once again become one with the Father.

The Kingdom of Heaven is at hand and the Church today has stepped into the third day, a day predestined to be one full of God's glory and supernatural power. The Word of God is clear that a thousand years equals one day to the Lord[447] and

---

[447] Psalm 90:4; 2 Peter 3:8

in the year 2000 we celebrated the 2000th-year anniversary of Jesus coming to earth to redeem us. That is, we have just completed the second day of the Church and have now entered into the third day of God's Church. God has established a principle for the power of the third day, and it is important for the Body of Christ to understand that the latter rain is beginning to fall! We were predestined for such a time as this to be harvesters, reapers of the lost and broken of this world. The principle of the third day is one that must be acknowledged and understood by believers.

> *After two days He will revive us; on the third day He will raise us up, that we may live in His sight. Let us know, let us pursue the knowledge of the LORD. His going forth is established as the morning; He will come to us like the rain, like the latter and former rain to the earth.*[448]

God also demonstrated the significance of the third day as one of preparation. When after three days of preparation for His people, the Lord appeared in thunder and glory at Mount Sinai.[449] On the third day God made the shadow go backward for Hezekiah.[450] It was the third day on which Abraham lifted his eyes and saw the place where his faith and trust in God would forever be established and a nation was borne out of that faithfulness, founded upon the truth that God will always provide.[451]

It was the third day when Pharaoh's butler's and baker's dreams were fulfilled based on Joseph's interpretation of them, demonstrating Joseph's utter faithfulness unto God.[452] Joseph easily could have hardened his heart from all the disappointment of not experiencing what God had promised through his earlier dreams. He could have turned down the chance to interpret the dreams of the butler and baker. In faithfulness, however, Joseph not only interpreted the dreams, he also gave God all the glory! God restored, delivered, and blessed Joseph because of his unwavering faithfulness and trust.

It was the third day after King Saul's death that David received word and became the King of Israel, restoring God's truth, order, power, and presence over the land.[453]

---

[448] Hosea 6:2,3
[449] Exodus 19:16,17
[450] 2 Kings 20:5-11
[451] Genesis 22:4-14
[452] Genesis 40:5-23
[453] 2 Samuel 1:2

None can compare, however, to the greatest event known to man, the greatest miracle ever recorded. And it happened on the third day, when Jesus the Christ was raised from the dead! The third day is established throughout history as the day of resurrection power, the day of restoration, arising from oppression, and victory. The third day is the day on which God releases an anointing, a glory that transforms man's heart and destroys the strongholds of death and sin. The third day is the day the Church will step into her glory and demonstrate the power and love of God throughout the world. The third day is the day that we, the sons and daughters of God, will see the prophesies of long ago fulfilled as God pours out His anointing presence upon all who hunger and thirst for Him.

The third day is the day that we as a Church prepare this world for the second coming of Jesus the Christ. For the Spirit of the Lord says,

> *The present-day wine skins will not be able to hold the "new wine," My greater glory that is being prepared for this time. The old wine skins of traditions, based off of man's doctrine will not be able to withstand the power and glory of the "new wine." The old wine skins of tradition and rituals will not be able to explain the supernatural phenomenon and miraculous power being experienced throughout the faith of My children. I say today, that the doubt and faithless doctrine that many cling today will in fact inhibit the ability to release this "new wine," this greater glory that I pour out upon My land. The Church is being called back to the essence and truth of My heart and woe to all those who do not heed My call.[454]*

Chuck Pierce, a true and proven Prophet of the Body of Christ, has said, "This will be a season when we will awaken to our latter-day blessings. The Lord will break discouragement, disillusionment and disinterest from our ranks. He will give us new strength to labor in our cities with a victorious mindset, and we will see His glory come. We are entering into a building phase like we have never experienced in the Kingdom. Pray and watch the Church change."[455]

As a Church, as the body of Christ, we are being called to prepare ourselves to receive a greater, better, more powerful presence of God in our lives. This is what Christianity is all about. We ought to be living in the supernatural, with miracles, signs and wonders happening all around us. No longer can we sit back and try to justify or question the truth of the Word of God. Far too many people are perishing at satan's hands because we Christians have failed to act – we have

---

[454] Prophetic Word spoken December 3, 2003

[455] C.D. Pierce, *The Future War of the Church*, Renew: Venture Ca. p. 76

failed to demonstrate our faith in the resurrection power and love of Jesus the Christ!

Jesus sent out His disciples saying, *"Go and preach the Kingdom of Heaven is at hand, heal the sick, cleanse the lepers, raise the dead, and cast-out demons. Freely you have received, freely give."*[456] Jesus has released every Christian to go and preach that the Kingdom of Heaven is at hand. We are to demonstrate its power. That the Kingdom of Heaven is at hand literally means the King's dominion is near.[457] Jesus has given us, His disciples, the power and authority to preach and demonstrate that the King's domain is here now and forever.

We cannot bury the good news of Jesus Christ and refuse to utilize the spiritual weapons, power, and authority freely given to us through the Holy Spirit. Jesus has clearly instructed us to go forth and demonstrate His Kingdom. Jesus said, *"You are the light of the world. A city that is set on a hill cannot be hidden. Nor do they light a lamp and put it under a basket, but on a lamp stand, and it gives light to all who are in the house. Let your light so shine before men, that they may see your good works and glorify your Father in heaven."*[458]

We must boldly step out in faith and demonstrate the resurrection truth through signs, wonders, and miracles. We must freely give to all in need that they, too, may be free to live in the victory and triumph of our Lord and Savior, Jesus Christ.

Jesus said, *"And these signs will follow those who believe: In My name they will cast out demons; they will speak with new tongues; they will take up serpents; and if they drink anything deadly, it will by no means hurt them; they will lay hands on the sick, and they will recover."*[459] After the Lord had spoken to them, He was received into heaven, and sat down at the right hand of God. *"And they went out and preached everywhere, the Lord working with them and confirming the word through the accompanying signs."*[460]

We have a responsibility to be light in this dark land, to be the examples of God's glory and promise. At some point, we must stand and rebuke the darkness that tries to destroy us. God's purpose is to create in man a real and recognizable awareness of God in all we do. The only way to possibly develop a church that

---

[456] Matthew 10:7
[457] Strong's Concordance Dictionary
[458] Matthew 5:14-16
[459] Mark 16:17-18
[460] Mark 16:19-20

will perpetuate such a truth is to bring awareness to the full measure of consciousness of God that Jesus Christ enjoyed.

Releasing God's power stems from a consciousness in man's soul of the overcoming Christ and the power residing in Him. Jesus said, *"Most assuredly, I say to you, he who believes in Me, the works that I do he will do also; and greater works than these he will do, because I go to My Father. And whatever you ask in My name, that I will do, that the Father may be glorified in the Son. If you ask anything in My name, I will do it. If you love Me, keep My commandments."*[461]

Jesus spoke the words, and they are words that cannot be denied. If we believe in Him and the works He performed, we are equipped to do the same and even greater. Jesus has given us a prophetic word and it must come to pass. The body of Christ has been given the power, authority, and love to do greater works even than Jesus during His earthly ministry.

Brothers and sisters, we have a calling to fulfill, a legacy to create, and a truth to acknowledge. Jesus suffered and died on the cross that you and I, and all the children of God, would be free from the curse of sin and death. Through the sacrifice of our Lord we have been perfectly redeemed – spirit, soul, and body – set apart unto God, chosen to be instruments of righteousness in this world, given a Promise and gift of the Holy Spirit to come alongside us to help and support us as we go forth restoring, healing, and delivering the land from the yoke of oppression that destroys man's faith in God. We have eternal life – a God kind of life, wanting and desiring nothing, forever! It is our responsibility to share this life with the lost.

Let us go forth with confidence and faith to fulfill the destiny of the Church. Let us step into this third day with a consciousness deep in our souls, one absolute and concrete in God's promises. This is a great time to be alive and to be called a Christian, because this is the time, this is the day, that the fullness of God's love and glory is going to be experienced. Let us go forth, preaching and demonstrating that the Kingdom of Heaven is NOW at hand!

Kingdom Living

Jesus did not just die, rise, and ascend to the right hand of the Father for us, He did all of it <u>as</u> us! Colossians 3:1-2 states, *"If then you were raised with Christ, seek those things, which are above, where Christ is, sitting at the right hand of*

---

[461] John 14:12-15

God. Set your mind on things above, not on things on the earth." The life of a Christian is a life of resurrection power, a life predestined to be lived in faith, trust, and dependence on God to fulfill the impossible, the extraordinary, when we set our minds on the things of above and not on the things of the earth. The eternal life we are called to experience, the Zoë Life, a God kind of life, a life of the extraordinary, is promised to the Christian now and forever.[462] Never should the promise of Heaven or Life after death or even the promise of the Millennial Kingdom replace the truth of the present-tense reality that the Kingdom of Heaven exists now in this world through Jesus' crucifixion.

When Jesus cried out *"It is finished,"*[463] He was declaring that His sacrifice, suffering, and death were fulfillments of the Father's will and the liberation of mankind from the devil's works. *"It is finished"* was a victorious cry piercing the heavens and tearing down the demonic stronghold over the lives of God's children and restoring what Adam had lost. Jesus was not just stating that His life was over – He was declaring that everything He had been sent to fulfill on the earth for mankind was fulfilled. He bore all sin, sickness, disease, turmoil, strife, and division. He bore all unrest and affliction becoming the curse for all of mankind. He destroyed *all* the works of the devil![464] The blood of the perfect Lamb of God was shed for mankind, and it is through His blood that we are encouraged to arise today and declare that the Kingdom of God is among us.

The truth of God's Word, promise, victory, and triumph through the suffering endured on the Cross has been completely overlooked and dismissed by many Christians today. We must ask the question why Jesus was crucified. If people around the world could receive the depth of the revelation of "why" Jesus was crucified, there would be a great outbreak of revival of God's Spirit in the world.

The most obvious reason for Jesus' crucifixion was to forgive mankind's sin. However, the crucifixion established much more than forgiveness of sin. It allowed man once again to have the position to enter the presence of the Father as Adam did in the Garden of Eden. The crucifixion of Jesus positioned man once again to have dominion over the world, both physically and spiritually! Adam gave the keys of the world's power and authority to satan when he defied God and ate of the Tree of the Knowledge of Good and Evil. God prophesied at that time that Jesus would come and bruise His heel on the head of satan and return to man all that Adam had lost.[465] The crucifixion of Jesus was the institution and fulfillment of that prophecy.

---

[462] John 3:16; 2 John 2:25
[463] John 19:30
[464] 1 John 3:8
[465] Genesis 3:15

Jesus' crucifixion broke the curse on this world and man once again was provided the ability to commune with the Father in a more intimate relationship. The New Testament reminds us time and again that we are not to fix our minds on the things of this world, but to keep our focus, attention, and faith on the promises established in the New Covenant.

If Jesus Christ is the Lord and Savior of your life then you are born again, translated into His Kingdom,[466] dwelling in the house of God forever,[467] and becoming a recipient of the blessings of Abraham.[468] Jesus Christ has redeemed us from the curse so that we, the Gentiles, might receive the blessings of Abraham and the promise of His Holy Spirit.[469] You are the seed of Abraham and heirs according to the promise through your faith and confession of Jesus Christ.[470] You are called to live and experience a Kingdom life today in and through your faith in Jesus Christ!

Colossians 3:3 states, *"For you died, and your life is hidden with Christ in God."* Our promise of abundant life, a life of divine health and prosperity, is hidden with Christ in God. As in this world, anything valuable must be searched out with diligence and perseverance. I have yet to find a watermelon-sized gold nugget in my garden during spring planting, or a basketball-sized, uncut diamond in my yard as I mow the lawn. Anything extremely valuable in this land must be searched out – and the same is true with the spiritual blessings given to us by our Father.[471] We must be willing, diligent, and persistent in our pursuit of the promise of abundance hidden with Christ in God.

The secret to finding the hidden promise of abundant life in God is simple. Jesus said, *"I am the vine, you are the branches. He who abides in Me, and I in him, bears much fruit; for without Me you can do nothing. If you abide in Me, and My words abide in you, you will ask what you desire, and it shall be done for you."*[472] The secret place where God's entire Kingdom dwells is found when we abide in Christ, having His words abide in us. We will not achieve the great blessings and promises of God without living in His Word and presence. In Jesus' words, *"I am the bread of life. He who comes to Me shall never hunger, and he who believes in Me shall never thirst.*[473] The secret to abiding in the secret place of God, where

---

[466] Colossians 1:13
[467] John 14:23; 1 Corinthians 3:9; 2 Corinthians 5:1
[468] Galatians 3:13-29
[469] Galatians 3:13,14
[470] Galatians 3:26-29
[471] Ephesians 1:3
[472] John 15:5-7
[473] John 6:35

all of our spiritual blessings rest, is not difficult to achieve; we must simply hunger for more of His Spirit.

Prayer and study of His Word elevate the believer to the place of faith and confidence where a rest is experienced. This secret place is reached when we are faithful and confident in God's promise fulfilled with the crucifixion of Jesus. Christians are called to abide in and live a Kingdom Life – a life full of the presence of God through His Word and Spirit. We have been exhorted to live in the Spirit and not in the flesh, and yet much of our confessions and faith are based on our flesh and worldly experiences rather than the truth of God's Word.[474] We must remember that the Christian life is established upon a foundation of redemption and the power and grace of God's Kingdom. This foundation is the revelation Rock we are to build our lives upon, allowing us to experience God's fullness.

I heard the testimony of a woman whose baby had drowned in the bathtub when she left to answer the phone. It was a testimony based on the mercy, love, and compassion of God to heal this woman's broken heart and bring her through the deepest, darkest depression of guilt and affliction a person could endure. I praise God for His continual love and compassion for His children. However, this woman proclaimed that for the rest of her life she will bear the same cross Jesus bore, a cross of suffering because of the loss of her child. Jesus did not suffer and die that we would have to bear the same cross He bore.

I could not help but think after hearing this message that something was missing in the Christian faith. Far too often we look to God to help us, when clearly, through the crucifixion of Jesus His Son, our Redeemer, He already has fulfilled that cry and is waiting for us to exercise our faith in His Word. I wonder if the circumstances for this woman would have been different if she had the knowledge of the supernatural power and authority dwelling within her to raise her child from the dead. We have been called to a life of the supernatural, one that experiences, expresses, and demonstrates the very essence and power of Kingdom living in our present-day reality. We are appointed to live the Kingdom Life. Imagine how different our lives could be today if we were to begin exercising the truth of Kingdom living.

"Seek first the Kingdom of God and His righteousness and all these things should be added to you."[475] Jesus did not tell us to seek God first, but to seek the Kingdom of God. When we seek the Kingdom of God with hunger,

---

[474] Romans 8:5
[475] Matthew 6:33

perseverance, diligence, and faith, we find the hidden place of God the secret place where all blessings, power, and love are experienced and released. When we seek the Kingdom of God we receive the fullness of God! The Kingdom of Heaven is at hand and we must be willing to open our minds to the truth of the power, authority, and responsibility we have been given through the crucifixion of Jesus.

At the beginning of this book I encouraged you to write down the desires of your heart, whether healing, deliverance, restoration, or reconciliation of a relationship, freedom from oppression, or whatever drew you to pick up this book. You were to write it down, to lay it, in faith, at the altar of God.

As you poured through the pages of this book, as you prayed and meditated on God's written Word, prayerfully you were able to claim a faith that would bring those desires to pass. Stand in glory today, because God is faithful in all He has promised!

Consecration Prayer

Please take the time right now to seek the Kingdom of God through this prayer. Make it your own prayer by consecrating your heart, soul, and body unto the Lord. The Father is committed to blessing you and releasing His Kingdom in your life. It is your turn to be completely committed to Him in all you say and do.

Heavenly Father,

I come to You in the name of Your victorious and triumphant Son, Jesus Christ. I thank you today, Father, that I have been created in Your image, redeemed from the curse of sin and sickness and filled with Your Holy Spirit to be more than a conqueror in all that I do.

I realize that Your very essence, Your very Kingdom, dwells in my being, that every day I am moving closer to being a perfect reflection of Your Son in this world. Father, I ask that You take me to a deeper place of fellowship with You, that You and I may truly be One in spirit, soul, and body and that I may experience Your presence, glory, and love every hour of the day.

In Jesus' name, I appropriate by faith Your promises today. I take authority over the tribulations in my life. In Jesus' name, I take authority over the mentalities of oppression and lack. To satan I say: you have no part in my family. My seed and I are going to be blessed because we serve and obey God!

Holy Spirit, I invite You to possess my nature, soul and body. Fill me to overflowing that Your presence may extend all around me and bring the Kingdom of God into my atmosphere. I know that through the blood of Jesus and through the power of the Holy Spirit in me, I can do all things, that greater is He who is in me than he who is in the world. I am empowered to heal the sick, raise the dead, and cast out demons, all in Jesus' name!

Today, right now, I take my stand for righteousness and surrender myself to becoming a compete demonstration of the Kingdom of God in this world. I will torment the demons and the demonic kingdom and not allow them to torment my loved ones or me. I am a soldier in God's army, and today I declare by faith that I am taking up the Sword of the Spirit and engaging the enemy. I am triumphant! Sickness, disease, torment, oppression, strife, and poverty -- you have no hold on my life! Jesus broke the curse and I am free! I recognize, Jesus, that You bled seven ways for my complete redemption:

1. You *bled through the brow in the garden of Gethsemane for the complete redemption of mental anguish, stress, anxiety, and pressure. (Luke 22:43; Hebrews 5:7,8)*

2. You were bruised for my iniquity, breaking the generational curse over my life now and forever. I realize iniquity is an internal force that causes me to do what is wrong, and, Jesus, you bled from the inside, through the buffeting and bruising You endured that the iniquity and handwriting on the wall of the generations be blotted out now and forever by Your precious blood! (Matthew 26:67; Mark 14:65; John 18:22; Matthew 27:31; Isaiah 53:5)

3. Through Your stripes I am healed! When You were scourged, whipped, and torn apart by the Roman soldiers, the blood, oh, Lord Jesus, that poured from Your body through the torn flesh was for my complete healing and restoration of my physical body. Jesus, You are the Bread of Life, broken, that I may be healed. I thank you. (Isaiah 53:5; I Peter 2:24; John 19:1)

4. You bled when they drove the crown of thorns upon Your head, pounding it into place with a rod. The blood pouring from the thorns redeemed and atoned me from the idolatry of my heart and the worshipping of false gods. The blood from the thorns also broke the curse of poverty over the land, and, therefore, today I can proclaim that my whole being prospers in Jesus' name and by Your precious blood. (Matthew 27:29; John 19:2; Matthew 27:27-31; Mark 15: 16-20)

5. You bled through Your hands when the nails tore through your wrists, causing extreme pain in Your entire arm, waxing Your heart in agony. Lord Jesus, You endured it all that I may be free today from the wrongs I have done with my hands. Thank you, Jesus! (Luke 24:39,40; Psalm 22:16)

6. You bled from Your feet when they pounded the nail through each foot, piercing the nerve endings and shooting great, arching pain through your legs and creating an inconceivable pain throughout Your whole body. Jesus, my Redeemer, You did this so I may be forgiven and atoned for all the wrong decisions I have made in my life that were contrary to You and the Word of God! (Isaiah 53:6; Psalm 22: 16)

7. You bled from Your side when they pierced You for my transgressions. When the spear pierced Your heart and blood and water gushed from Your body, I was then completely set free from all my sins, positioning me to be adopted into the

*God of the poor,
we long to see your face.
You tell us, "Whatever
you did for one of these
least brothers of mine,
you did for me."*

*May we recognize you
in each of our brothers
and sisters. May our
prayers unite us with
those who hunger.*

*May we share your
blessings with people
in need.*

Amen

Photo by Karen Kasmauski for CRS

Prayer
REQUEST CARD

Please remember my prayers for:

- ☐ Survivors of Typhoon Haiyan
- ☐ Pope Francis
- ☐ World peace
- ☐ Homeless refugees
- ☐ Hungry and sick children
- ☐ Unborn children
- ☐ Healing of an illness
- ☐ Departed loved ones
- ☐ Marriage
- ☐ Reconciliation
- ☐ Financial problem
- ☐ Employment
- ☐ Spiritual growth
- ☐ Peaceful death
- ☐ Other: _____

_____

_____

_____

*Your requests will be
remembered at Mass offered in
St. Stephen's Chapel
at Catholic Relief Services
world headquarters.*

Please fill in the information below:

Name   (Please Print)

Address

Kingdom family as a son or daughter of the Most High God. Jesus, I thank you today for my complete redemption and salvation in Your Awesome and glorious name! (Isaiah 53:5; John 19:34)

You have set me free, oh, Lord, free to live in the Kingdom of God and experience His full promise of life. I proclaim today, by faith, that I will no longer count the blood covenant established by my Lord and Savior Jesus the Christ a common thing. I repent from compromising the Word of God because of ignorance or fear. Today, therefore, I make that covenant my life. I commit my life to be a demonstration of the triumphant victory established through my Redeemer's perfect sacrifice.

Today, there is a breakthrough in my life and the miracle-working, healing power of the Holy Spirit of God is upon me. The Kingdom of God possesses me. I set my mind on things above, Your Kingdom, and not on this earth, and I know that where the Spirit of Lord is, there is complete, transforming liberty in everything that concerns me. You, oh Father, are faithful to Your Word and You have said that You are able to do exceedingly, abundantly, above all I could ever ask or think, according to the power within me. Today, I release the Holy Spirit power in me into every aspect of my life that Your extraordinary presence may saturate all that I do.

I commit myself today to learn to abide in the presence of Jesus Christ and to allow the Kingdom of God and all its wonder, power, and glory to abide in me. I am more than a conqueror through Him who loves me, and I will demonstrate today and every day that I am an ambassador for God's Kingdom. Thank you, Father, for loving me so much that You gave Your only begotten Son that I will not perish, but live a Zoë life of abundance, health, prosperity, peace, and joy, now and forever. Thank you, Father, for making me Yours.

Amen !

We want to hear from you!

Find other resources by Rev. Dr. David Carlson at:

www.info@josiahcenter.org

Please contact us with your testimonies of healings and deliverances. Also, if there is a stronghold in your life that you find difficult to break, even after reading this book, please contact us right away and we will join with you in prayer and faith to achieve the freedom and liberty you deserve through Jesus the Christ our Lord.